American Indian Workforce Education

In this collection of original essays, contributors critically examine the pedagogical, administrative, financial, economic, and cultural contexts of American Indian vocational education and workforce development, identifying trends and issues for future research in the fields of vocational education, workforce development, and American Indian studies.

Carsten Schmidtke is Assistant Professor of Human Resource and Workforce Development, University of Arkansas, USA.

Routledge Research in Education

For a full list of titles in this series, please visit www.routledge.com

138 **Aristotelian Character Education**
Kristján Kristjánsson

139 **Performing Kamishibai**
Tara McGowan

140 **Educating Adolescent Girls Around the Globe**
Edited by Sandra L. Stacki and Supriya Baily

141 **Quality Teaching and the Capability Approach**
Evaluating the work and governance of women teachers in rurual Sub-Saharan Africa
Alison Buckler

142 **Using Narrative Inquiry for Educational Research in the Asia Pacific**
Edited by Sheila Trahar and Wai Ming Yu

143 **The Hidden Role of Software in Educational Research**
Policy to Practice
By Tom Liam Lynch

144 **Education, Leadership and Islam**
Theories, discourses and practices from an Islamic perspective
Saeeda Shah

145 **English Language Teacher Education in Chile**
A cultural historical activity theory perspective
Malba Barahona

146 **Navigating Model Minority Stereotypes**
Asian Indian Youth in South Asian Diaspora
Rupam Saran

147 **Evidence-based Practice in Education**
Functions of evidence and causal presuppositions
Tone Kvernbekk

148 **A New Vision of Liberal Education**
The good of the unexamined life
Alistair Miller

149 **Transatlantic Reflections on the Practice-Based PhD in Fine Art**
Jessica B. Schwarzenbach and Paul M. W. Hackett

150 **Drama and Social Justice**
Theory, research and practice in international contexts
Edited by Kelly Freebody and Michael Finneran

151 **Education, Identity and Women Religious, 1800–1950**
Convents, classrooms and colleges
Edited by Deirdre Raftery and Elizabeth Smyth

152 **School Health Education in Changing Times**
Curriculum, pedagogies and partnerships
Deana Leahy, Lisette Burrows, Louise McCuaig, Jan Wright and Dawn Penney

153 **Progressive Sexuality Education**
The Conceits of Secularism
Mary Lou Rasmussen

154 **Collaboration and the Future of Education**
Preserving the Right to Think and Teach Historically
Gordon Andrews, Warren J. Wilson, and James Cousins

155 **Theorizing Pedagogical Interaction**
Insights from Conversation Analysis
Hansun Zhang Waring

156 **Interdisciplinary Approaches to Distance Teaching**
Connected Classrooms in Theory and Practice
Alan Blackstock and Nathan Straight

156 **How Arts Education Makes a Difference**
Research examining successful classroom practice and pedagogy
Edited by Josephine Fleming, Robyn Gibson and Michael Anderson

157 **Populism, Media and Education**
Challenging discrimination in contemporary digital societies
Edited by Maria Ranieri

158 **Imagination for Inclusion**
Diverse contexts of educational practice
Edited by Derek Bland

159 **Youth Voices, Public Spaces, and Civic Engagement**
Edited by Stuart Greene, Kevin J. Burke, and Maria K. McKenna

160 **Spirituality in Education in a Global, Pluralised World**
Marian de Souza

161 **Reconceptualising Agency and Childhood**
New Perspectives in Childhood Studies
Edited by Florian Esser, Meike Baader, Tanja Betz, and Beatrice Hungerland

162 **Technology-Enhanced Language Learning for Specialized Domains**
Practical applications and mobility
Edited by Elena Martín Monje, Izaskun Elorza and Blanca García Riaza

163 **American Indian Workforce Education**
Trends and Issues
Edited by Carsten Schmidtke

American Indian Workforce Education
Trends and Issues

**Edited by
Carsten Schmidtke**

LONDON AND NEW YORK

First published 2016
by Routledge

2 Park Square, Milton Park, Abingdon, Oxfordshire OX14 4RN
52 Vanderbilt Avenue, New York, NY 10017

Routledge is an imprint of the Taylor & Francis Group, an informa business

First issued in paperback 2018

Copyright © 2016 Taylor & Francis

The right of Carsten Schmidtke to be identified as editor of this work has been asserted by him/her in accordance with sections 77 and 78 of the Copyright, Designs and Patents Act 1988.

All rights reserved. No part of this book may be reprinted or reproduced or utilised in any form or by any electronic, mechanical, or other means, now known or hereafter invented, including photocopying and recording, or in any information storage or retrieval system, without permission in writing from the publishers.

Notice:
Product or corporate names may be trademarks or registered trademarks, and are used only for identification and explanation without intent to infringe.

Library of Congress Cataloguing-in-Publication Data
Names: Schmidtke, Carsten, editor of compilation.
Title: American Indian workforce education : trends and issues / edited by Carsten Schmidtke.
Description: 1st edition. | New York : Routledge, 2016. | Series: Routledge research in education ; 163 | Includes bibliographical references.
Identifiers: LCCN 2015042149 | ISBN 9781138959552 (hardback) | ISBN 9781315648873 (ebook)
Subjects: LCSH: Indians of North America—Vocational education.
Classification: LCC E97 .A456 2016 | DDC 370.113—dc23
LC record available at http://lccn.loc.gov/2015042149

ISBN: 978-1-138-95955-2 (hbk)
ISBN: 978-0-367-19622-6 (pbk)

Typeset in Sabon
by Apex CoVantage, LLC

Contents

Acknowledgements ix

Introduction: More Than Paraeconomic Survival 1
CARSTEN SCHMIDTKE

1 A History of American Indian Vocational Education 15
JON REYHNER

2 Education for Jobs, Education for Life 32
CHARLES T. SAUNDERS

3 From Boarding School to Tribal Colleges: The Rise of Retribalization Through Vocational Education 55
CHARLOTTE LEFORESTIER

4 "How Can We Change Without Destroying Ourselves?": Arguments for Self-Determination and Workforce Education Through Tribal Colleges and Universities 74
JOHN GOODWIN

5 The Role of Tradition in Education: Economic Development and American Indian Higher Education 96
AMY FANN, LINDA SUE WARNER, AND G. S. BRISCOE

6 Educating the Educators: Making Workforce Education Successful Through Understanding and Respect for Indigenous Cultures 116
DELILAH F. O'HAYNES

7 Career Development Counseling for American Indian Students 139
CARSTEN SCHMIDTKE

8 Young Native Men's Work Experiences 159
J. K. PAYDEN SPOWART AND E. ANNE MARSHALL

| 9 | Building Tomorrow's Tribal Public Health Workforce | 181 |

JENNIFER PHARR AND MICHELLE CHINO

Conclusion 202

CARSTEN SCHMIDTKE

List of Contributors 205
Name Index 209
Topical Index 211

Acknowledgements

This volume was a long time in the making from its inception to seeing years of work finally come to fruition. I thank my editors at Routledge, Christina Chronister, Katherine Tsamparlis, and Autumn Spalding for all their work in seeing this project through to completion and in their support through the entire process of assembling the collection. This has been a learning experience for me, but it has been more than worthwhile.

I also thank all the contributors to this volume for their patience and their willingness to stay the course and to not give up while this book went through the proposal and approval phases. In addition, I am grateful for everyone's cooperation in revising work quickly and providing me with all the information needed to submit the final manuscript.

Finally, my thanks go to all my colleagues who agreed to read parts of the manuscript as it was in preparation and provided useful feedback. They are, in no particular order, Deanna R. Davis, University of Nevada Las Vegas; Pamela B. Howze, Merck Vaccine Manufacturing; Paula E. Faulkner, North Carolina A&T University; Barton Washer, University of Missouri; Janet Louise Burns, Georgia State University; Niki Sandoval, Santa Ynez band of Chumash Indians; Howard R. D. Gordon, University of Nevada Las Vegas; Klara Bonder, University of Amsterdam, Netherlands; Earlene Washburn, University of Arkansas Ft. Smith; R. Kirby Barrick, University of Florida; Jacky Moore; Karl Held, Concordia University; Norena Norton Badway, San Francisco State University; Françoise Besson, University of Toulouse 2, France; Katja May; Tara Shollenberger, High Point University; Noémie Waldhubel, Ethnologie in Schule und Erwachsenenbildung, Münster, Germany; R. Saya Bobick, West Virginia University; Trellys A. Riley, Troy University; Michelle Conrad, University of Central Missouri; and John Gaal, Carpenter's District Council of Greater St. Louis and Vicinity. Thank you all for making this project a success.

Introduction
More Than Paraeconomic Survival

Carsten Schmidtke

> "Tribal people will continue to survive in a paraeconomic system without the independent and interdependent development of enterprises owned and operated for profit by tribal people living on reservations."
>
> (Vizenor, 1976, p. 115)

It may certainly strike readers as more than a little curious to see Gerald Vizenor cited in a collection of essays on workforce education for American Indians despite the fact that this quotation is taken from his earlier, journalistic writings. The connection between Vizenor and workforce development occurred to me when I presented a paper on workforce education at a conference on American Indian studies. During the question-and-answer session after the presentations given by the members of the panel I was on, one of the other panelists uttered the following retort to one of my answers to an audience question: "Vocational education is all good and well, but we need more doctors and lawyers." Apart from evoking visions of the old stereotype that vocational education is somehow inferior, closes doors instead of opening them, and is meant for people with less than average intelligence, the comment also made it clear that the panelist was more than happy to have American Indians continue to be paraeconomic survivors. Luckily, organizations such as the National Congress of American Indians (NCAI) (NCAI, 2013a) and National Indian and Native American Employment and Training Conference (NINAETC, 2015) would beg to differ very strongly. This realization that workforce training was still seen as something detrimental to tribal and community development today was the ultimate impetus to conceive of this volume and to ask scholars to contribute their views on issues and trends in workforce education for American Indians.

To be certain, there is no question that many tribes and their members face significant health issues that need addressing before economic development can be sustained and workforce education can be successful, and at the same time, competent legal counsel is certainly needed to ward off encroachment on tribal sovereignty and to ensure that the federal government will no longer be able to escape honoring its promises made toward tribal nations. At the same time, the NCAI is fully aware that development without workforce education is a losing proposition: "Tribal citizens with high-quality education and skills development are a critical ingredient to build strong tribal economies" (NCAI, 2013a, p. 12). Paraeconomic survival is the antithesis to this goal.

Vizenor (1976) defined *paraeconomic* as follows: "The meaning of paraeconomic is derived from the combined definition of being irregular and dependent on the dominant economic systems of production, consumption of goods and services, and the distribution of wealth" (p. 107). In other words, paraeconomics to Vizenor is a situation where money made on the reservation is spent making purchases in off-reservation businesses, thus injecting funds into the dominant economic system and ensuring continued dependence on this system for goods and services. That setup leaves tribal governments beholden to the business interests of outsiders if they wish to ensure that their members have access to needed goods, and it also encourages continued dependence on the federal government to help tribes and tribal members exert regulatory control on the off-reservation economic system on behalf of tribes. The real road to sovereignty, Vizenor asserted, is to create an economic system on the reservation in which businesses manufacture goods that they sell to reservation residents. That way, greater independence from the outside can be achieved, and the influence of local people on economic and policy decisions is likewise strengthened. To create such a tribal economy, as stated in the NCAI quote above, requires workforce education and skills development.

Skills development to benefit the local community is nothing new in Indian country. In fact, traditionally education for boys and girls has emphasized precisely this particular aspect of education and training. For example, Charles Eastman in *Indian Boyhood* (1971/1902) spoke to the nature of such education in a chapter appropriately titled "An Indian Boy's Training":

> He [the boy] is called the future defender of his people, whose lives may depend upon his courage and skill. . . . This sort of teaching [listening to and repeating traditional stories] at once enlightens the boy's mind and stimulates his ambition. His conception of his own future career becomes a vivid and irresistible force. Whatever there is for him to learn must be learned; whatever qualifications are necessary to a truly great man he must seek at any expense of danger and hardship. (pp. 42–43)

Eastman, a Dakota, clearly saw the connection between training and community survival; in fact, he made the point that being able to serve one's community is motivation to acquire the skills that are being taught. In modern terms, we might say that Eastman understood the role workforce education can play in achieving and preserving tribal sovereignty. Another early 20th-century writer, Luther Standing Bear, a Lakota, had this to say:

> All this was training for the boy. Just as the mothers were training the girls to be able to be good housewives, so the fathers were teaching the sons to become skillful hunters. Our parents were our only teachers. . . . But when our training was completed, we were prepared to face life.
> (Standing Bear, 1988/1931, p. 46)

While it took the progressive movement and educators like John Dewey to advance the idea that vocational or workforce education is more than just job training, the quotation from Standing Bear makes it clear that the Lakota had understood the connection between work skills and life for a long time. Therefore, it appears that workforce education should be celebrated as an integral aspect of tribal sovereignty rather than be vilified as something holding back people and their communities.

One of the biggest issues facing tribal communities is unemployment. In fact, the regional unemployment rates of American Indians in the first half of 2013 were between 1.2 to 3.3 times higher than the corresponding rates for whites (Austin, 2013). In the past (and still today), the frequent lack of reservation businesses often led to a situation where seasonal agricultural work was all that was available. If there were jobs, they tended to be low-paying because of a lack of skill and education among the local population (Olson & Wilson, 1984). This situation then led and still leads to a vicious cycle in what Grey and Herr (1998) have called the *skills-employability paradigm*: low-skilled workers attract only low-skill, low-wage jobs, which in turn removes the motivation to acquire more skills, which leads to more low-wage work, and so on ad infinitum. Furthermore, low-wage jobs mean low purchase power, which leads to a reluctance to provide goods and services on or near a reservation. Workforce education in conjunction with Vizenor's (1976) ideas of independent reservation economies could help break this cycle.

However, accomplishing this break may not be as easy as it seems. Champagne (2007) gave a rather bleak assessment of American Indian economic prospects:

> Many Native communities, especially isolated ones, will continue to rely on subsistence economic production and limited trade. . . . The effects of political and economic marginalization of most Native communities have left few viable subsistence or market economies. Especially in the lower forty-eight states, few reservation communities have the natural or economic resources to sustain their communities' needs. (p. 337)

What to do then? Champagne (2007) made Vizenor's (1976) ideas sound like so much pie in the sky when he provided a list of challenges: isolation, lack of resources, lack of capital, lack of support for individual entrepreneurship, and an unwillingness by tribal governments to support entrepreneurship and businesses that are independent of tribal government control. DeWeaver (2014) agreed and argued that these challenges had created a situation where American Indian individuals 40 years after Vizenor wrote his articles were still essentially limited to paraeconomic survival. Champagne advocated for small business development and participation in the outside economy as a possible solution as long as that participation does not run counter to community values and preservation. Issues surrounding tribal and reservation economies such as tribal resource development (hunting, fishing, agriculture, timber), energy exploitation (oil, gas, uranium, water), and gaming have been very controversial in many tribal communities, especially in terms of their relationship to sovereignty. In fact, the *Current Controversies* series of books published by Greenhaven Press in the 1990s has one volume on Native American rights (Roleff, 1998) that discusses the pros and cons of gaming, resource use, and limiting sovereignty.

Federal legislation and its attendant programs have over the past several decades attempted, with more or less success, to get American Indians into vocational and workforce training programs. A special program in 1946 for Hopi and Navajo students, an American Indian apprenticeship program begun in 1952, and the Adult Vocational Training Program begun in the 1950s were all designed to teach basic trades or technical skills to get people into employment, preferably in the cities as these programs were tied to relocation efforts (Fixico, 2008). The overall assessment of these programs was bleak: "Obtaining vocational training did not solve employment problems for many Indians" (Fixico, 2008, p. 26). The continued skills gap as a result of insufficient training led to low workforce participation and continued high unemployment rates, which in turn exacerbated poverty and forced many Indians into neighborhoods with substandard and dilapidated housing. To get a handle on such living conditions was one of the driving forces behind the Indian Manpower Program, which was part of the Comprehensive Employment and Training Act of 1973. Any gains made in employment rates as the result of workforce training, unfortunately, were soon negated by the high birthrate among American Indian women; there always seemed to be more young people needing jobs or training than was available (Fixico, 2008). Problems arising from the fact that the American Indian population tends to be young still exist today as evidenced by the NCAI brief on workforce development: "[E]nsuring job growth keeps pace with the growing Native youth population is an ongoing challenge. . . . Workforce development opportunities are particularly important because Indian Country has one of the youngest populations in the nation, with 42 percent of Native people under the age of 25" (NCAI, 2013b, p. 2).

The United States federal government, however, still persisted in its thinking that the next legislative initiative would finally be the panacea that put an end to the persistent problems of un- and underemployment as a result of a lack of skills. Another effort in that regard then was the Indian Employment, Training and Related Services Demonstration Act of 1992 as amended by the Omnibus Indian Advancement Act of 2000. Its purpose was to "demonstrate how Indian tribal governments can integrate the employment, training and related services they provide in order to improve the effectiveness of those services, reduce joblessness in Indian communities and serve tribally-determined goals consistent with the policy of self-determination" (Department of Labor Employment and Training Administration, 2010, para. 3). Programs such as the U.S. Department of Labor's Indian Welfare-to-Work (INA WtW) and Workforce Investment Act (WIA) Section 166 programs, the U.S. Department of Health and Human Services Native Employment Works (NEW) program, and the U.S. Bureau of Indian Affairs Tribal Work Experience (TWEP), Adult Vocational Training (AVT), Direct Employment (DE), and other programs were to be included in this attempt at integrating a patchwork of programs from different departments with different funding streams.

However, it appears that this effort once more was less than successful. Speaking about the Indian Employment, Training and Related Services Demonstration Act, DeWeaver (2014) arrived at this grim conclusion: "Although the initiative provided a significant way for tribes to adapt program resources to tribal goals, federal agencies have waged a determined campaign for over a decade to destroy the essential features of this initiative" (p. 15). The framers of the Workforce Investment Act (WIA) of 1998 seemed to think so as well and tried to rectify this situation. WIA Section 166, which dealt specifically with American Indians, created two new entities that were now supposed to coordinate workforce development in Indian Country. The first such entity was the Department of Labor's Employment and Training Administration's Office of Workforce Investment's Division of Indian and Native American Programs (DINAP), whose mission was to do this:

> [C]ontribute to the implementation of an integrated national workforce investment system that supports economic growth and provides workers with the information, advice, job search assistance, supportive services, and training in demand industries and occupations they need to get and keep good jobs and provide employers with skilled workers.
> (Office of Workforce Investment, 2013, para. 1)

More than this, the DINAP and the Department of Labor claimed to "share a vision of providing quality employment and training services to Native American communities that . . . are administered in ways that are consistent with the traditional cultural values and beliefs of the people they are designed to serve" (DINAP, 2015, para. 1). In addition to DINAP, WIA Section 166 also created the Native American Employment and Training Council (NAETC) as an advisory board for the Secretary of Labor on matters of "employment, training and economic self-sufficiency needs in their communities" (NAETC, 2009, p. 3). The language of the WIA and the mission and vision of DINAP are encouraging because they acknowledge that employment and training should not come at any cost but be mindful of tribal cultures and beliefs. The NAETC is very clear on this issue: "Native American workforce services are rooted in strong cultural values and family aspirations. They provide tools through education, skill training, employment services and support for job creation to address the chronic and severe joblessness in Native American communities on and off Indian reservation areas" (p. 4).

Despite such language, however, it appears that those statements were once again, as many would say who have knowledge of the relationship between tribes and the U.S. federal government, so much empty rhetoric. In its brief for Dr. Edward Montgomery, President Obama's transition team leader at the Department of Labor, the NAETC (2009) mentioned the "stalled progress of WIA Native programs" (p. 2) and had harsh words for the George W. Bush administration: "For the most part, NAETC advice, questions and policy development have been ignored by the current administration for the past eight years" (p. 5). Considering this state of affairs, the NAETC requested a more constructive relationship, including filling vacancies on the council and restoring its funding; the full restoration of DINAP, once again including better staffing; and a complete review of Section 166. In that same vein, Lorenda T. Sanchez, NAETC chair, used her 2009–2012 report to reframe the NAETC's goals: "Our goal now is to share with others how the Indian and Native American employment and training programs have developed a skilled Native workforce and helped launch Native businesses during these most stressed economic times . . ." (NAETC, 2009, p. 3).

The government's response to issues surrounding workforce development was to pass yet another piece of legislation, the Workforce Innovation and Opportunity Act (WIOA) of 2013 that creates one funding stream for WIA programs. WIOA Section 166(a)(2) speaks to its purpose of serving Native people to accomplish the following:

1) Develop more fully the academic, occupational, and literacy skills of such individuals [i.e., Native Americans];
2) Make such individuals more competitive in the workforce and equip them with entrepreneurial skills necessary for successful self-employment; and
3) Promote the economic and social development of INA [Indian and Native American] communities in accordance with the goals and values of such communities (NINAETC, 2015, p. 1).

Other WIOA provisions indeed restored some of DINAP's functions and strengthened the Tribal Employment Rights Office (TERO) program, which oversees and enforces tribal equal employment protection ordinances in dealings between tribes and outside contractors: "The work of TEROs has also enabled American Indian workers, contractors, and entrepreneurs through training and work experience to identify and successfully compete for opportunities off the reservation through the government or private sectors" (The Leadership Conference, 2015, para. 15). The WIOA, in fact, also expressly permits (and thus funds) tribes to engage in discussions about training and hiring with outside employers, partnerships with other service providers, and training for tribal administrators (NINAETC, 2015, p. 10). A further WIOA provision allows funding for the following services: workforce planning, job restructuring, recruitment and assessment of potential employees, pre-employment training, customized training, on-the-job training, post-employment services, work experience, and innovative forms of worksite training (NINATEC, 2015, p. 15).

Several federal, state, and Native organizations have tried and are trying their hand at remedying the confounded situation tribal communities often seem to find themselves in, and the realization that workforce education is one of the keys to breaking the combination of underdevelopment and un-/underemployment is to put an emphasis on workforce education. Rather than sovereignty being a requirement for successful workforce education, the latter is actually a component in strengthening and preserving sovereignty. This attitude can be seen in a statement by The Leadership Conference on Civil and Human Rights (2015), which makes a clear connection between workforce education and equal opportunity: "Equal opportunity has helped American Indians in the workforce, allowing American Indian women and men greater access to higher paying jobs and new employment fields" (para. 13).

At the national level, perhaps unsurprisingly, the Bureau of Indian Affairs (BIA) is a major service provider. In addition to administering services and programs offered by other government departments, the BIA Division of Workforce Development offers training in building trades in partnership with the Building Trades Association and highway construction training, manages the ironworker training program, and administers job placement and economic development opportunities (U.S. Department of the Interior, 2015). The National Indian and Native American Employment and Training Conference (NINAETC) bills itself as "the largest and most representative national Indian and Native American employment and training association" (NINAETC, 2015, p. 3). The association wishes to act as a sort of clearinghouse for information on employment and training, celebrate successes in workforce preparation, and serve as a place where workforce training providers can exchange ideas and work together for the benefit of their clients. Two other organizations, although not exclusively American Indian, also support tribal business and workforce development. The National Center for American Indian Enterprise Development (NCAIED) has the following mission: "Develop and expand an American Indian private sector which employs Indian labor, increases the number of viable tribal and individual Indian businesses, and positively impacts and involves reservation communities, by establishing business relationships between Indian enterprises and private industry" (NCAIED, 2015, para. 2). Through its Procurement Technical Assistance Center (PTAC), the NCAIED hopes to assist American Indian business in finding and responding to invitations to bid for contracts from federal, state, or private entities. In addition to the support provided by the NCAIED, the U.S. Chamber of Commerce's Native American Enterprise Initiative focuses on regulatory issues that may impede tribal businesses in Indian Country (U.S. Chamber, 2015).

At the tribal level, a number of tribes have programs and departments dealing with workforce development. The Navajo Nation Department of Workforce Development, for example, a WIA Section 166 grantee, provides work experience placements, vocational training, and other kinds of assistance through the administration of the Native Employment Works (NEW), WIA Youth, and WIA Adult programs (Navajo Nation Department of Workforce Development, n.d.). Cherokee Nation Career Services states its mission like this: "[T]o develop and encourage individuals to achieve and maintain work habits and skills that promote employability and self-sufficiency through programs encompassing education, training, rehabilitation and supportive services" (Cherokee Nation, 2015, para. 1). To that end, the department offers skills assessment; career literacy; training in building trades, business technology, child care, medical coding, and surgical technology; support for students enrolled in career programs at area colleges and CTE centers; daily on-the-job training to acquire occupational skills; and vocational rehabilitation. The Nation participates in the Talking Leaves Job Corps program that provides technical training to young people ages 16–24. Job placement through Cherokee Career Connections is also available (Cherokee Nation, 2015).

Smaller tribes offer such services as well. The Ketchikan Indian Community in Alaska, for example, wishes to "develop and expand vocational training opportunities in high-demand occupations relevant to our tribal community and Alaska; provide progressive classroom training to strengthen tribal members' basic employment skills, encourage professional development, and to foster entrepreneurship" (Ketchikan Indian Community, 2012, para. 2). Programs offered include career readiness training and preparation for the National Career Readiness Certificate, an apprenticeship program, vocational training grants, employment assistance, and a summer training and employment program for young people ages 14–17. Some small tribes unable to offer or administer programs themselves have formed workforce consortia such as the Inter Tribal Council of Arizona (ITAC), which represents 21 tribal nations and administers WIA funds for eight of them (ITAC, 2015). Another Arizona consortium is the Nineteen Tribal Nations Workforce Investment Board (NTNWIB), which wants to establish a connection between economic and workforce development to "support tribal economics, and improve the quality of life for Native Americans" (NTN-WIB, 2014, p. 4). Recognizing that tribal governments are often the only employers on or near reservations, the NTNWIB wishes to encourage all 19 tribes to collaborate in an effort to help tribal members avoid long-term paraeconomic survival.

Statewide initiatives exist as well. The North Carolina Commission of Indian Affairs, housed within the State of North Carolina Department of Administration, a WIOA grantee, wants to help American Indian residents of the state acquire workplace skills, make them able to be competitive applicants for work, and work toward community economic development and individual self-sufficiency (Commission of Indian Affairs, 2012). Another example of a state program that is also funded through WIOA are the State of Washington's Workforce Board's (2015) Native American programs, which feature the same WIAO approved goals as the North Carolina Commission of Indian Affairs. In a different kind of approach, the North Dakota Department of Commerce through its workforce development program offers grants to tribal colleges to build programs that teach students workplace skills and make them competitive for those jobs where shortages exist in the state (North Dakota Department of Commerce, 2015). Not all programs at the state level are offered through or administered by state governments, however. An example of a state-level non-governmental organization is the California Indian Manpower Consortium, Inc. Its Native American Workforce Investment Council exists to help the consortium develop and deliver skills training for American Indians and also helps qualified American Indian workers find and apply for jobs (California Indian Manpower Consortium, 2015).

As for local programs, Wascalus (2012) discussed several that are active within the Ninth District of the Federal Reserve Bank "to increase work preparedness, education levels, and employment rates in the communities they serve" (para. 3). Programs mentioned are the creation of a workbook by an organization from Havre, Montana, that helps people acquire so-called soft skills and understand workplace rules; the American Indian Opportunities Industrialization Center in Minneapolis, Minnesota, that offers training programs for a range of occupations and other employment services; fast-track programs at United Tribes Technical College (UTTC) in Bismarck, North Dakota; and the creation of reservation centers by Nicolet College in Rhinelander, Wisconsin, to help students overcome issues of geographic isolation. The purpose of any such program was best expressed by Dave Archambault, UTTC workforce director for the Tribal College Consortium for Developing Montana and North Dakota Workforce:

> Training people relatively quickly and getting them into the workforce allows them to become self-sufficient. We're building an American Indian workforce that will be less dependent and will have the ability to support themselves and their families. They'll have pride in who they

are and what they do. By developing this untapped workforce, we'll create change in Indian Country in a positive way.

(Wascalus, 2012, p. 4)

To say it in Vizenor's (1976) terminology, Archambault hoped to train people so that they could be more than paraeconomic survivors.

Additional examples of local programs can be cited as well. The Southern California Indian Center (SCIC) from Fountain Valley, California, wants to "assist individuals gain and retain employment" (SCIC, n.d., para. 1). To that end, it offers career assessments, resume writing, job readiness training, and job search and placement services. A similar center, the United Indians of All Tribes Foundation, exists in King County, Washington. Services include work experience placements, job and career counseling, job placement assistance, and vocational training (United Indians of All Tribes Foundation, 2015). Some programs can also be regional. The Tribal College Consortium for Developing Montana and North Dakota Workforce (TCC DeMaND Workforce) is a regional program funded by the U.S. Department of Labor to reduce unemployment among American Indians in the two states and work with colleges, employers, and communities to build training capacities and identify best practices in workforce preparation (Woodke, 2014).

Although many programs and initiatives exist to encourage and support workforce education for American Indians, Manzanares and Thaler (1998) cautioned that there is no easy solution to economic development and that each piece of a system must be built separately. To do so, workforce education professionals and planners must be familiar with the current conditions on reservations and in tribal communities and work to modify such conditions as to allow people to obtain skills and services. The chapters in this book want to supply some of the pieces of this puzzle by identifying the current conditions and focusing on how workforce education can be a boon to tribal sovereignty and help avoid a long-term quagmire of paraeconomic survival.

Jon Reyhner, a national expert on American Indian education, begins this volume with an overview of what vocational or workforce education for American Indians has historically been like and how this history still shapes negative perceptions today. Charles Saunders then extends this discussion by focusing on the challenges faced by American Indians interested in obtaining skills for better employment and how these challenges influence the choices people make about their education. Charlotte Leforestier takes this argument yet another step further, tying vocational education of the past to positive developments such as retribalization and pan-Indianism that are cornerstones of tribally controlled education and have influenced the tribal college movement.

Other contributors then focus on the role of tribal colleges in moving past paraeconomic survival and ensuring that workforce education is available to all American Indians, even those with major obstacles to access. John

Goodwin shows how workforce education, economic development, tribal sovereignty, and tribal educational control are linked and have contributed to the existence of tribal colleges. Amy Fann, Linda Sue Warner, and G. S. Briscoe then focus on another type of institution, the Native American-Serving Non-Tribal Institution (NASNTI), and show how the inclusion of tradition at a NASNTI in Oklahoma has helped strengthen workforce education and economic development. Delilah O'Haynes then, realizing that tribal colleges at present serve only 6.33% of all post-secondary American Indian students (American Indian College Fund, 2011; National Indian Education Association, 2015) and that many students will continue to be taught by non-Indian instructors, workforce education teachers, planners, and other professionals can be successful only if they have a deep understanding of the history on Indian-white relations and approach program development with a sensitivity regarding that knowledge.

Carsten Schmidtke continues the discussion by focusing on career counseling and development and reviewing approaches that professionals can use to provide appropriate and useful advice to American Indian students trying to decide on a career and career path. J. K. Payden Spowart and E. Anne Marshall then look at the specific life circumstances and experiences of young men as they search for work and for a career and discuss the implications of such experiences for career development. Finally, Jennifer Pharr and Michelle Chino discuss one specific example of workforce development, the public health workforce, and the challenges in training enough workers to serve the needs of tribes and communities.

This volume closes with a final chapter of my conclusions about the future of workforce development for American Indians and its role in tribal sovereignty and economic development.

A WORD ON TERMINOLOGY

A variety of terms has been used and is being used in research about American Indians. Depending on the preference of authors, publishers, and journals, terms such as Indian, American Indian, Native American, indigenous, tribal, aboriginal, Native, First Nation, and others may be found. In addition to the different terms, capitalization practices may also vary as the terms indigenous, tribal, aboriginal, and native appear variously as capitalized or not capitalized. Mihesuah (2005) stated that she prefers "Indigenous" or "Native" because of their political implications. She also referred anyone interested in issues surrounding terminology to an article by Michael Yellow Bird (see below for complete reference).

The chapter authors of this volume have used several of the terms mentioned above and at times used more than one term in the same chapter. To allow each contributor to this volume to use the terminology with which he or she is most at ease, the different chapters have preserved each contributors choice of terms, spelling, and capitalization.

REFERENCES

American Indian College Fund. (2011). *Facts about American Indian education.* Retrieved from http://www.collegefund.org/userfiles/2011_FactSheet.pdf

Austin, A. (2013, December 17). *High unemployment means Native Americans are still waiting for an economic recovery.* Economic Policy Institute. Retrieved from http://www.epi.org/publication/high-unemployment-means-native-americans/

California Indian Manpower Consortium, Inc. (2015). *Native American Workforce Investment Council.* Retrieved from http://www.cimcinc.org/NAWIC%20List.pdf

Champagne, D. (2007). *Social change and cultural continuity among native nations.* Lanham, MD: AltaMira Press.

Cherokee Nation. (2015). *Career.* Retrieved from http://www.cherokee.org/Services/Career.aspx

DeWeaver, N. (2014, August). *Indian workers and the reservation labor market.* Retrieved from https://doe.state.wy.us/lmi/LAUS/LM-dynamics-in-reservation-areas-9-1-14.pdf

Eastman, C. A. (1971). *Indian boyhood.* New York, NY: Dover. (Original work published in 1902)

Fixico, D. L. (2008). *American Indians in a modern world.* Lanham, MD: AltaMira Press.

Grey, K.C., & Herr, E.L. (1998). *Workforce education: The basics.* Boston, MA: Allyn and Bacon.

Inter Tribal Council of Arizona. (2015). *Workforce Investment Act program.* Retrieved from http://itcaonline.com/?page_id=120

Ketchikan Indian Community. (2012). *Workforce development.* Retrieved from http://kictribe.org/programs/chas/employment/index.html

The Leadership Conference on Civil and Human Rights. (2015). *Equal opportunity and American Indians—Fact sheet.* Retrieved from http://www.civilrights.org/equal-opportunity/fact-sheets/American-indians.html

Manzanares, E., & Thaler, D. (1998, April). *Toward a comprehensive workforce development system for the Oglala Nation.* Cambridge, MA: John F. Kennedy School of Government, Harvard University.

Mihesuah, D. (2005). *So you want to write about American Indians? A guide for writers, students, and scholars.* Lincoln, NE: University of Nebraska Press.

The National Center for American Indian Enterprise Development. (2015). *About the NCAIED.* Retrieved from http://ncaied.org/about-ncaied/

National Congress of American Indians. (2013a). *Securing our futures.* Washington, DC: Author.

National Congress of American Indians. (2013b). *Workforce development and job creation.* Washington, DC: Author.

National Indian and Native American Employment and Training Conference. (2015a). *Welcome to NINAETC.* Retrieved from http://www.ninaetc.net/index.htm

National Indian and Native American Employment and Training Conference. (2015b). *Subtitle D-national programs section 166 Native American programs: WIA/WIOA final rules side-by-side comparison.* Retrieved from http://www.ninaetc.net/WIA_Sec166_Final_Rules_v_WIOA_Proposed_07.pdf

National Indian Education Association. (2015). *Statistics on Native students.* Retrieved from http://www.niea.org/research/statistics.aspx

Native American Employment and Training Council. (2009). *Workforce Investment Act. Native American Employment and Training Council. Recommendation for Department of Labor transition team and Dr. Edward Montgomery*. Washington, DC: Author.

Native American Employment and Training Council. (2013). *2009–2012 chair report*. Washington, DC: Author.

Navajo Nation Department of Workforce Development. (n.d.). *Preparing the Navajo workforce for better and new jobs*. Retrieved from http://www.ndwd.org/

North Dakota Department of Commerce, Workforce Development. (2015). *Tribal college grants*. Retrieved from http://www.workforce.nd.gov/workforce/tcg/

Olson, J. S., & Wilson, R. (1984). *Native Americans in the twentieth century*. Urbana and Chicago, IL: University of Illinois Press.

Roleff, T. L. (Ed.). (1998). *Native American rights*. San Diego, CA: Greenhaven Press.

Southern California Indian Center, Inc. (n.d.). *Workforce Investment Act (WIA)/ workforce development and training program*. Retrieved from http://www.indiancenter.org/-workforce-developmentworkforce-investment-act-wia.html

Standing Bear, L. (1988). *My Indian boyhood*. Lincoln, NE: University of Nebraska Press. (Original work published in 1931)

State of North Carolina, Department of Administration, Commission of Indian Affairs. (2012). *Programs and services: American Indian workforce development program*. Retrieved from http://www.doa.nc.gov/cia/progr-aiwdp.aspx

United Indians of All Tribes Foundation. (2015). *Native workforce service program*. Retrieved from http://www.unitedindians.org/programs/daybreak-star-preschool/native-workforce-service-program/

United States Department of the Interior, Indian Affairs. (2015). *Division of workforce development*. Retrieved from http://www.bia.gov/WhoWeAre/BIA/OIS/DWD/index.htm

United States Department of Labor, Employment and Training Administration. (2010). *Indian Employment, Training and Related Services Demonstration Act of 1992*. Retrieved from http://www.doleta.gov/regs/statutes/pl477.cfm

United States Department of Labor, Employment and Training Administration, Division of Indian and Native American Programs. (2015). *Welcome to the DINAP "partnership" home page!* Retrieved from http://www.doleta.gov/dinap/

United States Department of Labor, Employment and Training Administration, Office of Workforce Investment. (2013). *Mission and function statements*. Retrieved from http://www.doleta.gov/etainfo/wrksys/dinap.cfm

United States Department of Labor, Employment and Training Administration, Office of Workforce Investment, Division of Indian and Native American Programs. (2013). *Charter for the Native American Employment and Training Council*. Washington, DC: Author.

U.S. Chamber of Commerce. (2015). *Native American enterprise initiative*. Retrieved from https://www.uschamber.com/native-american-enterprise-initiative

Vizenor, G. (1976). *Tribal scenes and ceremonies*. Minneapolis, MN: The Nodin Press.

Wascalus, J. (2012, Jul 1). Spanning the spectrum of Native workforce development. *Community Dividend*. Federal Reserve Bank of Minneapolis. Retrieved from http://www.minneapolisfed.org/publications/community-dividend/spanning-the-spectrum-of-native-workforce-development

Woodke, L. (2014, Dec.). *TCC DeMaND workforce project annual evaluation report: Year three*. Retrieved from http://demandworkforce.com/data/upfiles/media/DeMaND%20Evaluation%20Annual%20Report%20Y3_2.pdf

Workforce Training and Education Coordinating Board. (2015). *Native American programs*. Retrieved from http://www.wtb.wa.gov/NativeAmericanPrograms_Dir..asp

Yellow Bird, M. (1999). What we want to be called: Indigenous peoples' perspectives on racial and ethnic identity labels. *American Indian Quarterly, 23*(2), 1–21.

1 A History of American Indian Vocational Education

Jon Reyhner

American Indian education has been described as a "national tragedy," and some of the poorest counties and highest unemployment and poverty rates in the United States encompass Indian reservations (*KIDS COUNT*, 2012; Special Subcommittee, 1969). Sherman Alexie (2007) in his young adult novel *The Absolutely True Diary of a Part-Time Indian* fictionalizes his actual experience living on the Spokane Indian Reservation and leaving the underperforming school he attended there to go to a rural off-reservation school with a more demanding curriculum. Alexie's portrayal of the bleakness of reservation life and its lack of opportunities presents a daunting challenge to anyone seeking to improve life for America's Indigenous population.

The No Child Left Behind (NCLB) Act of 2001 passed in the United States sought to close the gap between the long-term academic performance of American Indians and other non-Asian minority groups. However, a decade later, after tens of millions of dollars have been spent, that gap still exists (National, 2012). A study by the National Indian Education Association found that changes made under NCLB that stressed teaching language and math were only leading to making schooling "increasingly boring and disconnected from student lives" (NIEA, 2005, p. 6). This is a serious charge given that boredom is the most frequent reason American Indians and other students give for dropping out of school, and American Indians have one of the highest dropout rates of any U.S. ethnic group (Faircloth & Tippeconnic, 2010; Reyhner, 1992). There is nothing new about the decontextualization of academic information in schools serving American Indians and others. Francis Leupp, U.S. commissioner of Indian affairs from 1905–1909, recalled this:

> [T]he more intelligent teachers in the Indian Service are ignoring books as far as they can in the earlier stages of their work. They are teaching elementary mathematics with feathers, or pebbles, or grains of corn; then the relations of numbers to certain symbols on the blackboard are made clear, and thus the pupils are led along almost unconsciously from point to point. Had a system like this been in vogue twenty years ago, an Indian who became a bank teller would have been spared a confession he once made to me, that he had reached a full man's estate before

he understood why he multiplied four by five in order to find out how much four pounds of sugar would cost at five cents a pound! Throughout his school life he had been an expert mathematician, yet figures meant nothing to him but so many pure abstractions which could be put through sundry operations mechanically; they bore no relation in his mind to any concrete object in nature.

(Leupp, 1910, pp. 127–28)

As Bruner (1996) points out, educators need to think about not just their subject matter but also how to teach in a way that answers student questions like, "What am I doing here anyway? What's this to do with *me*?" (p. 98 [emphasis in original]). Educators also need to consider the claims of Carnoy (1972, 1974) and others that schools and especially their vocational education programs are designed to keep the poor in their place and elites in power. Academically oriented education is the vocational education needed for business, law, medicine, and other higher-paying positions. Too often schooling was part of a program of "European settlers . . . [degrading] the Indian into an assigned state of savagery in order to delegitimize his right to stay on the land" (Carnoy, 1974, p. 271).

Brazilian educator Paulo Freire (1990/1968), among others (e.g., Cummins, 1992), describes a low-quality, passive transmission/banking/memorization model of education often provided to children living in poverty, including American Indian children, that is a one-way delivery of information from teacher to student. In contrast, students from wealthy families often receive an active "problem-posing" education where political and social issues affecting students and their families are integrated into the curriculum. The latter active approach is more likely to combat student boredom by engaging and motivating students through connecting what goes on in the classroom to their lives outside of the classroom as well as to their home culture through place-, community-, and culture-based curriculum (e.g., Reyhner, 2015; Reyhner et al., 2011).

HIGH EXPECTATIONS

Teachers are currently being told to have high expectations for their students and that all students should be prepared for and go to college. However, as far back as the 1950s it was pointed out by Orata (1953a) that "[i]n many countries today there are thousands upon thousands of high-school and college graduates who are good only for certain types of white-collar jobs, which are over-crowded" (pp. 277–278). United Nations Educational, Scientific and Cultural Organization (UNESCO) associate Orata, an immigrant from the Philippines educated in American universities, wrote *Fundamental Education in an Amerindian Community* (1953b), printed as part of the vocational program at the U.S. government's Indian Office's (renamed the Bureau of Indian Affairs in 1947) Haskell Institute. In it he described his experiences as principal of the Little Wound School on the Pine Ridge Reservation in South Dakota in 1936–37. He described fundamental education as "education for better living" and education as being the "process of transition from book learning to learning by doing" (Orata, 1953a, p. 277). Orata saw not only that there were too few jobs for youths who just got "book learning" in school but also that education often left them unfit for life in their home communities. In contrast, Paulo Freire's well-known efforts to educate the poor in Brazil and Chile focused on basic literacy and issues of immediate concern to illiterate adult students (Kirkendall, 2010).

High academic expectations can lead to everyone's aspiring for their children to be doctors, lawyers, or other well-paid prestigious professionals who do not get their hands "dirty" with manual labor. As a result, feelings of being discriminated against arise if education does not focus on academics. Vocational education is too often viewed as second-class and as a continuation of the historic discrimination against people of color and ethnic minorities. Because education provided by the U.S. government has been repeatedly criticized over the years for having racially motivated low expectations for American Indian students, pushing anything but an academic curriculum can be viewed as racist.

However, teachers, especially those with little or no understanding of the home life of their students, face a dilemma when ethnic minority students often enter their classrooms already far behind academically. This challenge is compounded when students are American Indians and their teachers have little or no understanding of Indigenous cultures and of what things can be used to motivate these students. The result can be racist low expectations based on disappointing experiences interacting with these students in class as Alexie (2007) describes. In the early years of Indian education, the challenges faced by teachers included students not speaking English. This is usually not a problem today, but students can still come from homes with few books or other reading material, and their vocabularies can be relatively small and reflect an "Indian English" dialect. High academic expectations, therefore, come into conflict with classroom realities and students who can be much more interested in basketball and other sports than academics (Colton, 2000; Peshkin, 1997).

AMERICAN INDIAN EDUCATIONAL HISTORY

In contrast to the English-only approach to schooling American Indian students that has been the prevalent practice since colonial times in the United States, the authors of the 1953 UNESCO monograph *The Use of Vernacular Languages in Education* took this position:

> We take it as axiomatic that every child of school age should attend school and that every illiterate should be made literate. We take it as

axiomatic, too, that the best medium for teaching is the mother tongue of the pupil.

(UNESCO, 1953, p. 6)

They thought that the mother tongue should be used as long as possible and that mother-tongue instruction leads to better understanding between home and school. However, where are the mother-tongue-literate teachers and mother-tongue curriculum materials to achieve this, especially with 300 or so Indigenous languages still spoken in North America? A recognition of the situation where American Indian students often started school not speaking English, even into the middle of the 20th century, has to be accompanied by the fact that most Indigenous languages lacked orthographies and written literature. Nor were there many teachers who were literate in these languages or spoke them. This fact made it difficult, to say the least, to offer non-English-speaking Indigenous children an education equal to what non-Indian students were receiving. In addition, even most non-Indian students did not go to high school in the 19th century and the first part of 20th century. However, what could be accomplished, at least for a time, can be seen in Hawaii where children in the 19th century were successfully taught with textbooks written in the Hawaiian language until American adventurers overthrew the Hawaiian monarchy and English-only instruction was mandated (Wilson & Kamanā, 2006).

Most colonists and missionaries who came to America saw Indigenous cultures as savage and Indigenous people as less intelligent, and their languages were viewed as incapable of expressing higher, complex thoughts. If Indigenous children were to get schooling at all, an English-only and simplified curriculum was seen as all that these simple people could handle. Thus the call for vocational education for American Indian students was too often associated with the idea that they are racially inferior and not capable of higher education. Some missionaries realized that if they wanted to convert Indigenous peoples, they would have more success teaching Christianity using their Native language, but many held to the idea that these "primitive" languages were the languages the Devil spoke (e.g., Perley, 2011) or could not handle sophisticated Christian concepts (e.g., Crews & Starbuck, 2010). Such an attitude, of course, could antagonize their potential converts.

In the 19th century there was an emphasis on "industrial schools" because American Indians, along with many other ethnic minorities, were often stereotyped as lazy, in need of discipline, and less intelligent by European immigrants and their descendants who through ethnocentric and racist lenses viewed the Indigenous peoples of the Americas as savages with nothing of value in their cultures. Missionary teachers tended to see that the purpose of schooling was to "civilize" Indians by converting them to their particular brand of Christianity and to dress, live, talk, and look as much as possible like the immigrants from Europe (e.g., Bowden, 1981; Reyhner & Eder, 2004).

As American Indians were confined by the U.S. army to reservations under the control of U.S.-government-appointed Indian agents in the 19th century, agency farmers and blacksmiths were supplied to help Indians shift from hunting to farming. European immigrants held an ideal of the industrious yeoman farmer along with the stereotype of the lazy savage Indian who would either vanish before the onslaught of "civilization" or learn the value of work and civilization in industrial schools that focused on teaching English and preparing Indian males to become farmers or work in farm-related vocations and Indian females to be homemakers.

The most famous of these schools was Carlisle Indian Industrial School established in Carlisle, Pennsylvania, in 1879. Richard Henry Pratt, an army officer and the school's founder, recognized that among Pennsylvania Quakers, Mennonites, and Moravians, his students would experience less racial prejudice than in other areas of the country. With Carlisle, the U.S. government began moving away from funding Christian denominational schools and to directly operating a school system that focused on removing American Indian students from what most educators, policy makers, and the non-Indian public saw as the regressive influence of their families and communities by putting them in boarding schools. Both to reduce the cost of educating and to give students practical skills, the curriculum at Carlisle and the subsequently established boarding schools had a half-day academic curriculum and a half-day vocational curriculum. Figure 2.1 shows an example of this curriculum. Just as it is hard today to get taxpayers to fund education programs, especially for other people's children, it was hard back then, and the half-day vocational education programs in Indian boarding schools often became just child labor to maintain the schools and feed and clothe the students (Reyhner & Eder, 2004).

Besides its on-campus academic and vocational programs and two nearby farms, Carlisle also placed older students in non-Indian homes where Pratt hoped they would be treated the same as the farmer's children and would directly experience civilization. Pratt was an ardent advocate of cultural assimilation and hoped Carlisle students would never return home. Mike Burns (Yavapai) is an example of Carlisle's Outing Program ideal until he went back home. Burns (2002) wrote in his autobiography how he volunteered to participate in Carlisle's Outing Program because then he could go to school all day at a public school rather than just getting half-day academics at Carlisle. In Ohio at his outing placement, he was offered land and a white wife if he stayed, but he chose instead to return west in 1884.

In 1887 the U.S. congress passed an allotment act to break up Indian reservations with the idea that with their loss of communal lands, allotted Indians would be forced to become farmers on 160 acres or less of land, and students needed to learn how to farm these allotments if they were not to live off government annuities and succumb to the accompanying demoralization that often went with dependence on the government. Agrarian America held a patriarchal ideal of a farmer who cultivated the land while

20   Jon Reyhner

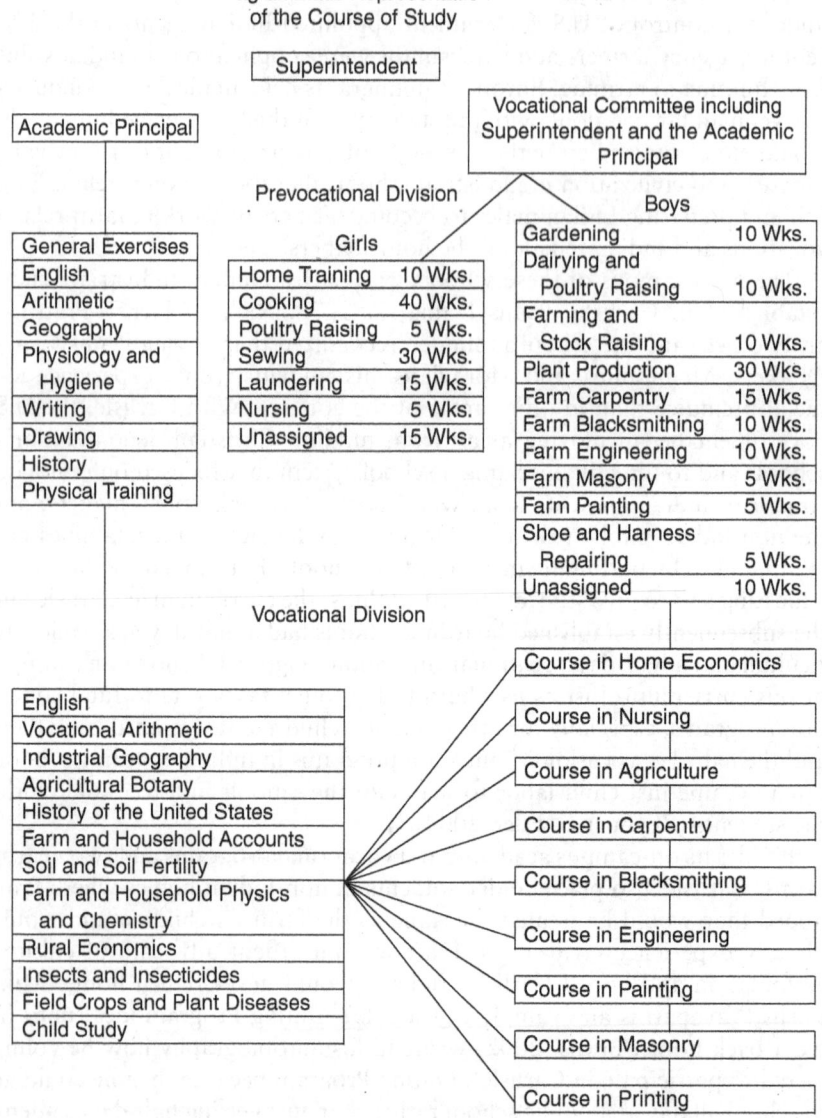

Figure 2.1 Diagrammatic representation of the Course of Study. From the 1917 *Annual Report of the Commissioner of Indian Affairs.*

a helpmate wife took care of his home and children. This ideal was promulgated in both Indian and non-Indian schools.

In 1901 Estelle Reel, superintendent of Indian schools in the Office of Indian Affairs, issued a 276-page "outline," *Course of Study for the Indian Schools of the United States: Industrial and Literary,* which was also exported to the new American colony in the Philippines when Dr. Orata was just entering school there. It was organized in alphabetical order, starting with agriculture and arithmetic and ending with tailoring, teachers' reading course, upholstering, and writing. It displayed the influence of the government's assimilationist policies and educational ideas of Froebel, Rousseau, Pestalozzi, and Comenius:

> The aim of the course is to give the Indian child a knowledge of the English language and to equip him with the ability to become self-supporting as soon as possible. . . . The value of education must be measured by its contribution to life interests, and it is our purpose to fit the Indian pupil for life. . . . The child learns to speak the English language through doing the work that must be accomplished in any well regulated home, and, at the same time is being trained in habits of industry, cleanliness, and system. He learns to read by telling of his daily interests and work with the chalk on the blackboard. In dealing with barrels of fruit, bushels of wheat, yards of gingham, and quarts of milk; in keeping count of his poultry and in measuring his garden, he becomes familiar with numbers in such a practical way he knows how to use them in daily life, as well as on the blackboard in the schoolroom.
> (*Course of Study*, 1901, pp. 5–6)

According to historian K. Tsianina Lomawaima (1996), the *Course of Study* reflected Reel's limited view of Indian capabilities in its concentration on domestic and manual labor training, and it received widespread praise from influential writers of the day, including Charles F. Lummis and George Bird Grinnell. However, former Commissioner of Indian Affairs T. J. Morgan condemned it: "Now why should the national government offer to its wards so much less in the way of schooling than is offered by the States to the pupils in the public schools" (as cited in Prucha, 1984, p. 828). Reel's curriculum not only underestimated Indian abilities but also did not reflect the rapid transition America was undergoing from a predominantly rural, agrarian country of farmers to an increasingly urban, industrialized society of factory workers.

However, even agricultural instruction in boarding schools could be problematic for Indian students who wanted to become farmers. Leo Crane, Indian agent for the Hopis, concluded that Hopi parents "know a thousand times more than the white instructor for agriculture, and have demonstrated it to his discomfiture; and therefore they are suspicious or contemptuous of all other white instructors" (RSS #24, 1917, p. 66). Because of climate and soil differences, farming in Carlisle, Pennsylvania, was very different from dryland farming in much of the western United States.

By 1902, the U.S. government had opened 24 boarding schools in the West and Midwest with a total enrollment of 9,736 students. The new schools had a curriculum similar to Carlisle's and were also run as military schools like Carlisle where students wore uniforms and were marched around, but they were not as well funded. In the new schools student outings tended to turn into menial labor in non-Indian homes for girls and on non-Indian farms for boys (Trennert, 1988).

In 1907 gendered training at Sherman Institute, a U.S. government Indian boarding school in Riverside, California, included having boys take landscape gardening, agriculture, stock raising, vegetable gardening, poultry, dairying, steam cooking, printing, shoemaking, harness making, baking, laundry, cleaning, tailoring, care of horses, carpentry, blacksmithing, and engineering. Girls were offered dressmaking, sewing, regular cooking, nursing, dining room service, laundry, housekeeping, farm housework, farm cooking, and art needlework (Paxton, 2006). In 1933 Sherman Institute was offering a cosmetology program that came to replace its nursing program.

Indian agents reported in 1917 that the equipment such as steam presses that students were trained to operate in off-reservation boarding schools was not available at home. They found that the individual craftsmanship in harness making, blacksmithing, printing, carpentry, masonry, and other trades offered at boarding schools was outdated. A student commented to the superintendent of the Taholah, Washington, agency, "I graduated in scrubbing and they teach nothing else" (RSS #24, 1917, p. 157).

Lomawaima (1994) offers a picture of the industrial training provided at government boarding schools in her history of Chilocco Indian School in Oklahoma. In 1927, 12 boys in Chilocco's bakery baked "2,000 loaves, 2,000 buns, 900 cinnamon rolls, 220 pies, 900 cookies, 900 slices of gingerbread and cake, and 1,800 pieces of cornbread" weekly. Its laundry in 1931 processed "475,000 towels; 98,000 sheets; 35,000 shirts; and tens of thousands of nightgowns, pillowcases, bloomers, and long underwear" (p. 68). She concluded from her study, "Much of the work subsumed under 'trades training' could fairly be called drudge work, with little or no educational value," but it did lower the cost of running the school (pp. 68–69). A Chilocco student in the 1920s recalled the following:

> I'll never know whether I volunteered or was assigned the Dairy Barn.... I found out later that was probably the least desired assignment as far as vocational was concerned. Really it wasn't that bad.... [I]t was a lot of fun, but it was a lot of hard work.... We milked forty-five cows, I believe, twice a day. We also fed 'em, put up feed and mended the fences, separated the cream, they had automatic milkers incidentally, and I guess the prize job down there was being a milker.... They put us in a dormitory of our own, and the night watchman would wake us up at 3:30 in the morning and we'd milk the cows.
> (Lomawaima, 1994, p. 74)

In the early 1920s Chilocco's school superintendent noted:

> Half of the vocational girls are detailed to the sewing room. Of the remaining half, five-eighths are assigned to the laundry, the balance

divided among kitchen, dining room and homes. Not more than one-fourth of the kitchen detail is vocational so that at all times there are enough prevocational girls to keep the work going. As a result, we have a large detail of vocational and a small detail of prevocational girls in the sewing room and laundry. . . . Prevocational girls entering Chilocco are always assigned to the kitchen/dining room if they are large enough. A double detail of kitchen/dining room girls work before breakfast, after breakfast and after supper.

(Lomawaima, 1994, p. 84)

Alumni interviewed by Lomawaima (1994) recalled Chilocco as a place where they "learned to work" (p. 71). Anne Phelps Kopta, who taught at Phoenix Indian School from 1908 to 1918, wrote in her introduction to the autobiography of one of her Pima Indian students:

Her experience with academic subjects was extremely satisfactory. The courses of study at the school were not designed to make whites of Indians, as is sometimes charged, but to give young Indian students a basic education in the three R's, to acquaint them with the rudiments of many different trades, and to introduce them to the world off the Indian reservation.

(Shaw, 1974, p. xiii)

While most students in Indian boarding schools never graduated, exceptionally talented students who learned in English quickly or who entered already knowing English were often encouraged to further their education. At Carlisle, for example, advanced students could take classes at nearby Dickinson College. The Indian Office's largest boarding schools had normal (teacher training) departments and commercial and nursing programs. To help find employment for graduates of these programs, the commissioner of Indian affairs started an employment bureau in 1905 headed by Charles Dagenett, a member of the Peoria tribe and a Carlisle graduate (Vuckovic, 2008).

In 1907 Sherman Institute in California started a three-year student nurses training program that lasted until 1956. Caring for sick students, nursing students learned about healthy living and spread their knowledge to fellow students through weekly public health articles in the school newspaper, *The Sherman Bulletin*, for many years. Because Sherman did not offer the chemistry and biology high school courses required for students to become registered nurses, the program had its limits. Sherman's program helped lead the way to Chemawa (in Salem, Oregon) and Haskell (in Lawrence, Kansas) Indian boarding schools getting nursing programs in 1921 and Chilocco (in Oklahoma) and Albuquerque (in New Mexico) in 1927. Through a cooperative agreement with the Minnesota Board of Nursing, Haskell's program was able to prepare students to be registered nurses (Keller, 2012).

With the closing of Carlisle in 1917, Haskell Institute became the U.S. government's flagship boarding school. An example of a student in

Haskell's Normal Department is Esther Burnett Horne, who participated in its teacher training program and was recruited in 1929 while still a student to teach at Eufaula Boarding School because of a teacher shortage. She went on to teach at Wahpeton Indian School from 1930 to 1965 where her husband, whom she met at Haskell, worked in the school's power plant, using training he received at Haskell. During the summer of 1936, she did demonstration teaching at Indian Office teacher inservices (Horne & McBeth, 1998).

THE INDIAN OFFICE'S EDUCATION PROGRAM UNDER REVIEW

Vocational education continued to be a major part of Indian education into the 1950s; however, boarding schools and the U.S. government's treatment of Indians generally came under intense criticism in the 1920s, leading to an independent study by the Brookings Institute, which published its results in 1928. Popularly called the "Meriam Report" after Lewis Meriam, the director of the study, it was critical of many aspects of the Indian Office's educational programs. This criticism included its half-day vocational education programs where students were taught to use machines that were not available back on their reservations and learn crafts that were rapidly being outdated. America was going through a radical change from a rural farming nation to an urban industrial nation at the end of the 19th and beginning of the 20th century. The report pointed out that no surveys were done to find out what skills the available jobs for Indian school graduates required, and it noted that harness making was still being taught in the 1920s, but not auto repair:

> Agriculture at an Indian school is rarely taught in terms of what the Indian boy will need when he gets out. The old notion persists that farming is a desirable occupation into which more people should be sent, whereas the Department of Agriculture has recently issued warnings to the effect that there are already too many persons engaged in certain kinds of agriculture; but in Indian schools institutional needs for farm products are so immediately pressing that production becomes almost the only aim.
> (Meriam, 1928, pp. 384–385)

AN INDIAN NEW DEAL

The election of Franklin D. Roosevelt as president of the United States in 1932 brought a shift in Indian policy known as the "Indian New Deal." Responding to the criticism of the Meriam Report, the Indian New Deal placed less emphasis on assimilating Indians into mainstream America and gave more support for Indian self-determination, including the freedom to maintain their traditional cultures. In addition, under Roosevelt there was more emphasis on "learning by doing" as advocated by John Dewey and other Progressive educators. Willard Beatty, president of the Progressive Education Association, who had attended a model vocational high school in San Francisco, was appointed Director of the Indian Office's education programs in 1936 (Stefon, 2009). Another example of the shift was the hiring of anthropologists who studied American Indians and were often admirers of their cultures to help guide Indian Office policies. Another example is the hiring of Pedro A. Orata for the 1936–37 school year to lead one reservation day school in a new direction, asking the Indian community what they wanted for their children and focusing education on what could be done for immediate community improvement, something Orata and others termed "fundamental education." This included the idea that a solely academic/textbook/lecture-oriented educational approach was too disconnected from the lives of students, which often led to students' not seeing its value and dropping out of school.

During World War II the U.S. government found that some Indians and many Navajos had never been to school at all and spoke little or no English, and after the war a special five-year program was started for teenagers who had not been to school. Navajo translators were provided in classrooms, and the curriculum was very beginning in nature. In their fourth year at Sherman, these students had 21 vocations to choose from, including agriculture, baking, dry-cleaning, home and general service, masonry, metalwork, painting, welding, operating a metal machine, and being a gas station attendant (Ille, 2012).

TERMINATION AND SELF-DETERMINATION

After World War II there was a conservative reaction to the Indian New Deal, and the government made an effort to relocate American Indians from reservations with high unemployment to cities where, it was hoped, they would find work. In addition, an effort was made to "set the Indians free" by eliminating their reservations (a policy called *termination*). Indians, like many other non-white people in the United States, continued to suffer from white prejudice. For example, in Minneapolis, Indians were excluded from entering some businesses, and newspaper want ads in the 1960s could be found stating, "Indians need not apply" (Davis, 2013, p. 25). In addition, jobs for unskilled workers were decreasing as more and more jobs required advanced education. According to the report of the Special Senate Subcommittee on Indian Education (1969) titled *Indian Education: A National Tragedy—A National Challenge,*

> It was the Bureau relocation program, begun in 1952 that spotlighted the deficiencies of the Bureau high school vocational program [where] the undereducated, poorly trained Indian with his rural background

and cultural differences had not been adequately equipped to compete in the labor market or make adequate social adjustment to his new environment. (p. 80)

This situation helped lead to three out of ten urban relocates' returning to the reservation between 1953 and 1957 and many after that. The report noted a "desperate shortage of trained guidance counselors" and "the limited prevocational program in BIA schools had no relevance to manpower needs or economic development of the Indian community" (Special Subcommittee, 1969, pp. 81, 83). In theory U.S. government-run boarding schools shifted to offering only prevocational education in 1963 (Special Subcommittee, 1969).

In contrast to the move towards cultural assimilation that powered the relocation and termination policies of the 1950s, the Subcommittee's report found "shocking" the absence of bilingual materials and recommended developing culturally sensitive teaching materials for Indian students (Special Subcommittee, 1969, p. 117). This cultural sensitivity was in line with a new interest in human and civil rights after World War II as shown by the founding of the United Nations and the flowering of the Civil Rights Movement and exemplified by the desegregation of American schools after the 1954 Supreme Court *Brown v. Board of Education* decision. For Indians this new interest in human rights led in the 1960s to a strong push for Indian self-determination, more community control of Indian education, and improvement of the quality of schools, which often meant de-emphasizing vocational education.

The first Indian-controlled school in modern times, Rough Rock Demonstration School, was founded in 1966, and the U.S. Civil Rights Commission went so far as to issue a report on the U.S.'s largest Indian reservation titled *The Navajo Nation: An American Colony* (McCabe & Lewis, 1975). In 1969, high dropout rates of Indian students in mainstream universities led to the founding of the first tribal college, Navajo Community College. In 2015 there were 38 tribal colleges, which often focused on preparing students for local jobs and brought back vocational education. These colleges take students where they are academically and bring them forward as much as possible. For example, Salish Kootenai College in Montana has done exemplary work to identify locally available job openings in health care and other professions, design programs to fill these shortages, and recruit and support students.

In 1971 the BIA established the Southwestern Indian Polytechnic Institute (SIPI) in Albuquerque, New Mexico, that continued to struggle for existence in 2015 with limited federal funding. Like Haskell Indian Nations University in Kansas, also funded by the federal government, SIPI offers an almost free education, including room and board, for Indian students, but with half the per-student funding of Haskell. Khachadoorian (2010) describes how "[a]s more and more technical fields become computerized, SIPI is finding that the vocational technical programs require math and language skills comparable to those necessary in the academic programs" (p. 15), which led to more and more of its students opting for a program of studies leading to transfer to a four-year college rather than choosing a straight vocational program of studies.

The American Indian Movement in the early 1970s helped open a few small "survival schools" in their push for sovereignty because many Indian students were failing in public schools that did not reflect Indian culture. They attracted "troubled, alienated Indian youth" whom staff worked with to provide "meaning for their lives" (Davis, 2013, pp. 160, 196). These schools supported student political activism and the teaching of traditional Indian cultures but apparently did not offer much vocational education, partly because they were not well funded. Davis (2013) in a study of two of these schools in Minnesota concluded that they helped make students "relatively resistant to the problems that continue to plague young Native people in the United States, such as high dropout, suicide, and teen pregnancy rates" (p. 212).

CONCLUSION

In a survey of 1,171 students in grades 5–12 attending an urban public school district, including 81 American Indians, Radda, Dawn, and Patrick (1998) found the Indian students were retained in grade at three times the rate of non-Indians. Similarly to what Deyhle (1992) found, Radda et al. determined that

> The students also perceive that the intention to complete high school has little to do with employability. There is a disconnection between the intention to complete school and the common perception that it will affect ability to work or get a job. This suggests, as does other data in the study, that the relevance of completing school in relation to employment and type of employment is lacking. These results support the importance of school being personally relevant to the student, the impact the parents can have in reinforcing that relevance, and the work teachers can do to connect schoolwork to the student's life. (p. 15)

Deyhle (1989), in a seven-year study of Navajo and Ute students in southeast Utah, found that they "complained bitterly that their teachers did not care about them or help them in school" (1989, p. 39). She further found that "a little less than half of the Navajo and almost two-thirds of the Ute [students] felt school was not important for what they wanted to do in life" (p. 42) and that the high school graduates had no better jobs than dropouts. As Ogbu (1995) noted in his study of "involuntary minorities," who on average have not done well in school, that attractive job opportunities for those youth who do stay in school are needed.

After giving Arnold, the Alexie character in *The Absolutely True Story of a Part-Time Indian* (2007), a well-worn math textbook used by Arnold's mother, the non-Indian teacher says,

> That's how we were taught to teach you. We were supposed to kill the Indian to save the child . . . We were supposed to make you give up being Indian. Your songs and stories and language and dancing. Everything. We weren't trying to kill Indian people. We were trying to kill Indian culture. (p. 35)

Because Arnold opts to leave the Indian reservation to get a better education, he is called derisively an "apple" (red on the outside and white culturally on the inside) by those he leaves behind. School success is viewed as only obtainable by assimilating into the dominant colonizing culture. Similarly, Stocker (2005) in her Costa Rican study *I Won't Stay Indian, I'll Keep Studying* found that "the label Indian had connotations of backwardness and even inferior intellect. . . . Being Indian automatically set students up for being treated as inferior" and that "for most students from the [Indian] reservation, projecting an Indian identity seemed incompatible with school success" (p. 2). A few talented and driven individuals like Sherman Alexie can overcome the odds that growing up in poverty, living with negative stereotypes, and receiving an often inferior education present, but for most the barriers are too high. Today it is cheaper to mouth "high expectations" and give students a desk and a commercial one-size-fits-all textbook/curriculum than to supply quality vocational education, let alone high-quality culture-, community- and place-based education that addresses issues of student identity and tackles the challenge of the growing number of American Indian and other children living in poverty in the United States.

The emphasis on test scores in the 2001 NCLB Act, Barack Obama's administration's "Race to the Top," the current push for a "Common Core" curriculum, and the "Tea Party" taxpayer revolt that affects public and Bureau of Indian Education funding do not bode well for either American Indian students or quality vocational or academic education. How the current emphasis on science, technology, engineering, and mathematics (STEM) will affect vocational education is just now playing out. For example, engineering can be a very practical application of mathematics and science to real-world problems; however, when I was an engineering student in the 1960s, I received a very theoretical education with limited hands-on opportunities to apply what I was learning, helping lead me to switch my major to history.

Despite popular beliefs to the contrary, just as Orata found in the 1950s, there are currently not enough jobs today for all engineers and other technical and scientific graduates from our colleges and universities (Berliner & Biddle, 1995). In addition, there are strong efforts to reshape immigration laws to allow the entering of high-tech graduates from abroad who can be paid less than American citizens. Overall, we live in a culture today that values some occupations more than others and even creates artificial scarcity through limiting access to medical schools and other routes to higher-salary, prestige occupations. Especially troubling for ethnic minority students, including American Indian students, is the relatively small but very visible number of high-paying careers in popular music and professional athletics that can make buckling down and studying in school less attractive. In addition, there is the opportunity to make quick money selling illegal drugs while there are few opportunities for other employment. In such an environment there are no easy answers as to how to improve the education of American Indians. However, it is clear that viewing academic and vocational education as antithetical will only make it harder to make improvements.

REFERENCES

Alexie, S. (2007). *The absolutely true diary of a part-time Indian.* New York, NY: Little, Brown.

Berliner, D. C., & Biddle, B. J. (1995). *The manufactured crisis: Myths, fraud and the attack on America's public schools.* Reading, MA: Addison-Wesley.

Bowden, H. W. (1985). *American Indians and Christian missionaries: Studies in cultural conflict.* Chicago, IL: University of Chicago Press.

Bruner, J. (1996). *The culture of education.* Cambridge, MA: Harvard University Press.

Burns, M. (2002). *The journey of a Yavapai Indian: A 19th century odyssey.* Princeton, NJ: Elizabeth House.

Carnoy, M. (Ed.). (1972). *Schooling in a corporate society: The political economy of education in America* (2nd ed.). New York, NY: David McKay.

Carnoy, M. (1974). *Education as cultural imperialism.* New York, NY: David McKay.

Colton, L. (2000). *Counting coup: A true story of basketball and honor on the Little Big Horn.* New York, NY: Warner Books.

Course of study for Indian schools of the United States: Industrial and literary. (1901). Washington, DC: Government Printing Office.

Crews, C. D., & Starbuck, R. W. (Eds.). (2010). *Records of the Moravians among the Cherokees* (Vols. 1 & 2). Tahlequah, OK: Cherokee National Press.

Cummins, J. (1992). The empowerment of Indian students. In J. Reyhner (Ed.), *Teaching American Indian students* (pp. 3–12). Norman, OK: University of Oklahoma Press.

Davis, J. L. (2013). *Survival schools: The American Indian Movement and community education in the Twin Cities.* Minneapolis, MN: University of Minnesota Press.

Department of the Interior (1917). *Annual Report of the Commissioner of Indian Affairs.* 65th Congress., 2d sess. H. doc. 915.

Deyhle, D. (1989). Pushouts and pullouts: Navajo and Ute school leavers. *Journal of Navajo Education, 6*(2), 36–51.

Deyhle, D. (1992). Constructing failure and maintaining cultural identity: Navajo and Ute school leavers. *Journal of American Indian Education, 31*(2), 24–47.

Faircloth, S. C., & Tippeconnic, J. W., III. (2010). *The dropout/graduation rate crisis among American Indian and Alaska Native students.* Los Angeles, CA: The Civil Rights Project at UCLA and The Pennsylvania State University Center for the Study of Leadership in American Indian Education.

Freire, P. (1990/1968). *Pedagogy of the oppressed.* (M. B. Ramos, Trans.) New York, NY: Continuum. (Original work published in 1968)

Horne, E. B., & McBeth, S. (1998). *Essie's story: The life and legacy of a Shoshone teacher.* Lincoln, NE: University of Nebraska Press.

Ille, John. (2012). A curriculum for social change: The Special Navajo Five Year Program 1946-1961. In In C. E. Trafzer, M. S. Gilbert & L. Sisquoc (Eds.), *The Indian school on Magnolia Avenue: Voices and images from Sherman Institute* (pp. 137–158). Corvallis, OR: Oregon State University Press.

Keller, J. A. (2012). Healing touch: The nursing program at Sherman Institute. In C. E. Trafzer, M. S. Gilbert & L. Sisquoc (Eds.), *The Indian school on Magnolia Avenue: Voices and images from Sherman Institute* (pp. 81–105). Lincoln, NE: University of Nebraska Press.

Khachadoorian, A. A. (2010). *Inside the eagle's head: An American Indian college.* Tuscaloosa, AL: University of Alabama Press.

KIDS COUNT Data Book. (2012). Baltimore, MD: Annie E. Casey Foundation.

Kirkendall, A. J. (2010). *Paulo Freire and the Cold War politics of literacy.* Chapel Hill, NC: University of North Carolina Press.

Leupp, F. E. (1910). *The Indian and his problem.* New York, NY: Charles Scribner's Sons.

Lomawaima, K. T. (1994). *They called it Prairie Light: The story of Chilocco Indian School.* Lincoln, NE: University of Nebraska Press.

Lomawaima, K. T. (1996). Estelle Reel, superintendent of Indian schools, 1898–2010: Politics, curriculum, and land. *Journal of American Indian Education, 35*(3), 5–31.

McCabe, C. J., & Lewis, H. (1975). *The Navajo Nation: An American colony. A report of the United States Commission on Civil Rights.* Washington, DC: U.S. Commission on Civil Rights.

Meriam, L. (1928). *The problem of Indian administration.* Baltimore, MD: Johns Hopkins Press.

National Indian Education Association (NIEA). (2005). *Preliminary report on No Child Left Behind in Indian country.* Washington, DC: Author.

Ogbu, J. U. (1995). Understanding cultural diversity and learning. In J. A. Banks & C. A. M. Banks (Eds.), *Handbook of research on multicultural education* (pp. 582–593). New York, NY: Macmillan.

Orata, P. T. (1953a). What is fundamental education? *Educational Theory, 3*(3), 276–280.

Orata, P. T. (1953b). *Fundamental education in an Amerindian community.* Haskell, KS: Bureau of Indian Affairs.

Paxton, K. A. (2006). Learning gender: Female students at the Sherman Institute, 1907–1925. In C. E. Trafzer, J. A. Keller & L. Sisquoc (Eds.), *Boarding school blues: Revisiting American Indian educational experiences* (pp. 174–186). Lincoln, NE: University of Nebraska Press.

Perley, B. C. (2011). *Defying Maliseet language death: Emergent vitalities of language, culture, & identity in eastern Canada.* Lincoln, NE: University of Nebraska Press.

Peshkin, A. (1997). *Places of memory: Whiteman's schools and Native American communities*. Mahwah, NJ: Lawrence Erlbaum Associates.

Prucha, F. P. (1984). *The Great Father: The United States government and the American Indians*. Lincoln, NE: University of Nebraska Press.

Radda, H. T., Dawn, I., & Patrick, C. (1998). Collaboration, research and change: Motivational influences on American Indian students. *Journal of American Indian Education, 17*(2), 2–20.

Returned Student Surveys #24. (RRS). (1917). Ayer Collection, Newberry Library, Chicago, IL.

Reyhner, J. (1992). American Indians out of school: A review of school-based causes and solutions. *Journal of American Indian Education, 31*(3), 37–56.

Reyhner, J. (Ed.). (2015). *Teaching Indigenous students: Honoring place, community, and culture*. Norman, OK: University of Oklahoma Press.

Reyhner, J., & Eder, J. (2004). *American Indian education: A history*. Norman, OK: University of Oklahoma Press.

Reyhner, J., Gilbert, W. S., & Lockard, L. (Eds.). (2011). *Honoring our heritage: Culturally appropriate approaches for teaching Indigenous students*. Flagstaff, AZ: Northern Arizona University.

Shaw, A. M. (1974). *A Pima past*. Tucson, AZ: University of Arizona Press.

Special Subcommittee on Indian Education, United States Senate Committee on Labor and Public Welfare. (1969). *Indian education: A national tragedy—A national challenge*. Washington, DC: U.S. Government Printing Office.

Stefon, F. J. (2009). Willard Beatty and progressive Indian education. *American Indian Culture & Research Journal, 33*(4), 91–112.

Stocker, K. (2005). *"I won't stay Indian, I'll keep studying:" Race, place, and discrimination in a Costa Rican high school*. Boulder, CO: University Press of Colorado.

Trennert, R. S., Jr. (1988). *The Phoenix Indian School: Forced assimilation in Arizona, 1981–1935*. Norman, OK: University of Oklahoma Press.

UNESCO—United Nations Educational, Scientific and Cultural Organization. (1953). *The use of vernacular languages in education, Monographs on Fundamental Education—VIII*. Paris, France: Author.

U.S. Superintendent of Indian Schools. (1901). *Course of study for Indian schools of the United States: Industrial and literary*. Washington, DC: Government Printing Office.

Vuckovic, M. (2008). *Voices from Haskell: Indian students between two worlds, 1884–1928*. Lawrence, KS: University Press of Kansas.

Wilson, W. H., & Kamanā, K. (2006). "For the interest of the Hawaiians themselves": Reclaiming the benefits of Hawaiian-medium education. *Hūlili, 3*(1), 153–181.

2 Education for Jobs, Education for Life

Charles T. Saunders

This chapter explores some of the problems affecting Native American students and the choices they make about their education, workforce development, and careers. Laing (2011) identifies education as one of the elements of human capital creation and the investment such creation requires:

> An investment is defined as any costly activity that potentially yields future benefits. . . . It follows immediately from the above definition that an extremely wide array of activities can be classified as human capital investments . . . Migration . . . Job Search . . . Education . . . Health . . . [The activity known as] Education [presumes that] [a]n individual exerts effort and pays for his [her] college tuition in order to improve [her or] his skills . . . In addition to the individual's own efforts, four great labor-market institutions are involved in the process of human capital creation: Family, Schools and colleges, Firms, Government. (pp. 141–142)

With regard to education, Laing (2011) emphasized that "one of the best known and most robust stylized facts in all of labor economics is the observation that average earnings increase with educational attainment levels. This result has been confirmed and reconfirmed in a vast corpus of empirical work that stretches back some 40 years or so, and that has covered almost every corner of the globe" (p. 166).

AN OVERVIEW OF NATIVE AMERICAN HIGHER EDUCATION

There are currently 36 tribal colleges and universities (TCU) in the United States. For the 2009–2010 school year (the most recent year for which complete statistics are available at the time of this writing), there were 19,070 students enrolled in the 36 U.S. TCUs, comprised of 15,994 American Indians and 3,076 non-American Indian students. In addition, because TCUs are chartered by one or more Native American tribes and also because they maintain close ties to the tribes and communities where they are located, TCUs enjoy a significant participation by community residents in various educational programs offered by the TCUs. During the 2009–2010 school year, 46,831 community residents participated in numerous TCU community education programs (AIHEC, 2012).

The 15,994 American Indian students enrolled in 36 TCUs in 2009–2010 comprise a small percentage of the American Indian/Alaska Native resident population of the United States (2,269,000) and an even smaller percentage of the total estimated resident population of the United States (309,326,000) as estimated for 2010 by the U.S. Census and reported by the National Center for Education Statistics (Snyder & Dillow, 2013). Perhaps the more important comparison of Native American college student enrollment is that the 15,994 American Indians enrolled in TCUs in 2009–2010 represent 7.7 percent of all American Indian/Alaska Native students enrolled (207,900) in all of the approximately 6,000 colleges and universities in the United States in 2009–2010 and 0.08 percent of total post-secondary enrollment (20,427,700 students) in the United States in 2009–2010 (Provasnik & Planty, 2008; Snyder & Dillow, 2013). Stein (1999) describes tribal colleges as "small tenacious institutions of higher education that serve the smallest and poorest minority in the United States (American Indians) under difficult and challenging circumstances" (p. 259).

Saunders (2011) examined issues surrounding American Indian higher education, focusing particularly on Native American TCUs located in the United States. The perspectives that will be shared here are based on an analysis of survey data from 398 students at eight TCUs during the 2010–2011 academic year. Demographically, survey respondents represented 7% of the enrollment of the eight TCUs they attended. Sixty-three percent were in their freshman or sophomore year in college, and 87% pursued either an Associate or a Bachelor's degree. The most popular fields of study were business, healthcare/nursing, education, arts and sciences, and tribal services/social work. Approximately 80% of the responding students self-identified as American Indian or Alaska Native, while 25.8% self-identified as White. Approximately 70% of the responding students were between 23 and 65 years of age, and 72.8% were female. The Sioux tribe was the largest tribal affiliation represented among respondents at 23.5%.

Perhaps most notable for the purposes of this chapter are the survey findings related to education for jobs and life. TCU students reported in the survey that their highest levels of agreement were in response to statements such as, "This college will help me pursue my educational and career goals," and "[My TCU education will help me] to get a better job after college." Furthermore, when all survey results were analyzed using factor analysis techniques, two of the highest-rated groupings of 47 survey content questions that resulted in the strongest levels of agreement among students contained questions pertaining to education for jobs (i.e., "career/work expectations" statements) and education for life (i.e., "self-actualization" statements) (Saunders, 2011).

Many Native American students are college-bound or would like to be according to the National Center for Education Statistics' (NCES) 2009 National Assessment of Education Progress and National Indian Educational Survey. When surveyed about their future education goals, more than 55% of eighth-grade students indicated they planned to go to college or another school full or part time in their first year after high school (NCES, 2010).

SETTING THE STAGE—A PEOPLE IN HISTORY

The history of the United States; its political, economic, social, and cultural development; and its current state of domestic affairs in the twenty-first century reflect more than simply involvement and coexistence with Native Americans. It is a history of political struggle, an economic juggernaut, and a confrontation of diverse peoples and their social and cultural perspectives that has spanned more than five centuries. This chapter is not about Native or non-Native American history, anthropology, sociology, political science, or economics per se. However, it is essential to understand the past, to know where we have come from and how we arrived here, in order to comprehend the present context of American Indian higher education today. Without that comprehension, an understanding of the educational issues confronting American Indians in the twenty-first century is not possible.

In 1492, Christopher Columbus "discovered" America, which is to say that he brought the fact of its existence to the realization of the people of Western Europe. Prior to 1492, other explorers from Northern Europe had arrived and left. But before any of the discoverers and adventurers came to the Western Hemisphere from elsewhere, America was known and inhabited. Those indigenous, original inhabitants are referred to today as the First Nations, the First People, or the Native Americans in what is now North America. Once, the First People were numerous and diverse. Snipp (2004) conservatively estimates the North American indigenous population in 1492 to be in the range of 3–5 million. By 1900, the indigenous population had declined to approximately 250,000. They comprised many nations, spoke many languages, and lived in many diverse cultures. They had their own distinctive social structures, they educated their children, and they governed their lives through the means of formal governments that represented individual members, families, clans, tribes, communities, and nations (Begaye, 2008).

The indigenous peoples were never owners of the land and its resources but users of them, with respect for the abundant and various resources it contained and in adoration of the Spirit that made life possible. They occupied the land and survived on it in every ecological region from Arctic to tropical, from ocean shores to forests to plains to deserts and mountains. They were hunters and gatherers, people who followed the seasons and the animals on which they depended for their sustenance. They were agrarian, masters of agriculture in the regions where they lived. They lived in relative peace and prosperity—until the arrival of the discoverers, the white Western Europeans.

The discoverers brought with them their views of society, culture, civilization, religion, and life as well as of democracy, government, and education (Begaye, 2008). They sought ownership of land and resources and the rights to use and dispose of them to achieve the goals of their civilizations to further their own prosperity and to support their way of life. They believed that they were obligated, whether by religious fervor or by allegiance to their sovereign, to convert the indigenous "savages" from indigenous beliefs to believe in and worship the god of the discoverers. The discoverers were obliged to make the indigenous productive members in support of the society from which the discoverers came and which they were bound to replicate in the newly discovered land. At first, the discoverers feared the indigenous, not knowing them or what to expect from them, unable to communicate with them, unable to understand the indigenous way of life. But the discoverers were also needy when they arrived. Many arrived unprepared to survive in the conditions of the New World. Many perished. Others managed to communicate with the indigenous to seek and obtain help from them, to learn survival from them. The indigenous extended their help and friendship to the discoverers. They helped them find food and shelter. They taught them to survive.

The discoverers also brought with them diseases to which the Europeans were largely immune but to which the indigenous were not. Widespread epidemics resulted in widespread decimation of the indigenous population. The discoverers brought firearms and gunpowder, ostensibly for hunting, then later for self-defense, and ultimately for warfare and genocide. They brought alcohol and the habit of abusing it without restraint to the point of intoxication.

Most importantly, the discoverers brought their greed and lust for the riches and wealth of the land that the indigenous inhabited. With their greed and lust came a sense of urgency to dominate, to attain ultimate control, to claim ownership. They were colonizers and conquerors who believed that to assert their claims to the land on which the indigenous lived was indeed their right, even their "Manifest Destiny," in effect subordinating the rights of the indigenous.

The history since the fifteenth century of the political relationships between the European discoverers—who eventually established the American colonies and later became the citizens of the United States of America—and Native Americans is a sad and often tragic story. Since the beginning of their presence in North America, European Americans have steadily increased in wealth, power, influence, dominance, and control. Begaye (2008) observed:

> While the U.S. population, industrialization, and wealth flourished tremendously in the White mainstream, little has changed over time in

other ethnic/racial or cultural groups who are as much participants and citizens with access in a democratic society . . . The urban poor and Native reservations in the isolated and remote corners of the United States are missing out on the social and economic benefits of a democratic society because of their status and position within the broader social economic hierarchy. (p. 462)

As they progressed westward from their initial foothold on the Eastern seaboard of North America, European Americans encountered the Native American people who lived in North America prior to their arrival. European Americans grew in their demand for the land and resources of North America and in their inability to accommodate the interests of the Native American residents of the land they desired. It became the "Manifest Destiny" of Americans to expand in population and control from the Atlantic seaboard to the Pacific Ocean, pushing the frontier ever westward, displacing the Native American people from their traditional homelands. During their history on the North American continent, European Americans changed in the nature of their relations with Native Americans. Relationships that began in wonder and tentative friendship were later characterized by fearful repulsion, curiosity, collaboration, dependence, independence, rejection, removal, extermination, assimilation, and most recently, to self-determination. Democracy, a model of governance founded on the concepts of participation, inclusion, and equality of the governed, became a government of social control, exclusion, unequal treatment, and loss of voice in the American version of the model, concepts that were foreign to and in opposition to the indigenous governmental models and ways of the Native Americans (Begaye, 2008). Relationships among indigenous and discoverers have evolved through periods of cooperation, domination, physical genocide, cultural genocide, and laissez-faire coexistence. Throughout this relationship history, the emerging dominant European American hegemony has used its institutions—including educational institutions—to promote its purposes and achieve its goals and interests (Urban & Wagoner, 2009).

PRESENT-DAY NATIVE AMERICAN PEOPLE—A FEW SNAPSHOTS

By 1900, the indigenous population in the United States had declined to approximately 250,000 (Snipp, 2004), but U.S. Census figures in recent years indicate a gradual recovery of the population of American Indians and Alaska Natives (i.e., AI/AN), numbering 1.9 million in 1990 (Snipp, 2004). Lobo, Talbot, & Morris (2010) stated that there were 4.5 million AI/AN counted in the 2000 U.S. Census (this amount most likely represents members who self-identified as AOIC, "race alone or in combination with one or more other races," as explained below). As of 2012, the most recent data published by the U.S. Census American Community Survey indicates that the population of AI/AN people in the United States was 2,529,100 or 0.8 percent of the total U.S. population using the "one-race" U.S. Federal criterion. In the AOIC, i.e., alone or in combination census category, the total AI/AN population in 2012 was 5,049,092 or 1.6 percent of the U.S. population (Norris, Vines, & Hoeffel, 2012). The AI/AN population grew by 1.1 million (26.7 percent) from 2000 to 2010, compared to the overall population growth of the United States of 9.7 percent during the same period.

Who are American Indians, and where are they in the United States of the twenty-first century? Native Americans are organized in 566 federally recognized tribes and nations (U.S. Department of the Interior, 2014), including 200 Native villages in Alaska and approximately 68 state-recognized tribes (National Conference of State Legislatures, 2014). The largest percentage of the AI/AN population resides in the West region of the United States with more than 2.1 million residents (40.7 percent), followed by the South with more than 1.7 million (32.8 percent). California, Oklahoma, Arizona, Texas, New York, and New Mexico are the states with the largest (200,000 or more) AI/AN populations (Norris et al., 2012). Comparing the populations of the tribal groups, the ten most populous tribes are the Cherokee, Navajo, Latin American Indian, Choctaw, Sioux, Ojibwe, Apache, Blackfeet, Iroquois, and Pueblo. By 2050, the total AI/AN AOIC population is projected to number 5.2 million and will then comprise two percent of the total U.S. population (U.S. Census Bureau, 2011). "Approximately 28.1% of the [AI/AN] population is below 16 years of age . . . 64.8% are between 16 and 64 . . . . [and] those ages 65 and older represent only 7.1% of the population . . ." (U.S. Department of the Interior, 2014, p. 10). The median age of Native Americans living on reservations is 29.0 years, compared to the median of 37.2 years for the United States population as a whole (U.S. Census Bureau, 2011). Thirty-one percent of AI/AN people lived on reservations, and 69 percent lived in urban areas in 2010 (Norris et al., 2012).

Some statistical results for 2010 reflect conditions that, in general, do not paint a particularly encouraging picture of Native American life or of the prospects for Native American education. Consider the following, according to the U.S. Census Bureau (U.S. Census Bureau, 2012):

1) Seventy-seven percent of American Indians and Alaska Natives had a high school diploma or alternate credential, and 13 percent had a Bachelor's degree or higher, compared to 86 percent and 28 percent, respectively, of the U.S. population as a whole; 67,444 AI/AN people had a graduate or professional degree.
2) The median household income of AI/AN was $35,062, compared with $50,046 nationally.
3) The poverty rate was 28.4 percent for AI/AN families, compared with 15.3 percent nationally.

Regarding the AI/AN workforce, the U.S. Department of the Interior (2014) reports the following median estimated employment statistics:

1) Approximately 49.52 percent of AI/AN people ages 16 and over were working in civilian jobs (compared with the U.S. national average of 67.25 percent of all persons 16 and older who were "available for work");
2) Approximately 17.73 percent of AI/AN people ages 16 and over were available for work but not working; and,
3) The poverty rate varies across all United States regions and states; however, South Dakota was particularly hard-hit with a relatively low level of employment (40.2 percent) and the highest proportion of poverty among Native American families of between 43 percent and 47 percent.

Furthermore, Lobo et al. (2010) observed that compared to the U.S. population in general, American Indians and Alaska Natives had a significantly greater incidence of and mortality from AIDS, heart disease, diabetes, tuberculosis, infant mortality, alcoholism, motor vehicle accidents, unintentional injuries, and suicide. Unfortunately, American Indians and Alaska Natives often did not receive quality health care due to cultural barriers, geographic isolation, and low income.

It is of course impossible to generalize by assuming that all Native Americans exist in one particular circumstance, whether economically, educationally, socially, culturally, or politically. The educational status of any Native American in particular depends not only on the impact of historical and cultural events that have brought Native Americans generally to their status today but also to a great extent on the location and environment in which they live and work and the lifestyle they have chosen to pursue. Furthermore, the non-Native American reader should be cautioned about the potential for personal stereotypes and prejudice based on romantic images and misinformation readily available from the popular press, television, Hollywood, and the Internet. For example, the Choctaw Nation lies primarily in Southeastern Oklahoma, in the geographic region of the United States formerly known as "Indian Territory" to which the Choctaws and many other Native American tribes were removed by the federal government during the mid-19th century. For example, Lambert (2007) describes the "great differences in wealth and lifestyle" among today's Choctaws as evident in their clothing, occupations, and wealth (pp. 114–115).

NATIVE AMERICAN EDUCATION—A PLACE IN HISTORY

Education as an institution has been one of the means by which European American interests, as reflected in United States federal policies and actions towards Native Americans, have been served directly and indirectly. Grande (2008) notes that three prominent American colleges—Harvard University (founded in 1654), the College of William and Mary (founded in 1693), and Dartmouth College (founded in 1769)—were "established with the express purpose of 'civilizing' and 'Christianizing' Indians" (p. 235). However, Grande writes that the real purpose of American education was never to civilize or even to deculturalize indigenous peoples, but rather to ". . . colonize Indian minds as a means of gaining access to indigenous resources . . . material exploitation [by] the forced extraction of labor and natural resources in the interest of capital gains" (p. 235).

Cremin (1980) used the term "discordant education—an education in which at least two conflicting configurations of education sought to inculcate in the same individuals quite different sets of values and attitudes via quite different pedagogies" (p. 243)—to describe education that purports to "civilize" a group of people who are actually thought to be "unassimilable" into the dominant society. African American slaves; Native Americans; immigrants from Ireland, Germany, Norway, Sweden, Mexico, China, and Japan; and many other ethnic groups in the United States have encountered discordant education. However, "the crucial variable" (p. 245), according to Cremin, is race. Cremin concludes:

> Put otherwise, the assumption was that white ethnic immigrants were assimilable and indeed needed to be assimilated as rapidly as possible. Clearly, however, the assumption of the dominant white community with respect to blacks and Indians, and indeed with respect to all peoples of color, was that they were essentially unassimilable . . . In the end, whatever the unclarities, the prevailing assumption was clear: people could be educated to transcend the barriers of ethnicity and religion in order to become full-fledged members of the American community, but they could not be educated to transcend the barriers of race. (p. 245)

In his later writing, in which he chronicled the history of American education during the period from 1876 to 1980, Cremin (1989) discussed further the impact of discordant education:

> The discordant education that had characterized black, Native American, and immigrant communities during the nineteenth century . . . became even more complicated, as social diversity increased and as so-called Americanization programs were launched with the intention of assimilating one or another of the myriad ethnoreligious minorities more fully into the dominant American community. The dynamics of discordant education were manifest in Native American resistance to federal assimilation programs . . . The outcome of this extraordinarily complex education was a variegation characteristic of metropolitan American society . . . strengthening both the cosmopolitanism and the particularity suggested by the metaphor of a "kaleidoscope." (p. 150)

The involvement of Native Americans in white Euro-American education since 1869 has included day schools on reservations, boarding schools on reservations, and boarding schools far removed from reservations. Often, the tactics of "enrolling" Native American children in schools have included such draconian measures as round-ups, man- (i.e., child-) hunts, separation from families and homes and removal by force, and brutal enforcements including physical and psychological punishments, mistreatment, incarceration, and worse treatments (Adams, 1995). In 1869 and for much of the next 100 years, the commonly accepted immediate goal and purpose of providing education to American Indians was to enable their assimilation into the dominant white culture of the United States.

However, the larger purpose of education was to exterminate the Native American people, not through warfare (which was never ethical or successful) but through the removal and erasure of Native American culture. For example, Richard Henry Pratt, founder and first director of Carlisle Indian School, Carlisle, Pennsylvania, believed that education should solve the "Indian problem" by "kill[ing] the Indian and sav[ing] the man" (Adams, 1995, p. 52). This phrase came to represent the guiding strategy for educating American Indians. It was often repeated and practiced. Education consisted of teaching American Indians to speak the white man's language, adopt the white man's culture and behaviors, and learn the menial trades and occupations acceptable in the white man's economy. Education was accomplished by extinguishing Native American languages, cultural and religious practices, and ways of life. The history of Native American education at the hands of the Euro-Americans has not been lost on present-day Native Americans. Their history has shaped who they are today, how they have survived, how they live, and how their perspectives on their lives in the white society have evolved.

THREE ERAS OF NATIVE AMERICAN EDUCATION

Historically, there are three eras of Native American higher education: the Colonial Era (approximately 1492 through the Revolutionary War), the Federal Era (from the American Revolution into the mid-20th century), and the Self-Determination Era (from approximately World War II to the present day) (McClellan, Fox, & Lowe, 2005). During the Colonial Era, nine colleges were established in several of the American colonies. Of these nine colleges, three colleges (Harvard, William and Mary, and Dartmouth) included the education of Native Americans in their original mission or purpose statements; however, only 47 Native American students enrolled, and only four graduated (McClellan et al., 2005). Several reasons for this failure to educate Native Americans have been proposed, including greater interest in the fundraising appeal of educating Native Americans than in its accomplishment, a perceived lack of apparent value of European-American higher education by Native Americans, and a lack of acceptance of educated

Native Americans into white society on the one hand and a lessening of traditional skills, resulting in unfitness for tribal life, on the other (McClellan et al., 2005).

The Federal Era is characterized by the politics of treaties and related legislation that affected trustee relationships between the federal government and many Native American nations. Many colleges and universities were established in the United States during this era, but very few of these "mainstream" institutions focused on Native American education. Vocational education became the dominant mode of education for Native Americans. Essentially, educational services provided by the federal government to Native Americans during the Federal Era were based on the continued Colonial Era philosophies of "Christianization, forced acculturation, and assimilation" (McClellan et al., 2005, p. 10).

The Self-Determination Era may be characterized by several trends that, in many instances, seem to contradict one another. The Progressive movement in education brought about a renewed appreciation of and emphasis on Native American culture along with the inclusion of Native American culture in curricula rather than the suppression and eradication of it. However, while the federal government enacted the Indian Reorganization Act of 1934, affirming Native American sovereignty and self-determination, federal legislation and termination policies during the 1940s and 1950s sought to end treaty and trust relationships with many Native American tribes, to end federal recognition of some tribes, to shift service responsibilities from Federal government to State governments, and to relocate Native Americans from their reservation homes to urban areas, often with disastrous consequences (McClellan et al., 2005).

The modern concept, need for, emphasis on, and availability of workforce development is most likely a trend that became a reality of modern life during the era following World War II. Throughout the United States, there was a tremendous need for trained men and women to go to work and go to war. Later, as American soldiers, including Native American soldiers, returned from World War II, they began to use their educational benefits under the GI Bill. Scholarship money from the Bureau of Indian Affairs and from tribal governments became more available to Native Americans. Jobs were plentiful, and trained workers were in great demand; workforce development programs came of age out of social and economic necessity. Later, in the 1960s, as a response to protests from both Native and non-Native Americans, the federal government changed its policies from termination and relocation to self-determination in the form of the Indian Education Act of 1972, the Indian Self-Determination and Assistance Act of 1975, and the Education Amendments of 1978. Other federal legislation and actions during this era that positively affected Native American higher education include the Navajo Community College Act of 1971, the Tribally Controlled Community College Act of 1978, and the extension of the Morrill Act, granting land grant status to tribal colleges in 1994 (McClellan et al., 2005). Significantly, the Self-Determination Era brought a renewed recognition among Native Americans of the value of, even the necessity for, post-secondary education for Native Americans. Boyer (1997) observed, "The value of higher education became clear to many American Indian leaders in this new era . . . A college degree did not have to be synonymous with assimilation. Now it could be used to strengthen reservations and tribal culture. This belief that higher education could serve the practical needs of a tribe was [a necessary ingredient] for the founding of the tribal college" (p. 23).

PRESENT-DAY ISSUES AND PROBLEMS—IMPLICATIONS FOR EDUCATION AND WORKFORCE DEVELOPMENT

In personal correspondence with this author, administrators of several Native American tribal colleges and universities identified numerous barriers to workforce development and education faced by Native American students. Remote geographic locations, high unemployment, scarcity of jobs, and lack of opportunities for on-the-job training and mentoring are some of the challenges that continue to confront Native American residents of reservations and trust lands in the twenty-first century. Serious issues and threats affect the capabilities of TCUs to meet the needs of their constituents, i.e., the students, tribal governments, and communities they serve. Some of these issues include:

1) Remediation, retention, student financial support, and economic shifts (both local and regional).
2) Funding (lack of), federal bureaucracy, hiring of personnel.
3) Financial issues, lack of financial resources, constraints upon the services the colleges can offer.
4) TCUs typically serve the students most in need, yet they are expected to maintain the same standards as other institutions of higher education including accreditation, student services, academic integrity, etc.
5) Underfunding; federal appropriations are less than amounts authorized by federal law (e.g., the Tribally Controlled Community College Act of 1978).
6) No funding for non-Indian students who attend TCUs (approximately 20 percent of all TCU students enrolled).
7) No tax base for tribal colleges.
8) State governments generally do not provide any funding for TCUs.
9) Faculty salaries are low, instructional supplies minimal, facilities basic, housing in short supply, etc.
10) Overdependence on grants to fund many TCU initiatives and infrastructure. (Grant funding also requires enormous energy to develop, administer, and implement even though many are aligned with institutional policies.)

11) Student issues, such as lack of preparedness for college resulting in need for remedial coursework in math and English.
12) Students are often the first generation of their families to attend college and need additional orientation towards the higher education process and protocol.
13) General education levels are low in the families of prospective college students
14) Educational opportunity in the schools is often disrupted by socio-economic need and deprivation.
15) Success of workforce development efforts is often limited by the availability of private sector employers, jobs, role models, internships.
16) Lack of administrative training programs for development of leadership and management resources. Absence of residents, absence of competency-based recruitment models, and lack of succession planning in many tribal colleges.
17) Failure to adequately provide for leadership succession. Lack of financial support from the financial environment, i.e., impoverished communities with unemployment reaching 70 percent to 80 percent during the winter months.
18) Workforce development success may also be hampered by the nature of post-secondary education itself, especially when textbook knowledge has been emphasized more than knowledge of practical, real-world applications in leadership and project management.

The issues listed above impact students directly by diminishing the ability of the institutions to provide high-quality, culturally and socially meaningful education that students want and deserve. Tribal college administrators report that Native American students at tribal colleges and universities are in need of remedial course work, financial aid, housing, and employment. They are also facing poverty and deprivation, being ill-prepared for college study, and being "first generation" college students. There are scarce employer role models and few opportunities for internships. Native American colleges and universities struggle with problems such as the shortage of funding from federal and state sources, the federal funding bureaucracy and appropriations process, meeting and maintaining accreditation and educational standards on severely restricted budgets, inadequate funding for hiring and developing faculty and administrators, limited funding for operating expenses including salaries and instructional supplies, and limited capital funding to provide basic facilities and housing.

In their appraisal of challenges facing tribal colleges and universities in the new millennium, McClellan et al. (2005) described tensions between preserving tribal culture and promoting tribal economic development, conflict between Native American and non-Native American professionals employed by the tribal colleges, physical facilities that are insufficient or deteriorating, lack of adequate funding, lack of public support for minority issues, the need to meet accreditation requirements in order to qualify for federal funding, and the inability of federal allocations to keep pace with inflation. The Tribal College Act of 1983 originally specified an allocation of $5,280 per full-time equivalent Native American student; that amount would have to have been $8,450 in 1998 to keep up with inflation, but the actual allocation in 1998 was only $2,900 per student (McClellan et al., 2005).

The Carnegie Foundation for the Advancement of Teaching issued two special reports (Boyer, 1997; The Carnegie Foundation, 1989) that described the major issues facing Native American tribal colleges and universities and the progress that had been made in the interim. The 1997 special report repeated and updated the status and recommendations of the earlier special report. The ten recommendations made by the Carnegie Foundation are summarized as follows:

1) The federal government [should] adequately support tribal colleges by providing the full funding authorized by Congress [in the Tribally Controlled Community College Assistance Act of 1978] . . . Federal appropriations should keep pace with the growth of Indian student enrollment.
2) 1989 and 1997: The libraries, science laboratories, and classroom facilities at tribal colleges should be significantly improved through federal government appropriations and private foundation grants. 1997: Full appropriation of Land Grant funds under the Land Grant Act of 1862.
3) 1989: Connections between tribal colleges and non-Indian higher education should be strengthened. 1997: Tribal colleges should enrich their curricula—and build even stronger collaboration with non-Indian institutions—through the expanded use of distance learning technology.
4) Programs linking tribal colleges to their communities should be significantly increased.
5) 1989: Tribal colleges should expand their important role of preserving the languages, history, and cultures of the tribes. 1997: Tribal colleges should continue to expand their important work in preserving the arts, philosophy, science, and religious studies of their tribes.
6) State governments should more adequately support tribal colleges, especially community service programs.
7) A comprehensive program for faculty development at tribal colleges should be implemented.
8) Private foundations should collaboratively support the Tribal College Institute (in 1997, the American Indian Higher Education Consortium].
9) The national awareness and advocacy programs for tribal colleges should be strengthened through private philanthropies' collaboration.

10) 1989: The newly established tribal college endowment should be supported. 1997: Foundations, corporations, the federal government, and individuals should continue their support of the American Indian College Fund.
11) 1997: Funding of the journal *Tribal College: Journal of American Indian Higher Education* should be continued. (Boyer, 1997; The Carnegie Foundation, 1989)

Although great progress had been made as indicated by comparing the results of the 1989 (Carnegie) and 1997 (Boyer) reports, many of the issues identified by the tribal college presidents as described above are continuations of issues identified in 1989 and 1997. Issues such as these have developed over time. Solutions will likely require equally long periods of time during which concerted, focused efforts must be made to bring about resolutions.

IMPACT OF RACIAL PREJUDICE: ADAPTING, ASSIMILATING, SURVIVING

In a review of the research on racial issues in American higher education, Bennett (2004) provides an assessment of trends in higher education among ethnic groups with regard to their preparation, access, recruitment, admission, retention/persistence, attrition, and attainment/achievement during the period from 1976 to 1997. During this time period, college enrollments grew steadily for all ethnic groups except Whites. Although American Indians have increased their college enrollments, graduation rates of American Indians remain the lowest of all ethnic groups. Graduate school enrollments have slowly increased for all ethnic groups during this time period but have increased least for American Indians. American Indians have gained slightly in undergraduate education but have maintained approximately the same proportion of graduate and professional school enrollments since 1976 (Bennett, 2004).

Racial and ethnic differences impact all ethnic groups to some extent, but different groups are affected in different ways. According to Bennett (2004), factors may include background and external factors, academic integration/segregation, social integration, institutional factors, and the financial aid mix (loans vs. grants, scholarships, and fellowships). One of the most serious factors impacting all students is the prevalence of poor pre-collegiate academic preparation in the face of rising entrance exam standards, a lack of counseling, and a lack of remedial support. These factors particularly impact Alaska Natives, American Indians, African Americans, Mexican Americans, and Puerto Ricans who, as groups, are often overrepresented in vocational tracks, classes for the mentally retarded, and in schools that have outdated books and inadequate facilities (Bennett, 2004). Furthermore, Bennett states, "Traditional criteria for college admission, such as standardized test scores and high school grades, are not good predictors of college potential for many minorities . . . yet alternatives have not been developed" (p. 853).

Disrespect for or denial of the cultural, community, and family values of some ethnic groups, along with the expectation that ethnic students must assimilate into the white cultural milieu in order to succeed, also adversely affect ethnic students and their success in college (Bennett, 2004). In his study of the experiences of three Native American students attending Ivy League schools in the 1990s, Brayboy (2004) found that the students encountered negative, degrading attitudes and attention, "were seen variously by their classmates, administrations, and institutions as romantic 'Others,' welfare mongers, whiners who need to get over past injuries, affirmative action babies, and noble savages" (p. 129). As a result, Native American students adopted strategies that enabled them to hide from, avoid, and be invisible to their classmates and others. Brayboy concluded that American Indian students in predominantly white institutions are often forced to enter into a "brutal bargain . . . [which] essentially asks American Indian students to assimilate, accommodate on others' terms, or suffer marginalization" (p. 137). Additionally, students who enroll in a community college program as a means to qualify for transfer to a four-year college program may often face a difficult transfer process into the senior college as well as additional and new barriers due to language, culture, the historical orientation of the receiving institution, and the degree of acceptance of ethnic students—these factors tend to negatively impact the rates of completion of American Indian, African American, and Latino students in particular (Bennett, 2004).

In their review of the literature of Native American student retention issues in higher education, Larimore and McClellan (2005) proposed drawing from the models and frameworks of several authors "to develop a culturally rooted and culturally responsive plan for enhancing success for students who are Native American" (p. 26). The plan that Larimore and McClellan propose would consider representation, climate and intergroup relations, education and scholarship, institutional transformation, financial aid, financial resources, cultural identity, resilience, recruitment and admissions, academic services, student services, curriculum and instruction, respect, relevance, reciprocity, and responsibility.

EDUCATION FOR EMPLOYMENT: WORKFORCE DEVELOPMENT

Workforce development has been defined as "the coordination of public and private sector policies and programs that provides individuals with the opportunity for a sustainable livelihood and helps organizations achieve exemplary goals, consistent with the societal context" (Jacobs & Hawley, 2009, p. 2543). There are several forces or vectors of social change that may be considered as drivers of workforce development. These include globalization, technology, the economy, political change, and demographic shifts.

Workforce development policy seeks to address, among other issues, the educational preparation of individuals to enter or re-enter the workforce and the responses of individuals to life transitions and other changes that impact their participation in the workplace (Jacobs & Hawley, 2009). Education for employment can be thought of as a life-long endeavor, one that begins at a very early age in many societies but that is often thought of as an effort most characterized by formal education in schools. In the United States, formal education usually occurs for youth approximately 5–18 years of age in school grades K–12. Education for work often extends into postsecondary education in the form of career and technical education, academic education, and professional education pursued at two- and four-year colleges, universities, or trade school programs.

Throughout the history of the efforts of European Americans to use education as a means of preparing Native Americans to become contributing members of American society, there has been fierce debate and controversy about exactly what Native Americans should be educated to do or become. In an account of the development and implementation of U.S. Government policy regarding education for Native Americans, Szasz (1999) describes the attempts of early administrators of the U.S. Department of the Interior, Bureau of Indian Affairs (BIA), to resolve this dilemma:

> . . . what the child learned was unconnected to the reality of his life. A child taken from a nomadic, home-oriented life of herding sheep on the Navajo Reservation could make no connection between this and the white middle-class stories of "Dick and Jane" he read in school. A child who had hunted wild horses or ridden after cattle in the hills of the Yakima Reservation could not comprehend why he should learn to distinguish between a noun and a verb or why he should study American history when all it discussed was what the whites had done. Nor did this education enable the child who chose an off-reservation life to support himself adequately. (p. 55)

Willard Wolcott Beatty, BIA Director of Indian Education, 1936–1952, wrote that when encouraging a child to attend boarding school or college, "let us be sure that the experience won't unfit him for return to life among his own people, while failing to fit him for making a living anywhere else" (Beatty, 1944, p. 14).

World War II had a lasting impact on all people and all nations. One might say that almost nothing was the same after World War II as it was before the war. The war's impact was also felt among Native American peoples, and changes in American society during and after World War II also wrought changes in American education, including Native American education. More than 24,000 Native Americans served in the U.S. Armed Forces during the war, while more than 40,000 Native Americans left their reservations to work in war-related jobs and industries in other parts of the United States. Native Americans who had participated in government-sponsored work programs before the war, such as the Depression-era Indian Civilian Conservation Corps, were prepared to go to work in shipbuilding, aircraft production, mining, railroad work, and farming. Such jobs were located primarily in urban areas of the United States, far from the reservations. The pull of Native American workers from their reservations to urban centers of industry often resulted in the neglect of resource development on the reservations as well as the social fracture of uprooted homes and families (Szasz, 1999).

In addition, Native American leaders became more aware of the need for education to enable their people to effectively compete for and succeed in new employment opportunities. Whereas before the war, the Education Division of the U.S. Bureau of Indian Affairs had "discouraged vocational training for nonexistent jobs in the city [during the Depression] . . . postwar students [were urged] to train for jobs in the growing metropolitan areas" (Szasz, 1999, p. 106). As a result of the national experience during World War II,

> A significant number of tribes emerged from the war with a new outlook on the priority of their needs and a new awareness of how the federal government could assist them in filling those needs. Within a number of tribes education had leaped to the forefront. In widely scattered areas, from the Plateau country to the central Plains and thence south, Indian leaders and parents, Indian elders, and returning Indian veterans faced the postwar period with a deep conviction that education for their children was imperative. A number of tribal councils passed compulsory education ordinances even before the war was over and others began to enforce similar regulations that they had neglected. One of the most promising developments was tribal support of higher education. Many tribes began to encourage their high school graduates to go on to college by setting aside tribal funds for scholarships.
> (Szasz, 1999, p. 115)

As noted earlier in this chapter, a comment by one tribal college president indicated his concern that successful performance on the job often depends on successful past experience and the learning that comes from practical, real-world experience rather than from academic study. He stated, "A college degree has to be coupled with practical, empirical application" (R. E. Littlebear, personal communication, July 16, 2010) to ensure success at work. Marsick and Watkins (1990) documented their case study of a tribal community college that attempted to address this problem through an innovation in which students could earn a Bachelor's degree in management through a combination of academic and individualized studies, including obtaining college credit for their competencies in a program known as "Credit for Prior Learning." In this program, "a student identifies relevant learning outcomes and documents them" under the "implicit assumption that students can define their learning and that learning need not take place in a traditional college course . . . The program was to be competency-based, reflecting competencies needed for reservation jobs" (pp. 157–158). Problems occurred in the training of faculty and staff, the identification and documentation of job competencies, the governance of the program by traditional tribal patterns, and the strain on the college's existing system, procedures, and scarce faculty resources. In addition, this non-traditional program became further complicated by assigning administrative responsibility for it to a manager without direct and comparable experience, by efforts to meet the needs of students without the knowledge of what students' needs are, and by attempts to force the implementation of the program through the use of curriculum materials developed by a third-party provider, which was not entirely appropriate to the program or its needs.

Among people of racial and ethnic differences, finding employment is more complicated than education and experience, even having "the right" education and experience. Employment is often taken for granted among members of the workforce who are not considered the marginalized members of society. However, Brown, Yamini-Diouf, and Ruiz de Esparza (2005) describe what the literature on career development refers to as "potentially salient and 'differentiating' dimensions . . . risk factors . . . 'dimensions of differentiation'" (p. 233). Brown et al. describe the following categories:

1) Dimensions of differentiation from the majority (cognitive and physical ability; wealth, poverty, socioeconomic capital, and hardship; psychological manifestations of social status; skill and efficacy for managing racism, ethnocentrism, sexism, and classism; worldview perspectives (i.e., cultural values and perspectives); societal estrangement, isolation, and acculturation; language use and facility);
2) Dimensions of differentiation from same social circle (cognitive ability; racial and ethnic identification and within-group involvement or isolation; and traditionality of occupational interests); and,
3) Dimensions of familial responsibility (primary caregiver status and primary economic provider status) (pp. 233–234).

At the core of the heart-rending issues of unemployment and poverty, both of which are endemic among Native Americans, is the success of economic development that makes jobs available. Education, workforce development, job training, and the ability to successfully negotiate employment opportunities fraught with "dimensions of differentiation" by which workers may be screened, discriminated, selected for hire, or refused/denied employment are meaningless if jobs are not available. Grubb and Lazerson (2004) wrote about the "work-family-schooling dilemma" (p. 115), elucidating multiple barriers and problems that often inhibit people from taking advantage of training and obtaining employment. Perhaps the most difficult barrier to overcome in addressing the role of workforce development in eliminating unemployment and poverty is the fiction that education and training alone can correct these and other economic ills. In order to obtain the "sustainable livelihood" that results from employment as contemplated by Jacobs and Hawley (2009), workers must not only be qualified for the work they seek but jobs must also be available. This can be a severe limiting factor in many areas where reservations and tribal communities are located.

Joe L. Graham, as a doctoral student at New Mexico State University and a member of the Pueblo of Laguna, New Mexico, lamented the ". . . obstacles, incentives, distractions, or alternative opportunities that Laguna college graduates encountered on their academic paths that influenced their perceptions about working for the tribe. The significance is that several challenges were identified. If addressed, the tribe could increase retention of tribal graduates for the professional roles for which they were academically trained." Graham's research found ". . . that significant rifts existed between the arenas of tribal professional employment opportunities, college level academic attainment, and the existing secondary school system. On the other hand, notions of tribal student loyalty and an intense desire to contribute to community were confirmed." Graham "recommended that several critical decisions regarding the future of the Pueblo's higher education priorities be made [and] . . . that the tribe increase their efforts to capitalize on the intrinsic community connectedness demonstrated by the Laguna graduates" (Graham, 2013, p. 1).

DISCUSSION—BRIGHT, SHINING LIGHTS

Stein (1999) observed, "The positive impact of tribal colleges on the American Indian people and communities they serve is phenomenal, particularly as represented by the successes of their students in the workplace and in the mainstream institutions to which they transfer. The impact seems even more powerful considering the pride and hope the colleges have spread throughout Indian country" (pp. 267–268).

Perhaps the brightest light rising on the horizon of modern-day Native American education, one that will benefit not only individual members of Indian nations but also the larger societies of the United States and the world, is the emergence of American Indian TCUs, community colleges, and universities (Lomawaima, 2004). Tribal colleges and universities are founded and controlled by individual Native American tribes and reflect not only the governance of the founding tribe but also the spirit, philosophy, ontology, and epistemology of the native peoples. Larimore and McClellan (2005) reviewed several studies that "have documented that retention rates for Native American students enrolled at TCUs are higher than those for Native American students enrolled at mainstream institutions" (p. 22). Native American students who graduated from tribal colleges also experienced successful educational outcomes in terms of employment, transfer rates, and continued studies (Boyer, 1997).

In addition, tribal colleges provide opportunities for addressing the needs of the members of their tribe in the context of the society in which they live. Boyer (1997) observed that tribal colleges have helped to shape the movement toward economic development, cultural survival, and community health. Boyer wrote, "In many communities, [tribal colleges] were the first to address economic, cultural, and social issues . . . Tribal colleges are part of a movement for fundamental social change within reservations. Their mission is to rebuild cultures and, in the end, create new and stronger nations" (pp. 56–57). Tribal colleges often offer programs, curricula, and research opportunities related to their native language and culture in addition to education and training to enable graduates to achieve employment and higher education goals. However, as Lomawaima (2004) suggests, "History, politics, and education have always been and will forever be inextricably bound up with one another in Indian America" (p. 455). The vision of many Native Americans, expressed by those who occupied Alcatraz Island, San Francisco Bay, on November 20, 1969, to plan and control their own futures and the education of their own children, ". . . flourishes today on the . . . campuses of the tribal community college system. Education, politics, and history still walk hand in hand across Indian country" (p. 455).

*****

For many Native American youth who can find the means and wherewithal to attend, a college education offers perhaps the best and highest hope for obtaining a job, pursuing a career, and establishing a way of life. This chapter has drawn on research about Native American tribal colleges and universities to explore some of the issues and problems affecting Native American students and the choices they make about their post-secondary education and workforce development. Issues and problems of education and workforce development have been shown to stem from the historical setting of Native American people, their education, politics, and present-day conditions of poverty and racial prejudice.

Perhaps the larger issues in this chapter address the perspectives of peoples seeking education and jobs as a means to ensure their cultural and ethnic survival, i.e., the survival of the Native American people, their identity, and their ways of life. The issues and problems facing Native American TCUs today have to do with the specific needs and particular circumstances of people who need jobs and education that will result in jobs—essentially, education for economic survival. Native American youth and adults need and want employment and jobs, and tribal community members of all ages can benefit from TCU programs and services, but they also want much more than this—they want successful careers and lives that are personally meaningful within the context of their heritage, their culture, their beliefs, their traditions, and their values. Many Native American students want to serve their people, their communities, and their sovereign nations. Native Americans want their people to survive.

Education is a means to pursue ambitions, goals, and dreams. Tribal colleges and universities have become available to Native American students as a way for them to achieve the education they need, demand, and deserve. Achieving educational goals and applying one's education to the achievement of even greater goals are never easy paths to follow. The paths are long, and the travel is arduous. When the path is strewn with seemingly insurmountable barriers such as racial discrimination, poverty, and health issues, the path to achievement can be as rugged and as desolate as some Native American reservation lands themselves. It is the hope of this author that the readers have gained knowledge that may help them to light their path and the paths of other travelers who journey toward achieving society's goals of growth, change, and improvement for all people.

REFERENCES

Adams, D. W. (1995). *Education for extinction: American Indians and the boarding school experience, 1875–1928*. Lawrence, KS: University Press of Kansas.

American Indian Higher Education Consortium. (2009a). *AIHEC AIMS fact book 2007: Tribal colleges and universities report*. Retrieved from http://aihec.org/resources/documents/AIHEC_AIMS_Factbook2007.pdf

American Indian Higher Education Consortium. (2009b). *Tribal colleges and universities*. Retrieved from http://aihec.org/colleges/index.cfm

American Indian Higher Education Consortium. (2012). *2009–2010 AIHEC AIMS fact book: Tribal colleges and universities report*. Retrieved from http://www.aihec.org/resources/documents/AIHEC-AIMSreport_May2012.pdf

Beatty, W. W. (1944). *Education for action*. Chilocco, OK: U.S. Department of the Interior, United States Indian Service, Education Division.

Begaye, T. (2008). Modern democracy: The complexities behind appropriating indigenous models of governance and implementation. In N. K. Denzin, Y. S. Lincoln & L. T. Smith (Eds.), *Handbook of critical and indigenous methodologies* (pp. 439–458). Thousand Oaks, CA: Sage.

Bennett, C. I. (2004). Research on racial issues in American higher education. In J. Banks & C. Banks (Eds.), *Handbook of research on multicultural education* (2nd ed., pp. 847–868). San Francisco, CA: Jossey-Bass.

Boyer, P. (1997). *Native American colleges: Progress and prospects*. Princeton, NJ: The Carnegie Foundation.

Brayboy, B. M. J. (2004). Hiding in the ivy: American Indian students and visibility in elite educational settings. *Harvard Educational Review, 74*(2), 125–152.

Brown, M. T., Yamini-Diouf, Y., & Ruiz de Esparza, C. (2005). Career interventions for racial or ethnic minority persons: A research agenda. In W. B. Walsh & M. L. Savickas (Eds.), *Handbook of vocational psychology: Theory, research, and practice* (3rd ed., pp. 227–242). Mahwah, NJ: Lawrence Erlbaum.

The Carnegie Foundation for the Advancement of Teaching. (1989). *Tribal colleges: Shaping the future of Native America*. Princeton, NJ: Author.

Cremin, L. A. (1980). *American education: The national experience, 1783–1876.* New York, NY: Harper & Row.
Cremin, L. A. (1989). *American education: The metropolitan experience, 1876–1980.* New York, NY: Harper & Row.
Graham, J. L. (2013, June). *Laguna graduates assessment of utilization of Laguna academic capital.* Paper presented at the meeting of the Native American and Indigenous Studies Association, Saskatoon, Sasketchewan, Canada. Retrieved from http://www.naisa.usask.ca/program/schedule.php?t=24
Grande, S. (2008). Red pedagogy: The un-methodology. In N. K. Denzin, Y. S. Lincoln & L. T. Smith (Eds.), *Handbook of critical and indigenous methodologies* (pp. 233–254). Thousand Oaks, CA: Sage.
Grubb, W. N., & Lazerson, M. (2004). *The education gospel: The economic power of schooling.* Cambridge, MA: Harvard University Press.
Jacobs, R., & Hawley, J. (2009). Emergence of workforce development: Definition, conceptual boundaries, and implications. In R. MacLean & D. Wilson (Eds.), *International handbook of education for the changing world of work* (pp. 2537–2552). Bonn, Germany: Springer Science and Business Media. doi:10.1007/978-1-4020-5281-1_XV_2
Laing, D. (2011). *Labor economics: Introduction to the classic and the new labor economics.* New York, NY: W.W. Norton.
Lambert, V. (2007). *Choctaw Nation: A story of American Indian resurgence.* Lincoln, NE: University of Nebraska Press.
Larimore, J. S., & McClellan, G. S. (2005). Native American student retention in U.S. postsecondary education. *New Directions for Student Services: Serving Native American Students, 109,* 17–32.
Lobo, S., Talbot, S., & Morris, T. L. (Eds.). (2010). *Native American voices: A reader* (3rd ed.). Upper Saddle River, NJ: Pearson.
Lomawaima, K. T. (2004). Educating Native Americans. In J. Banks & C. Banks (Eds.), *Handbook of research on multicultural education* (2nd ed., pp. 441–461). San Francisco, CA: Jossey-Bass.
Marsick, V. J., & Watkins, K. E. (1990). *Informal and incidental learning in the workplace.* New York, NY: Routledge.
McClellan, G. S., Fox, M. J. T., & Lowe, S. C. (2005). Where we have been: A history of Native American higher education. *New Directions for Student Services: Serving Native American Students, 109,* 7–15.
National Center for Educational Statistics. (2010). *Data snapshot.* Retrieved from http://nces.ed.gov/
National Conference of State Legislatures. (2014). *State recognized tribes.* Retrieved from http://www.ncsl.org/research/state-tribe-institute/list-of-federal-and-state-recognized-tribes.aspx#State
Norris, T., Vines, P. L., & Hoeffel, E. M. (2012). *The American Indian and Alaska Native population: 2010.* U.S. Census Bureau. Retrieved from http://www.census.gov/prod/cen2010/briefs/c2010br-10.pdf
Provasnik, S., & Planty, M. (2008). *Community colleges: Special supplement to The Condition of Education 2008 (NCES 2008–033).* Washington, DC: National Center for Education Statistics, Institute of Education Sciences, U.S. Department of Education.
Saunders, C. T. (2011). *Native American tribal colleges and universities: Issues and problems impacting students in the achievement of educational goals* (Doctoral dissertation). The Ohio State University, Columbus, Ohio.

Snipp, C. M. (2004). American Indian studies. In J. Banks & C. Banks (Eds.), *Handbook of research on multicultural education* (2nd ed., pp. 315–331). San Francisco, CA: Jossey-Bass.

Snyder, T. D., & Dillow, S. A. (2013). *Digest of education statistics* (NCES 2014–015). Washington, DC: National Center for Education Statistics, Institute of Education Sciences, U.S. Department of Education.

Stein, W. J. (1999). Tribal colleges: 1968–1998. In K. C. Swisher & J. W. Tippeconnic III (Eds.), *Next steps: Research and practice to advance Indian education* (pp. 259–270). Charleston, WV: Appalachia Educational Laboratory, Inc.

Szasz, M. C. (1999). *Education and the American Indian: The road to self-determination since 1928* (3rd ed.). Albuquerque, NM: University of New Mexico Press.

Urban, W. J., & Wagoner, J. L., Jr. (2009). *American education: A history* (4th ed.). New York, NY: Routledge.

U.S. Census Bureau. (2011). *Facts for features: American Indian and Alaska native heritage month: November 2011*. Retrieved from http://www.census.gov/newsroom/releases/archives/facts_for_features_special_editions/cb11-ff22.html

U.S. Census Bureau. (2012). *DP05: ACS demographic and housing estimates 2008–2012 American community survey 5-year estimates*. Retrieved from http://factfinder2.census.gov/faces/tableservices/jsf/pages/productview.xhtml?pid=ACS_12_5YR_S0101

U.S. Department of the Interior. (2014). *2013 American Indian population and labor force report: January 16, 2014*. Retrieved from http://www.bia.gov/cs/groups/public/documents/text/idc1-024782.pdf

3 From Boarding Schools to Tribal Colleges
The Rise of Retribalization Through Vocational Education

Charlotte Leforestier

Since the 1970s and the passage of the Indian Education Act (1972) and the Indian Self-Determination and Education Assistance Act (1975), the American government has encouraged "maximum Indian participation in the Government and education of the Indian people" (S. 1017–93rd, Sec. 1). These acts, passed during the Civil Rights Movement of the 1960s, granted Native American tribes greater power of decision in the field of education, allowing them to direct it toward their specific needs. Education has had an essential place in Native American history, not only because of the unceasing efforts to educate Natives since the arrival of early missionaries on the American continent but also because these constant attacks created a trauma. The various policies implemented by the missionaries and colonial governments first and the American government later to deal with Native Americans all had provisions for their education with different orientations (removing them, eliminating them, assimilating them, etc.). In fact, the evolution of education for Native Americans can be divided into three major periods: (1) missionary schools with the conversion of Native American populations as a major objective from colonial times to the middle of the 19th century; (2) boarding schools working for assimilation until the 1950s; and (3) tribal colleges attempting today to achieve retribalization.

This chapter does not seek to dwell upon the experiences of the off-reservation boarding schools. The purpose here is to attempt to understand why Native Americans have dedicated a special place for vocational education in tribal colleges, which respond to tribal needs in terms of cultural and linguistic preservation—when knowing that the trauma inflicted by the boarding school system and the educational policies still affects Native American communities today. That is why it seems essential to study how Native Americans succeeded in being in charge of their own education, how the transition from government-run education with the establishment of boarding schools to Native American-run education with tribal colleges was achieved, and how pan-Indianism allowed the transition from trauma to hope for a better future. Thus, this chapter will initially present the historical perspective on vocational education by looking at the implementation not only for Native Americans but also for the rest of the American population. The second section will focus on the transition from boarding schools to tribal colleges, and the third will offer a reflection on vocational education in tribal colleges.

It is unnecessary to start this chapter by reviewing once more the history of the boarding school system in the United States as a great deal of comprehensive research has been published on the topic and on the policy of assimilation implemented in the boarding schools (Adams, 1995; Coleman, 1993). Rather I argue that even though the boarding school model had a detrimental impact on Indian communities, today Native American tribes insist on incorporating components of it in their educational systems. The boarding school model will be used to analyze the process which has made it possible today for Native American communities to place education at the core of their priorities. At the center of this study stands vocational education, which needs to be defined.

VOCATIONAL EDUCATION THROUGH TIME

The term *vocational education* used in this chapter is the one that applied to American society at the end of the 19th and throughout the 20th century and that is defined as an instruction oriented toward job or career skills. As such, "A variety of components fall under the vocational education umbrella: agricultural, business education, health occupations, home economics, marketing education, technical education, technology education, and trade and industrial education" (Miller, 1993, p. 4).

Such vocational training was common practice especially at the end of the 19th century and coincided with the development of the American Industrial Revolution. Needing to grow the labor force more and more, the government decided to implement this training for all but privileged white children (African Americans, Native Americans, immigrants, and mainstream white children). In 1910, for instance, 90 percent of the United States population made their living through industrial pursuits (Cohen, 1968). In fact, the first laws relative to workforce education date back to the 1860s when the Morrill Act, also known as the Land Grant College Act, was passed in 1862. It provided federal financial grants for state colleges interested in developing programs in agriculture, home economics, mechanical arts, and other professions that were practical for the period (Tindall & Shi, 1999). Academic and industrial training were integrated to enable students to read, write, and speak English in order to have a basic knowledge and understanding of user manuals (Cohen, 1968).

Following the trend of vocational training, African Americans after the abolition of slavery became interested in education and founded two well-known institutes devoted to academic and manual training, Hampton Normal and Industrial Institute in Virginia in 1868 and Tuskegee Institute in Alabama in 1881 (Atkins, 1933; Moton, 1933). The model African Americans used for Hampton actually served to establish the off-reservation boarding schools through which the assimilation of Native Americans into American mainstream society would be possible. From the 1870s to the 1950s, high priority was placed on vocational education for American Indians.

Today, vocational education or what is now called career and technical education has had a different scope, specifically since the passage in 1990 of the Carl D. Perkins Vocational Education Act. This law, which amended the Vocational Education Act of 1963, was meant to "make the United States more competitive in the world economy by developing more fully the academic and occupational skills of all segments of the population" (Public Law 101–392, Sec. 2). It focuses on the development and the funding of vocational education. As such, it defines the term "vocational education" as this: "Organized educational programs offering a sequence of courses which are directly related to the preparation of individuals in paid or unpaid employment in current or emerging occupations requiring other than a baccalaureate or advanced degree" (Public Law 101–392, Sec. 521 [41]).

BOARDING SCHOOLS AND VOCATIONAL EDUCATION

At the end of the 19th century, the education provided by the American government to assimilate Native Americans into mainstream American society also emphasized the need for industrial training. A key element for the boarding school system to succeed in its assimilationist goal was the division of the school day into two parts. The mornings, for instance, when the children learned reading, writing, and speaking English as well as arithmetic, geography, religion, and history, were dedicated to academic teaching while the afternoons were dedicated to industrial training. Agriculture was greatly emphasized because the government considered it to be one of the only types of work Indians could secure on the reservation and a means to ensure the success of the Dawes Act (1887). Turning them into farmers meant training them to have "good manners and morals" (Annual Report of the Commissioner of Indian Affairs, 1889, p. 341) and to help them find a job on the reservation as the Commissioner of Indian Affairs explained in his report (1889):

> On their return to the reservation they will find agriculture the most convenient and profitable vocation. We cannot too much emphasize this habit of industry as one of the greatest factors in the development of Indian youth—not simply to know how to plough, plant, sow, etc., but to form a habit and acquire a love for work.
> (ARCIA, 1889, p. 322)

Agriculture was available in all on- or off-reservation boarding schools. Other trades were also offered to students, but they varied based on the school. Criteria for the implementation of such trades were not centered on the needs of the reservation but rather on the size of the school, its equipment, and its funding. Boys learned, for instance, to become tailors, wheel makers, blacksmiths, or carpenters. As for girls, they were trained in domestic sciences and learned to iron, clean, cook, and sew to become good "housekeepers, faithful and worthy wives" (ARCIA, 1887, p. 350). Indeed, the purpose of that vocational education was supposed to enable them to find a job on or off the reservation and to earn a living. However, throughout the system, testimonies of children and reports of inspectors or Commissioners of Indian Affairs revealed that the trades learned served more as a source of profit for the schools than an efficient educational tool.

In reality, workshops were either too crowded (ARCIA, 1889) or often lacked instructors (ARCIA, 1892) or the proper equipment (RG 75, Box 638). At the beginning of the 20th century, some of the trades even became "outmoded by mass-production in factories" (Reyhner & Eder, 2004, p. 182). Besides, a chronic underfunding of the boarding school system pushed the schools' officials to use these workshops as sources of profit. Everything the students manufactured (harnesses, wheels, saddles, shoes, shirts, etc.) was sold, and the money collected was reinvested in the school in an attempt to make up for the constant underfunding (ARCIA, 1897). As a consequence, the children's testimonies were, for the most part, unhappy ones as they underline how much vocational work they had to do in the schools:

> Getting our industrial education was very hard. We were detailed to work in the laundry and do all the washing for the school, the hospital, and the sanatorium. Sewing was hard too. We learned to sew all clothing, except underwear and stockings, and we learned to mend and darn and patch. We canned food, cooked, washed dishes, waited on tables, scrubbed floors, and washed windows. We cleaned classrooms and dormitories. [. . .] I have never forgotten how the steam in the laundry mad me sick; how standing and ironing for hours made my legs ache far into the night. By evening I was too tired to play and just fell asleep wherever I sat down.
>
> (Stewart, 1980, p. 17)

Therefore, vocational education meant to teach American Indian children the values and morals of work and to fight their idleness was not centered on the needs of the reservation and on the jobs that could be found there. Still, the problem of what was referred to as "returned students" and the possibility that they returned "to the blanket" was omnipresent in the annual reports:

> What becomes of the Indian pupils who graduated from the schools and return to the reservations? This question is variously answered. I have seen many painful cases of returned students who have lapsed into gross conditions of the old-time India life. [. . .] The falling away

of the graduate pupils so often referred to is not the fault of the schools but the condition of the agencies and reservations.

(ARCIA, 1889, pp. 333–334)

However, stating that American Indian children could not find a job after their instruction in an off-reservation boarding school is inaccurate. In 1897, 37% of the 1,774 employees of the Indian School Service were Indian (ARCIA, 1897). By the end of the 19th century, returned students had secured 45% of some 2,562 positions in the Indian School Service (Adams, 2006). However, these figures need to be analyzed with caution, first because they only represent Indians employed by the government and second because it was difficult at the time to collect and find information about returned students.

CONSEQUENCES OF BOARDING SCHOOLS

Almost a century of assimilation through education and the use of vocational education that has not been adapted to Indian needs affected Indian communities socially and culturally. One of the consequences of the boarding schools was the loss of tribal languages and traditions:

> I spoke Indian when I went to school. I could speak some English because my sisters went to school. So you learnt. They told you when they came back . . . "You can't speak Indian; you got to speak English. If you speak Indian, you get whipped." It took them a long time to get it out of me. And to this day . . . I speak some words . . . But I don't speak it fluently. I used to be able to speak it fluently before I went to school.
> (Haig-Brown, 1988, p. 121)

The schooling of Indian children far from their families and communities for up to five years in some instances created a cultural shock and a moral trauma. For instance, the relationship between parents and children was often broken because of the long separation, which affected both deeply:

> Children returning home were often alienated within their communities and experienced uncomfortable relationships with guilt-ridden parents. Low self-esteem and self-hatred were commonplace. Many Natives turned to alcohol and violence as ways to express their anger and despair. The damage done to Native families and individuals through the boarding school program left a legacy of rage, and delivered children back to their communities ill-prepared to raise their own children.
> (Bowker, 2007, p. 6)

Parenting skills were indeed modified as children learn how to become parents by following the model of their own parents and the way they are educated. As a consequence of sending children to boarding schools, the parents were unable to perform their role as parents. Later, the children who became parents found themselves in the same situation as their parents and were also unable to take on their parenting skills as they had no model to reproduce:

> For me, I just did all of the things that I wanted to ... maybe that helped me in my parenting, because I had no skills and you don't know how to function in a family with a mom and dad. You never seen that role growing up, so for me it was all new. Not just being a parent, but what is a parent. I had to learn all those things on my own.
>
> (Bowker, p. 76)

In fact, the schools took away the responsibility of the parents because the parents were separated from their children all year long (Haig Brown, 1988). Finally, schooling strongly impacted Indian cultures and languages. Indeed, parents and grandparents played a significant role in transmitting cultural and linguistic heritage. Just as the link between parents and children was broken, so, too, was the transmission of cultural and traditional knowledge.

SELF-DETERMINATION AND THE RISE OF PAN-INDIANISM

After decades of a Western-centric educational system based on an Anglo-conformist assimilationist approach, the basic role of Indian education remains at the core of self-determination issues. The answer has pointed in two directions: assimilating into mainstream American society or following separate economic and social activities based on tribal cultures and traditions. The reality, however, suggests a middle ground with some form of cultural pluralism (Havighurst, 1978). How then did American Indians succeed in coping with and overcoming the experiences of the boarding schools to create an educational system responding to their specific needs while also focusing on vocational education?

A part of the answer lies in the analysis of the consequences of the boarding school system. Even though no one can deny that the system was detrimental to Indians overall, positive elements emerged in the long run. First, the efforts undertaken to assimilate by educating Indians failed. Second, in gaining an education, many students left the school system having mastered the English language. Finally, instead of replacing their students' Indian identity with an American one as planned, the schools reinforced it while creating a pan-Indian identity alongside older tribal identities. Howard (1955), an American sociologist, was the first to coin the term: "By Pan-Indianism is meant the process by which certain Indian groups are losing their tribal distinctiveness and in its place are developing a generalized non-tribal 'Indian' culture" (p. 215). Historically it takes its roots primarily in political and religious expression and solidarity with, according to Thomas

(1965), the birth of pan-Indianism at the end of the 18th century. Indian tribes started to see themselves as having a common interest in opposing the white man, and the political alliance that was born was accompanied by a pan-Indian religious movement.

To understand how the off-reservation boarding school system played a significant role in the emergence of pan-Indianism, it is necessary to have a closer look at the identity of Indian people, which can be synthesized into a three-layer hierarchy. Tribal identity is the most important one: Indians first belong to a specific tribe with its culture, language, and traditions. "Most Indians in the pan-Indian area conceive of themselves as let's say, Sioux and Indian and American" (Thomas, 1965, p. 81). Pan-Indianism, according to Thomas, creates "a new identity, a new ethnic group, [. . .] a new 'nationality' in America" (p. 82).

Tribal identity, having the greatest significance for Indians, was meant to be erased or eradicated by educational efforts. However, while tribalism was attacked on one side, pan- Indianism on the other side was slowly emerging. And it did so for two reasons: the constant attack on tribalism and the boarding school system that provided Indians with the tools for developing pan-Indianism. Off-reservation boarding schools, where pan-Indianism emerged initially, enrolled mostly children from Plains tribes in contrast to day schools and on-reservation boarding schools (Thomas, 1965). As a result, hundreds of children with different traditions, backgrounds, languages, and religions came into contact and lived together every year. As students were forbidden to speak their native languages, communication inside the school with classmates was made possible only through the use of English, which, as a vehicle of American culture and a tool to educate and assimilate Indians, became in reality a tool for future unity and cohesion among Indians. At first, it became the universal Indian language inside the schools and once schooling had ended outside of them as well. Additionally, it allowed students to understand how the American government worked and how they could best fight it.

When pan-Indianism emerged as a demonstration of resistance in the 1960s, it did not replace tribalism but complemented it (Hertzberg, 1971). Whenever Indians needed to resist or fight for their rights, they repressed tribal identities and became pan-Indian. In fact, a simple shift occurred in their main identity, although one does not disappear in favor of the other. This creation of a pan-Indian identity, for example, can be tied to the founding of the American Indian Movement (AIM). Created in Minneapolis in 1968, this pan-Indian organization "was founded to turn the attention of Indian people toward a renewal of spirituality which would impart the strength of resolve needed to reverse the ruinous policies of the United States [. . .]. At the heart of AIM is [. . .] a belief in the connectedness of all Indian people" (Wittstock & Salinas, para. 4). The various actions taken by AIM attracted the attention of the media and of the American public and contributed among other things to the passage of the Indian Education Act in 1972 and the Indian Self-Determination and Education Assistance Act in 1975, which ceded greater governmental and administrative powers to Indian tribes in terms of education. As a result, American Indians created their own higher education system, i.e., tribal colleges, which are a way of expressing tribal sovereignty.

TRIBAL COLLEGES AND VOCATIONAL EDUCATION

Tribal colleges have become a reality thanks to a combination of three factors: the rise of pan-Indianism, the awareness in the Indian world that higher education was necessary for their survival, and finally self-determination granted by the government. The attempts to eradicate native cultures and languages, the attacks on tribalism, and the boarding school system contributed to how American Indians have conceived their own educational alternatives (Flora & Emery, 2011). Tribal colleges, through a combination of academic and vocational courses, attempt to solve the various issues linked to American Indian higher education. They were created "as a way to increase access to higher education for youth growing up on reservations" (American Indian Higher Education Consortium, 1999, p. A-1).

The first, Navajo Community College (Diné College today), was founded on the Navajo Reservation in Arizona in 1968 (Oppelt, 1993). It set a precedent in the establishment of more tribally controlled colleges and four years later, five new tribal colleges opened (Haskell, KS; Oglala Lakota College, SD; Sinte Gleska University, SD; Southwestern Indian Polytechnic Institute, NM; and United Tribes Technical College, SD). In 1972, the presidents of the first six tribal colleges founded the American Indian Higher Education Consortium (AIHEC) to share information and develop federal subsidies. Despite the tribal character of each institution, the American Indian Higher Education Consortium became a reality thanks to solidarity among the six institutions whose mission and actions contributed to the creation of more post-secondary institutions. Stein (1992) studied the creation and the evolution of tribal colleges and justly points out that "tribal unity among the small number of tribally controlled colleges was essential to promoting the tribal colleges as viable options for Indian people in higher education" (p. 18).

In 1978, the Tribally Controlled Community College Assistance Act, also known as the Tribal College Act, facilitated the creation of more tribal colleges as it guaranteed "to provide grants for the operation and improvement of Tribal Colleges and Universities, to insure continued and expanded educational opportunities for Indian students, and to allow for the improvement and expansion of the physical resources of such institutions" (Public Law 95–471, 25 U.S.C. 640c—1[c]) (Tribal College Act, 1978).

As a result, more institutions were able to open. In 1980 there were 19 tribal colleges; by 1990 there were 27; and by 2000 there were 31 (AIHEC, 1999, p. A-5). The increase in their number reflects the reality of tribal colleges, the state of Native American education, and more generally the current state of Native Americans. The Indian community succeeded in creating and maintaining these institutions even though many were unstable and at high risk of closing due to a lack of funding despite governmental grants. This is why AIHEC in 1989 created the American Indian College Fund, whose mission is to collect money from various foundations, companies, and individuals (Boyer, 1997) for the following purpose:

> Transform Indian higher education by funding and creating awareness of the unique, community-based accredited tribal colleges and universities, offering students access to knowledge, skills, and cultural values which enhance their communities and the country as a whole.
> (American Indian College Fund, 2015, para. 7)

Despite funding issues, tribal colleges have become progressively stable institutions by providing Native American students with academic and vocational programs aimed at "increasing the student's ability to increase their income and contribute to their community" (Flora & Emery, 2011, p. 3). Today, AIHEC counts 37 tribal colleges, serving some 300 tribal nations and enrolling some 20,000 Native American full-time and part-time students (AIHEC AIMS Fact Book, 2012, p. 3). In its brochure, AIHEC (2015) defines itself as being "a unique community of tribally- and federally-chartered institutions working to strengthen tribal nations and make a lasting difference in the lives of Indians and Alaska Natives" (p. 1). In fact, since its creation, AIHEC helps its member institutions "through public policy, advocacy, research, and program initiatives to ensure strong tribal sovereignty through excellence in American Indian higher education" (AIHEC, 2015, para. 1).

One of the most significant objectives of tribal colleges is improving Native Americans' access to higher education, as explained by AIHEC:

> TCUs [Tribal Colleges and Universities] were created in response to the higher education needs of American Indians and generally serve geographically isolated populations that have no other means accessing education beyond the high school level. TCUs have become increasingly important to educational opportunity for Native American students and are unique institutions that combine personal attention with cultural relevance to encourage American Indians—especially those living on reservations—to overcome the barriers they face to higher education.
> (AIHEC, 2015, para. 2)

Indeed, tribal colleges give American Indians living on reservations opportunities to gain skills and qualifications that enable them to attend higher education, and the statistics illustrate the success of this encouragement. For instance, from 2001 to 2006, academic enrollment in general has increased by 23 percent (White House Initiative on American Indian and Alaska Native Education, 2010).

In terms of curricula, tribal colleges present academic programs that are quite similar to the ones at other North American universities. Tribal colleges offer a total of 350 programs, including apprenticeships, diplomas, certificates, and degrees. That last category is comprised of 181 Associate degrees at 23 tribal colleges; 40 Bachelor's degrees at 11 institutions; and five Master's degrees at two colleges in 36 disciplines (AIHEC, 2012, p. 3).

All the degrees offered at tribal colleges integrate vocational education, not because it is part of the trends in national education in the United States but because it helps foster individual and tribal economic and social improvements. Its significance goes beyond that of the individual to focus on reservations as well. It is resorted to more and more nowadays to attempt to improve the economic situation of reservations where the unemployment rate is extremely high. For instance, the Sokaogon Chippewa Community or the Oglala Sioux Tribe of Pine Ridge have unemployment rates of 93 percent and 89 percent, respectively (Schilling, 2013).

The objective is to help reservations in different areas. Economically, they try to increase employment, improve the skills of workers, attract businesses, and develop entrepreneurship. Politically, they attempt to develop leadership skills, and socially, they provide services such as continuing education, health care and counseling, and cultural programs (AIHEC, 2001). To make sure the programs correspond to local needs, some institutions have surveyed local communities and leaders to find out what skills are needed the most. For instance, Salish Kootenai College opened a forestry program as forestry is the dominant industry in Montana. Oglala Lakota College offers courses in natural resources management, agri-business, and entrepreneurship as agriculture and small businesses are the major industries in local communities (AIHEC, 2001). Besides, the statistics concerning tribal colleges' enrollment by program reveal first that these programs are quite successful among students as enrollment has been increasing over time. For instance, the business programs offered in tribal colleges enroll 11 percent of the students, while courses for the preservation of cultures and languages and American Indian studies offered in 28 institutions have grown by 101 percent from 2003 to 2010. STEM programs (science, technology, engineering, and mathematics) have grown by 92 percent, and vocational careers enroll 12 percent of the entire student population (AIHEC, 2010).

Besides, the holistic dimension of vocational education in tribal colleges is echoed in the work of AIHEC, which has throughout the years developed different partnerships with large governmental agencies such as the Peace Corps, the United States Department of Agriculture (USDA), and the National Aeronautics and Space Administration (NASA). In fact, its partnership with the lattermost has resulted in the AIHEC Facilitator/Broker Corps project. It is designed to accomplish the following goal:

> Bridge individual Tribal College academic and student support programs and NASA science education and research resources in a synergistic

manner, enhancing the educational and career development resources available to the college, while increasing the effectiveness of NASA education, research, and workforce development programs to engage and recruit American Indian students.

(AIHEC, 2010)

If one of the realities of education is comprised of the different issues linked to the economic and social condition of Indians living on reservations (alcohol dependence, poverty, unemployment, and others), the other reality presents offers of hope, signs that the living conditions of Indians can be improved partly through education. Tribal colleges are key to the future of Indian communities because they are institutions run by Indians for Indians with minimal interference from the government concerning curriculum and because they offer various programs adapted to the needs of the Indian communities.

Nonetheless, American Indian communities still have to deal with many obstacles in post-secondary education. For example, the legacy of cultural and linguistic destruction or repression in the boarding schools is still present. Many former students have retained the idea that English, the language of the mainstream society, was to be learned to the detriment of the "inferior" native languages, which explains why still today some parents are reluctant to allow bilingual education for their children (Reyhner & Eder, 2004). Besides, many Native people are still suspicious of any government-funded programs. This is mostly true for elementary education as education is compulsory; tribal colleges have the advantage of being institutions of higher education, targeting adult Indians who have enrolled in such institutions because they made that choice.

Another issue tribal colleges face is a high dropout rate. Although more and more students enroll in tribal colleges these days, the percentage of students who do not graduate is high. In 2012 for instance, 39 percent of American Indian students who started in 2005 as first-time, full-time students at four-year institutions graduated compared with 60 percent of White students (Knapp, Kelly-Reid, & Ginder, 2012). Linked to the dropout rate are efforts to attract people to go to tribal colleges. Potential students do not reject an Indian college outright, but the problem is that they do not want to pursue higher education for the following reasons: financial problems, a lack of aptitude in reading and math, single-parent families, limited knowledge of English, parents not involved in their children's education, another dropout student in the family, or being alone at home for more than four hours every day. In 1995, 34 percent of Indians met two or more of the above criteria (Juhel, 1995). That is why a lot of tribal colleges try to improve the retention rate of American Indian students.

Finally, funding remains another major issue. The American Indian College Fund continues to help by granting scholarships to students and encouraging cultural preservation. For instance, they fund cultural and language preservation courses, try to develop leadership among Indian communities, and encourage people to become faculty members (AIHEC, 2010).

DISCUSSION ON THE TRANSITION FROM BOARDING SCHOOLS TO TRIBAL COLLEGES

Considering the past use of vocational education in boarding schools and the trauma it inflicted on Native Americans, one could legitimately wonder why tribal colleges center their curricula on such courses. There are various answers to that question. First and foremost, vocational education at the time of the boarding schools did not have the same significance for tribal development as it does now. The assimilationist policy had focused on delivering agricultural and industrial instruction, thus limiting the access of American Indian children to higher education and restricting the kinds of jobs they could find if any were even available on the reservation at all. Second, tribal colleges establish their curricula and adapt them to the needs of individuals and communities. It is important to keep in mind that the United States government does not interfere in the programs offered by tribal colleges. Finally, vocational education used in other mainstream postsecondary institutions is not used in an assimilationist or a detribalization approach but as revitalization, as a retribalization process serving Indian communities and their members.

To understand how retribalization operates today, it is necessary to briefly explain how detribalization was carried out in the off-reservation boarding schools. It became the tool chosen by the government to carry out the policy of assimilation through the displacement of children from the reservation to schools exclusively for one race and through physical transformation with the objective of achieving cultural transformation. Inside the schools, detribalization was achieved in many ways like cutting the children's hair, giving them clothes typically worn by white people, forbidding them to speak their native language, giving them a new American name, and, most of all, requiring them to speak English only (Adams, 1995). In the Annual Reports of the Commissioner of Indian Affairs (ARCIA), there are numerous comments on the benefits of forcing the pupils to speak English:

> I venture the assertion that in no other institution are there as many different nationalities and languages as are gathered here with the object of molding all into one people, speaking one language and with aims and purposes in unison with the civilization of the day and its government.
> (ARCIA, 1897, p. 370)

However, the objective of assimilation was doomed to fail from the start because the U.S. government and the reformers have always refused to consider Indians in their diversity. To them there was one national Indian community with one problem and one solution, yet belonging to a tribe implies traditions, languages, and cultural features specific to that tribe. As a result, education for Lakota students was not suitable for Navajo children. This lack of understanding partly explains why the policy of assimilation failed even though the constant efforts to detribalize Indians worked (loss of culture, tradition, and language).

Despite the failure of the policy of assimilation through education, tribal cultural specificities were deeply affected. Indians had trouble relearning their mother language or even just integrating with their families and communities. However, it is because assimilation failed that Indians were able to reverse the trend and regain self-determination acquired partly thanks to pan-Indianism, itself developed because of assimilation through education. Retribalization therefore becomes a tool to reverse the consequences of many decades of bad decision-making. Promoting retribalization is a major asset for Indians in the perpetuation, the development, and the revitalization of tribal linguistic and cultural specificities through educational programs:

> The impact of forced displacement of Indian people to attempt to eradicate native religions and the boarding schools experiences all contributed to how tribes have worked to create their own educational alternatives particularly tribal colleges and universities.
> (Flora & Emery, 2011, p. 3)

The phenomenon of retribalization operates at two levels. First, tribal colleges participate in the retribalization of individuals, the members of a community, by providing courses on Native American culture (e.g., literature, history, religion, arts and crafts, or languages), which enable Indians to learn about their culture and reacquire their tribal identity, which had been lost, repressed, or put aside. It represents a major asset for Native Americans as it allows them to maintain and perpetuate, among other things, cultural specificities as it narrows the gap between the different generations by preserving tribal languages. For instance, Bay Mills Community College in Michigan has developed a language program to produce new speakers of Ojibwe. This is achieved through an immersion program where the instructors only speak Ojibwe and teach cultural traditions. Classes "are not taught by rote memorization, but rather via a dynamic and practical method that relies upon social and cultural contexts, storytelling, skits, and word games" (AIHEC, 2012, p. 7).

Tribal colleges have also understood that for education to succeed, reciprocity is essential. It is undeniable that it is significant to focus these curricula on reservations; therefore, reservation communities should be involved in the development of this curriculum. Northwestern Indian College in the state of Washington, for instance, establishes initiatives that are developed on an as-needed basis and as such offers programs at the invitation of local tribes (Akweks, Bill, Seppanen, & Smith, 2009). This reciprocity holds true especially when it comes to achieving cultural, historical, and language preservation:

> Elders work with many of the TCUs, including Lac Courte Oreilles Ojibwa Community College (Hayward, WI), Stone Child College (Box Elder, MT), Sisseton Wahpeton College (Sisseton, SD), Tohono O'odham Community College (Sells, AZ), and Wind River Tribal College (Fort Washakie, WY). Elders teach classes or workshops in language, traditional crafts, and history; provide guidance and counseling; pray with and for students; and translate materials.
>
> (AIHEC, 2010, p. 6)

Second, by providing academic and, more specifically, vocational courses, tribal colleges participate in the retribalization of the community as well. This reinvestment can be done in different ways on reservations: setting up wireless networks, opening libraries that archive documents concerning Native Americans, and operating childcare centers (AIHEC, 2010). Fond du Lac Tribal and Community College offers students and community members counseling services. They include educational, career, and personal counseling (mental health issues, domestic/sexual violence, and grief issues) (Fond du Lac Tribal College, 2015). Giving back to their community and being involved in its improvement and development allow students and graduates to find their identity again. Tribal colleges actively participate in the retribalization process by offering cultural activities as well. Leech Lake, Fond du Lac, and Haskell organize powwows, for instance, inviting all community members.

Pan-Indianism, which spread thanks to the boarding school system, is necessary in the process of retribalization, which seems paradoxical as one pleads for Indian unity on the one hand and for tribal individuality on the other. But in fact, being stronger as Indians allows people to be stronger as a tribe and as individuals.

> Boarding schools embodied both victimization and agency for Native people and they serve as sites for both cultural loss and cultural persistence. These institutions intended to assimilate Native people into mainstream society and eradicate Native cultures, became integral components of American Indian identities and eventually fueled the drive for political and cultural self-determination in the late 20th century.
>
> (Davis, 2001, p. 20)

In its holistic approach, the American Indian Higher Education Consortium also embodies how pan-Indianism served the cause of retribalization. Brought forth from the gathering of tribal institutions to form a national association that also has a pan-Indian dimension, AIHEC through its actions provides financial and organizational help to develop the network of tribal colleges and as such promotes both pan-Indianism and retribalization.

In fact, the change from detribalization to retribalization could be developed around another similar paradigm: the change from assimilation to cultural pluralism, thus achieving exactly the opposite of past government policies. Havighurst (1978) defines cultural pluralism as having three main characteristics: mutual respect and appreciation, collaboration in government and economic affairs, and self-determination. Cultural pluralism can only be achieved through a combination of pan-Indianism and retribalization, hence the significant role of tribal colleges today.

The best illustration of the evolution from boarding schools to tribal colleges is Haskell Indian Nations University, located in Lawrence, Kansas. Haskell began as an off-reservation boarding school and was one of the first federal boarding schools to open its doors to Indian children in 1884. It remained open and became a high school even after the government officially abandoned the boarding school system and its assimilationist policies. Then in 1970, the institution was transformed into a tribal college, enrolling an average of 1,000 students every semester (Haskell Indian Nations University, 2015).

Haskell's motto reflects on the will of Native Americans today to move on and look toward the future while at the same time keeping their traditions through education. "Building our future . . . Preserving our tradition . . . through academic excellence" (Haskell Indian Nations University, 2015). Haskell is proof that Native Americans have become strong enough to overcome past traumatic experiences and take their fate into their own hands.

Today, tribal colleges are more than just higher education institutions; they are symbols of hope, signs that the conditions of Native Americans can be improved with education.

FURTHER RESEARCH

Though the topic of vocational education's impact is the focus of some scholars' research, a great deal still remains to be done because it is a relatively new topic. Research producing qualitative and quantitative data is showing good progress, but the implementation of findings remains an issue because tribal colleges continue to lack significant funding. There are many projects institutions may wish to implement in response to tribal needs, but without proper funding, implementation is often partial at best, making the validity of any results doubtful.

As part of the many topics that still remain to be explored in the field of Native American education, one should not forget that Canada's First Nations were also the target of assimilation through education and were also educated in boarding schools (called residential schools). In fact, Canada and the United States have had very similar Indian policies, especially concerning education. Boarding schools existed in both countries, and tribal cultures and languages were also eradicated in both. It would be interesting to compare both countries' progress since the end of the boarding school systems (Leforestier, 2012).

Besides, the links established in this chapter between identity and education and between education and self-determination could be broadened to include all Aboriginal people around the world. In recent years the situation of Indigenous people has been brought to the international scene with the rise of Indigenous forces from all over the world. In the past decades, the pan-Indian movement has evolved into a pan-Indigenous one where many Aboriginal groups now cooperate. This pan-Indigenous movement has distinct advantages. By jointly working on common problems, solutions such as self-determination, economic development, and protection of sacred land can be proposed at the international level. The emergence of pan-Indigenous movements increases the power of aboriginal communities and their strength both as unified entities and as separate ones. Pan-Indigenous movements are mostly associated with political issues. What about education? The governments of Australia, New Zealand, and Canada, for instance, have had the same assimilation policies concerning the aboriginals for even longer than the U.S. What about today? Has the Aboriginal community succeeded in securing greater responsibilities and control of its education?

*****

It is undeniable that off-reservation boarding schools were detrimental to Native Americans, but it is also important to focus on the positive outcomes that in the end allowed Native Americans to survive as a people and as independent tribal nations. Tribal colleges have shown that Native Americans are able to take control of their education and use it to improve their condition. They are signs that an appropriate education can lead to positive consequences even though tribal colleges today still need to make a place of their own in the American educational system. The key element to a successful future is not just education. It is also a matter of identity, and to be more specific, finding and restoring that repressed tribal identity. Once Native Americans have overcome the trauma of the boarding schools, which destroyed or undermined their tribal identity, they will be able to strengthen it through education. In fact, "education for extinction," the expression used by Adams (1995) in one of the first comprehensive books about Native American boarding schools, is now becoming education for survival.

Are we witnessing an *Indian renewal* as Rostkowski (2001) put it, or are we witnessing a complete transformation, the birth of *new Indians*? This expression implies that American Indians are the main actors of the retribalization process, which gives them a proper tribal identity different from pre-Columbian times as they have adapted and integrated some of the white man's way of life and thinking through the policy of assimilation. In both the former and the latter, we are witnessing a radical or evolutionary movement directed toward the future for American Indian populations. Nevertheless, the definition of Indian identity is still unclear for the government and for Native Americans. Who can be identified as Indians nowadays? What are the main criteria of this identity: blood quantum, self-identification, or way of life? These questions will find answers with the joint efforts and collaboration of the American government and the Indian tribes involved.

REFERENCES

Adams, D. W. (1995). *Education for extinction: American Indians and the boarding school experience 1875–1928*. Lawrence, KS: University Press of Kansas.

Adams, D. W. (2006). Beyond bleakness: The brighter side of Indian boarding schools, 1870–1940. In C. E. Trafzer, J. A. Keller & L. Sisquoc (Eds.), *Boarding school blues: Revisiting American Indian educational experiences* (pp. 35–64). Lincoln, NE: University of Nebraska Press.

Akweks, K., Bill, N., Seppanen, L., & Smith, B. L. (2009). *Pathways for Native American students: A report on colleges and universities in Washington State*. Olympia, WA: Evergreen State College.

American Indian Higher Education Consortium (AIHEC). (2012). *AIHEC AIMS fact book 2009–2010: Tribal colleges and universities report: Sharing our stories-strengthening our nations through tribal education*. Alexandria, VA: Author.

American Indian Higher Education Consortium (AIHEC). (2015). *Tribal colleges: Educating, engaging, innovating, sustaining*. Retrieved from http://www.aihec.org

American Indian Higher Education Consortium (AIHEC) and the Institute for Higher Education Policy. (1999). *Tribal colleges: An introduction*. Washington, DC: Authors.

American Indian Higher Education Consortium (AIHEC) and the Institute for Higher Education Policy. (2001). *Tribal college contributions to local economic development*. Washington, DC: Authors.

Annual Report of the Commissioner of Indian Affairs (ARCIA). (1887). Washington, DC: U.S. Government Printing Office.

Annual Report of the Commissioner of Indian Affairs (ARCIA). (1889). Washington, DC: U.S. Government Printing Office.

Annual Report of the Commissioner of Indian Affairs (ARCIA). (1892). Washington, DC: U.S. Government Printing Office.

Annual Report of the Commissioner of Indian Affairs (ARCIA). (1897). Washington, DC: U.S. Government Printing Office.

Atkins, R. C. (1933). Tuskegee's vocational program for men. *Journal of Educational Sociology*, 7(3), 175–183.

Bowker, K. M. (2007). *The boarding school legacy: Ten contemporary Lakota women tell their stories*. Bozeman, MT: Montana State University.

Boyer, P. (1997). *Native American colleges: Progress and prospects*. Princeton, NJ: Carnegie Foundation.

Carl D. Perkins Vocational and Applied Technology Education Act Amendments of 1990, 20 U.S.C., § 2301 (1990).

Cohen, S. (1968). The industrial education movement, 1906–1917. *American Quarterly*, 20(1), 95–110.

Coleman, M. C. (1993). *American Indian children at school, 1850–1930*. Jackson, MS: University Press of Mississippi.

Davis, J. (2001). American Indian boarding school experiences: Recent studies from Native perspectives. *Magazine of History*, 15(2), 20–22.

Flora, C., & Emery, M. (2011). Vocational learning by and for Native America in the United States of America. In R. Catts, I. Falk & R. Wallace (Eds.), *Vocational learning: Innovative theory and practice* (pp. 111–126). New York, NY: Springer Science & Business Media.

Fond Du Lac Tribal Community College. (2015). *Counseling services*. Retrieved from http://fdltcc.edu/student-support/counseling-services/

Haig-Brown, C. (1988). *Resistance and renewal: Surviving the Indian residential schools*. Vancouver, British Columbia, Canada: Tillacum Library.

Haskell Indian Nations University. (2015). *Onward Haskell*. Retrieved from http://haskell.edu

Havighurst, R. J. (1978). Indian education since 1960. *Annals of the American Academy of Political and Social Science, 436*, 13–26.

Hertzberg, H. W. (1971). *The search for an American Indian identity: Modern pan-indianism movements*. Syracuse, NY: Syracuse University Press.

Howard, J. H. (1955). Pan-Indian culture of Oklahoma. *The Scientific Monthly, 18*, 215–220.

Indian Self-Determination and Education Act of 1975, 25 U.S.C. §450 (1975).

Juhel, J.-M. (1995). *Les centres universitaires tribaux et l'effort d'autodétermination des indiens d'Amérique dans l'enseignement supérieur, 1968–1993* [Tribal colleges and the American Indian effort at self-determination in higher education] (Unpublished doctoral dissertation). Université de Bordeaux III, Bordeaux, France.

Knapp, L. G., Kelly-Reid, J. E., & Ginder, S. A. (2012). *Enrollment in postsecondary institutions, fall 2011; financial statistics, fiscal year 2011; and graduation rates, selected cohorts, 2003–2008: First look (provisional data)* (NCES 2012-174rev). Washington, DC: U.S. Department of Education. National Center for Education Statistics.

Leforestier, C. (2012). *L'assimilation des Indiens d'Amérique du Nord par l'éducation: Une étude comparative* [The assimilation of North American Indians through education: A comparative study] (Unpublished doctoral dissertation). Université de Bordeaux III, Bordeaux, France.

Miller, M. T. (1993). *The historical development of vocational education in the United States: Colonial America through the Morrill legislation*. Retrieved from ERIC Database. (ED360481)

Moton, R. R. (1933). The scope and aim of Tuskegee Institute. *Journal of Educational Sociology, 7*(3), 151–156.

Oppelt, N. T. (1993). *The tribally controlled Indian college: The beginnings of self-determination in American Indian education*. Tsaile, AZ: Navajo Community College Press.

Reyhner, J. A., & Eder, J. (2004). *American Indian education: A history*. Norman, OK: University of Oklahoma Press.

Rostkowski, J. (2001). *Le renouveau indien aux États-Unis: Un siècle de reconquêtes*. [The renewed Indian in the United States : A century of reconquest]. Paris, France: Albin Michel.

Schilling, V. (2013, August 29). *Getting jobbed: 15 tribes with unemployment rates over 80 percent*. Indian Country Today Media Network. Retrieved from http://indiancountrytodaymedianetwork.com

Stein, W. J. (1992). *Tribally controlled colleges: Making good medicine*. New York, NY: Peter Lang.

Stewart, I. (1980). *A voice in her tribe: A Navajo woman's own story.* Socorro, NM: Ballena Press.
Thomas, R. K. (1965). Pan-indianism. *American Studies, 6*(2), 75–83.
Tindall, G. B., & Shi, D. E. (1999). *America: A narrative history.* New York, NY: W.W. Norton.
Tribally Controlled Community College Assistance Act of 1978, 25 U.S.C., §1801 (1978).
White House Initiative on Tribal Colleges and Universities. (2010). Retrieved from http://www2.ed.gov/about/inits/ed/indianed/docs.html
Wittstock, L., & Salinas, E. J. (n.d.). *A brief history of the American Indian Movement.* Retrieved from http://www.aimovement.org/ggc/history.html

4 "How Can We Change Without Destroying Ourselves?"
Arguments for Self-Determination and Workforce Education Through Tribal Colleges and Universities

John Goodwin

For the past several decades, American Indian communities have striven to take advantage of opportunities to exert self-determination over the various facets of their political, social, and cultural livelihoods. This chapter in particular examines the historical roots and early expressions of American Indian self-determination in higher education as a fundamental step in the larger effort to promote independent, healthy communities across Indian Country. The central goal of this chapter is to show how the fundamental philosophy of American Indian self-determination has been combined with the concrete goals of workforce education through the work of tribal colleges and universities (TCUs).

In order to fully understand what impact TCUs have had, how they operate today, and what challenges they still seek to overcome, it is necessary to examine how the era of self-determination overlaps with the tribal college movement. Without an understanding of the recent history of American Indian higher education, positive development for many Native communities is hard to envision theoretically or enact pragmatically. The historical background of tribal colleges and universities is especially important because these institutions represent one of the first true expressions of American Indian self-determination in the realm of education in that they are run by and are designed to serve their immediate tribal communities. Furthermore, a historical understanding of TCUs and the principles that have informed their founding and the construction of their curricula reveals that these schools have often performed multiple intertwined community functions that cannot be separated from one another.

Workforce education has been one of the most important of these functions, but its presence in TCUs must be understood as one part of a larger educational movement in American Indian communities. This movement has roots that stretch back to previous generations of Native leaders, but the context of the 1960s and 1970s provided a spark that launched an entirely new and exciting form of education in the United States. Through conference speeches, educational research papers, journal and newspaper articles, and tribal newsletters, educational leaders in American Indian communities developed a more powerful presence in the conversation on education than they ever had before. For the first time, self-determination over American Indian education began to gain true momentum, and the principles behind it became tangible in tribal colleges and universities.

This educational discourse comprises a powerful Native voice that gained increasing influence over time, was shaped and strengthened by widespread debate and collaboration, and became a key factor in affecting policy toward workforce development for American Indians. American Indian tribes and communities sought their own balance in an approach to education. They sought to engage mainstream American educational and workforce developments while at the same time protecting their unique tribal and cultural identities. Indeed, they came to argue that successful workforce education was inseparable from the protection of tribal and American Indian identities. As a result, their institutions often purposely embraced multiple simultaneous goals—workforce development *and* cultural renewal, for instance.

This chapter highlights the fact that a fundamental continuity exists between the educational philosophies and goals of the early tribal college movement and the continued efforts to advance workforce development and self-determination in education today. Indeed, the theoretical language and practical goals of self-determination and workforce education as part of tribal community development have remained remarkably intact from the 1960s until today. Embracing a long-term framework allows present-day educational leaders to distinguish which philosophies remain the most important for Native people and which strategies have had the most promising results. This framework can also show that tribal colleges and universities have in fact brought tangible, positive results to their communities' workforces. With a long-term perspective, today's supporters of self-determination and workforce development can be reassured that their efforts continue to align with a decades-long intellectual tradition in Native communities.

On the other hand, a broad temporal framework also underscores the fact that today's challenges—such as the fight for greater student retention and higher levels of funding—have deep histories and remain difficult to overcome. The recognition of these problems' origins and developments keeps the discussion of workforce education focused on long-term goals while opening up more fruitful conversations about what exactly terms like *success* can and should mean in Native communities according to Native people themselves.

Finally then, this chapter seeks to give a human face and a human voice to the philosophies that have become important principles in the workforce education strategies of American Indians today. So often the development of strong educational models depends on effective implementation of ideas that have come from years of empirical research and applied theory. This chapter seeks to show the vital intersections between these models, the institutions where they have been implemented, and—most importantly—the human beings they have affected on a ground-level basis. For American

Indian workforce education, tribal colleges and universities have been key sites of these interactions.

CONCEPTUAL FRAMEWORK: WORKFORCE EDUCATION AND THE PERSPECTIVES OF NATIVE COMMUNITIES

As mentioned above, tribal colleges and universities have acted as tangible and practical sites for combining the goals of self-determination and workforce education. However, in order to see how these two come together, it is first necessary to arrive at a clear understanding of what each term signifies. Regarding self-determination, Harris et al. (2011) have defined the movement as "the returning of Indigenous peoples and people to effective sovereignty, self-sufficiency, and harmony, that they may revert to living well in their own communities while partnering with their neighbors, the nation, and the world for mutual advancement" (p. vii). This contemporary philosophy of self-determination matches well the practical efforts of tribal colleges and universities, which from the beginning have sought to protect tribal identity and tribal sovereignty while also collaborating with mainstream American institutions for educational support and economic growth (Stein, 1992). Brayboy, Fann, Castagno, and Solyom (2012) have similarly argued that for American Indian self-determination to be successful, it must be "manifested" (p. 29) by Native people, not simply theorized. As the remainder of this chapter will show, TCUs today still maintain this complementary relationship between the philosophy and the manifestation of self-determination.

Unlike the literature on self-determination, traditional definitions of workforce education can represent a particular view of the relationship between education and society that does not always reflect the outlook of an American Indian reservation community. For instance, Gray and Herr (1998) envisioned workforce education as a specific subset of formal education, distinct from other forms of general learning. In the reservation setting, American Indian groups have often viewed formal education in a more integrated and holistic sense, recognizing the need within the community to have all systems from childhood through adult education working together for the economic and social welfare of the tribe. They have necessarily developed programs to target different segments of the community, but the goal was for *all* of these programs to collectively address the needs of communities that were often poor and suffered from high unemployment. As early as the 1950s, for instance, Navajo leaders called for higher education as a means to "supplant" non-Indians as lawyers, land managers, doctors, and nurses within their communities and as a way to improve the state of poverty on reservations. Young Native students themselves also saw universal relevance in education. One student endorsed a "message of acculturation, but also a concern for realizing individual . . . potential" based on tribal identity (Iverson, 2002, pp. 108–109).

In order to see workforce education in a way that more readily combines with the goals of Native communities, this chapter utilizes a broader conceptualization of workforce education and workforce development. Jacobs and Hawley (2009) have embraced the idea of a more general definition, emphasizing the goal of "provid[ing] individuals with the opportunity for a sustainable livelihood" that is "consistent with the societal context" (p. 2543) rather than focusing on a narrowly defined model of workforce education.

This more holistic approach to workforce education better aligns with the realities of American Indian communities. It not only complements the concept of self-determination as defined by Harris et al. (2011) but has been reflected in efforts to improve tribal colleges and universities in particular. In a twenty-first century context, His Horse Is Thunder (2012) reported on the *Breaking Through* initiative within TCUs. This initiative was designed to work with community colleges to address under-skilled workforces and "break through the barriers that get students stuck in remedial education and accelerate them through pathways" (Jobs for the Future, n.d., para. 3) to careers that support their families and communities. In her report on this initiative, His Horse Is Thunder emphasized the importance of culturally relevant family and community support for students as a factor in higher retention rates. An approach such as the Family Education Model, the author argued, holds great potential for balancing a student's need for individual responsibility with the necessary support that comes from extended family membership and a connection to tribal culture (HeavyRunner & DeCelles, 2002; His Horse Is Thunder, 2012). The significant finding from the Family Education Model is that, for TCUs in particular, "replicating the extended family structure within the college culture enhances the student's sense of belonging and leads to higher retention rates" (HeavyRunner & DeCelles, 2002, p. 29). In recent years, this type of model has been aided by organizations like Jobs for the Future and the National Council for Workforce Education through programs such as the *Breaking Through* initiative. These programs work to improve student retention, offer students the most promising job prospects possible, and overcome challenges such as poverty-stricken communities and low levels of funding for education. Still, these efforts and challenges regarding American Indian workforce education have deeper roots, which stretch back to the very foundations of TCUs.

Tribal colleges and universities have been working through the concepts that underpin approaches like the Family Education Model for decades. Tribal leaders and their advocates have long viewed workforce education as part of a holistic type of learning that includes positive concepts of tribal and American Indian identity. Indeed, the argument they developed from the 1960s and 1970s onward has posited that workforce development is *only* possible if fundamental concepts of students' identities are protected and nourished in a culturally relevant manner.

The American educational context of the 1960s and 1970s also provided an environment concerned with notions of student self-actualization, which complemented the educational philosophies of the early tribal colleges and universities. This combination of factors proved supportive of TCUs in developing their own ideas of curricula and general educational approaches, providing the potential for self-determination in education. Over time, TCUs continued to battle critics who saw American Indian communities as lagging behind mainstream Americans in terms of educational and economic success. Even today, some view the impact of TCUs on workforce development as inefficient and ultimately unable to ameliorate economic and social ills on reservations (Burnett, 2013). This chapter seeks to build on both historical and contemporary sources to form a coherent, long-term image of these developments. With a broad temporal framework, educators today can more clearly see the continuity between past and present goals of self-determination and workforce education, the successes that TCUs have achieved in pursuing these goals, and the ways in which TCUs today continue to innovate in order to overcome persistent challenges.

SECONDARY LITERATURE ON AMERICAN INDIAN EDUCATION

Unfortunately, secondary literature on American Indian education has largely failed to connect self-determination, workforce education, and the role of tribal colleges and universities in a broad temporal framework from the 1960s to the present day. The lack of such a connection will be addressed briefly here, and the remainder of this chapter will serve as one response to that void.

For the most part, tribally controlled institutions have appeared in secondary literature as part of one of two larger contexts. First, many recent works have focused on overall Native nation-building and self-determination efforts in the mid-to-late 20th century where higher education of American Indians plays a supporting role. However, this scholarship has generally focused either on activist groups such as the American Indian Movement (AIM) or on the legal and legislative battles between tribes and the U.S. government. In this sense, tribally controlled institutions of education serve as brief illustrations of a larger movement (Cobb, 2008; Shreve, 2011; Wilkinson, 2005).

In a second context, Native control of education has appeared in longer histories of education from the point of European contact until the present. With such a wide range temporally, authors can rarely devote in-depth analysis to any one segment of the history (e.g., DeJong, 1993; Reyhner & Eder, 2004; Szasz, 1999). Stein (1992, 1999) has been one of the few scholars to explore American Indian–controlled education—and specifically TCUs—as a central topic in book-length form. Stein's experience working closely with several TCUs as an administrator and educator is invaluable, providing insight into the origins of the colleges that few other secondary sources can offer. His framing of the issue has rested largely on legislation that provided funds for the institutions, which he has persuasively argued is the constant concern of the colleges. This focus gives clarity to the sequence of milestone moments for TCUs, yet it provides less analysis of the arguments surrounding the very idea of Native control. Indeed, Stein (1992) himself has pointed out that "no one has fully explored the reasons for [tribal colleges'] genesis and continued existence" (p. 1). Even since the publication of his assessment, few major projects have examined the topic in detail (Brayboy et al., 2012).

The intellectual debates surrounding the emergence and early years of TCUs—found in many of the sources examined in this chapter—can thus offer a more vibrant and more focused picture of how these institutions address concerns in the present while connecting to a rich past. The remainder of this chapter will illustrate how TCUs have combined the philosophies and goals of self-determination and workforce education over a period of nearly five decades. Utilizing this long-term framework displays a fundamental continuity in TCUs not only in terms of their guiding purposes but also in terms of the most difficult challenges they still face today, such as community poverty and consistent underfunding. The two sides of this continuity explain how a discourse can develop wherein some observers see inspiring results for American Indian workforce education while others portray Native communities as perpetually lagging behind. Furthermore, the disparate views of this discourse prompt a deeper conversation about what exactly "progress" or "success" can and should mean. By focusing on how ideas of self-determination and workforce education overlap within TCUs in a broad temporal framework, this chapter illustrates that these schools have in fact achieved significant successes according to the goals and standards established by the communities they serve. Just as importantly, they continue to test and refine the philosophies of self-determination and the tangible strategies for greater workforce education.

HISTORICAL DEVELOPMENT OF TRIBAL CONTROL IN WORKFORCE AND HIGHER EDUCATION

In order to understand how tribal colleges and universities operate today and which fundamental philosophies guide their overall mission, it is necessary to understand how and why they developed in the first place. In June 1961, Clarence Wesley, then-Chairman of the San Carlos Apache Tribe, wrote the opening article for the inaugural edition of the *Journal of American Indian Education* (*JAIE*). Wesley's (1961) call for new forms of education that would respect and protect Native "songs, tribal dances, arts and crafts" (p. 7), and other forms of culture served as an early indication of the discourse that would soon develop around the connection between education and community prosperity for American Indians. This discourse would eventually help fuel the movement toward TCUs as sites of self-determination and greater practical direction of workforce education.

That same month, 500 Native leaders from over 90 tribes assembled for the American Indian Chicago Conference, organized by University of Chicago anthropologist and activist Sol Tax (Ablon, 1962; Cobb, 2008). Though this conference failed to develop a unified endorsement of a "formal statement of what Indians want for their future" (Ablon, 1962, p. 17), it did encourage intense debate and create a lively forum for information-sharing. One Native woman who attended related, "[W]hen I came here, I thought only of my people and our problems, and now I think of *all the Indian people and all their problems* [emphasis added]" (Ablon, 1962, p. 22). Many ambitious Native students learned from their experience at the Chicago conference and soon formed the National Indian Youth Council (NIYC) (Cobb, 2008). This body built upon previous regionally based councils and aggressively pursued improvements in American Indian healthcare, economic conditions, and especially education (Minton, 1961; Shreve, 2011). The Chicago conference thus served as a spark for an expanding discourse on American Indian education and its role in Native communities. The *JAIE*, the publications of the NIYC, and numerous other forums then fed off one another in a nationwide momentum that carried this discourse well beyond the summer of 1961.

American Indian leaders and their supporters began by focusing on the desirability of gaining control of their own educational institutions as a centerpiece for meaningful change in terms of economic and workforce development. In much the same way that Jacobs and Hawley (2009) did, Native educators and their advocates viewed all levels of education as ultimately feeding their tribal workforces and the effort to strengthen the economic development of their communities. Dillon Platero, for example, spoke as the chairman of the education committee for the Navajo Tribe in 1960 about the realization among his people "that education is, and will be, the livelihood of the Navajo people in the future" (quoted in Iverson, 2002, p. 110). While he praised vocational training, he also implored his fellow educators to recognize the importance of the relationship between educational institutions, the students, their families, and tribes in general: "As the years pass we have seen that programs that were not sanctioned by the Navajo people have been rather unsuccessful" (quoted in Iverson, 2002, pp. 111–112).

What leaders like Wesley and Platero sensed in the early 1960s was a troubling lack of harmony between American Indian communities and the institutions responsible for educating their future workforces. This interpretation was backed up by a growing body of educational research on many fronts, in part spurred on by the emerging National Indian Youth Council. The NIYC encouraged an informative, accurate discussion of education as a path toward the correction of problems like poverty and other social ills in American Indian communities (Shreve, 2011).

The research and related commentary in the NIYC's early publications described education for American Indians as inadequate for fostering confidence among students and their communities. An Emory University study of

Oglala Sioux youth in South Dakota schools commented on "an appalling and frightening separation and lack of communication between teachers and students, school and community, administrators and teachers, and parents and the school" ("Oglala Sioux," 1963, p. 9). Without a fundamental level of trust between the schools, the students, and the community, educational development was often stymied at a very young age, making the idea of a motivated body of students in higher levels of workforce development difficult to imagine.

Further research showed that Native students also struggled in quantifiable ways that translated to students' economic prospects in the American workforce. For instance, among 11th and 12th graders tested in New Mexico, American Indian students in the early 1960s were approximately five grade levels below average in reading (Townsend, 1963). These numbers undoubtedly spoke to a language divide that could not be blamed entirely on public schools or their teachers. Still, in an environment with a high percentage of Native students, the schools showed a general lack of innovation in meeting the problems experienced by these students. Most teachers (80%) had no professional training in the teaching of reading skills, and this dearth of appropriate attention became in the eyes of American Indians another sign of "public schools fail[ing] to function equally well for all students" (Townsend, 1963, p. 10).

Poor educational achievement meant high dropout rates for Native students. Disheartening graduation and retention rates represented one of the most frequently expressed problems in the discourse of American Indian education throughout the 1960s. Kutsche (1964) studied Cherokee high schools and concluded that "the Cherokee feel their system does not now serve them in important ways, [as] the dropout data eloquently testify" (p. 27). If students did move on to college, success was elusive. At the University of New Mexico in the early 1960s, education professors noted that nearly 75 percent of all American Indian students dropped out before graduating (Charles, 1962). Wesley (1961) noted a similar rate at the University of Arizona. As years passed, results in higher education showed few signs of improvement; Dr. Robert Roessel Jr., who worked for years to improve Navajo education, argued that Navajo dropout rates in college approached 90 percent into the last years of the decade (as cited in "Navajo College," 1969). Similarly, Forbes (1966) plainly saw the connection between the state of American Indian education and the resulting workforces, which "lack[ed] prerequisite educational skills for meeting the challenges posed by poverty, poor organization, [and] rapid social change" (p. 1). Forbes recognized that even college-educated American Indians were disillusioned by the disconnect between their formal training and the real-life conditions on reservations, and were left "ill-prepared . . . for leadership among their own people" (p. 1).

The observations here reveal the state of American Indian education in the 1960s. The discourse surrounding it offered multiple voices and angles, but all approaching a generally agreed-upon problem: the lack of meaningful connections between schools and their Native students and, in turn, alienation, poor performance, and high dropout rates. All of these factors, revealed at multiple levels of education and in multiple types of institutions, contributed to generally ill-prepared workforces in American Indian communities. Fortunately, educators and Native leaders recognized these issues and worked toward new approaches—namely, the philosophy of American Indian self-determination in education as a means to improved workforce development.

Calls by Jack Forbes and other Native leaders for greater American Indian autonomy in education coincided with key changes in United States government positions toward poverty in general and toward American Indian communities in particular. For instance, Lyndon B. Johnson's "Great Society" opened up opportunities for communities to enact their own plans for addressing poverty, and Native people did not hesitate to take advantage. Wilkinson (2005) argued that although the term *self-determination* itself did not take off in popular usage until the 1970s, the federally funded Community Action Programs (CAP) under Johnson's Office of Economic Opportunity (OEO) allowed Native people to put the philosophies of self-determination into practice by the mid-1960s.

The shining example of this effort was the Navajo-controlled Rough Rock Demonstration School, which used OEO funds to open in 1966 as the first tribally controlled school on reservation land in the United States (Reyhner & Eder, 2004). Although Rough Rock served young children, its tribally controlled administration and creative curriculum stood as examples that translated to higher education and workforce education as well. After only six months of operation, Rough Rock had already attracted attention from visitors across the country. Over 50 American Indian tribes were represented among the visitors—the clearest sign available that Native educators throughout the country were engaged in a powerful and widespread discourse about the possibilities of taking charge of their educational systems for the benefit of their communities.

Rough Rock showed in practical terms how the philosophy of self-determination in education could utilize some of the basic methods of mainstream American educational systems while also protecting tribal identity and cultural expression (Reno, 1967). As Roessel (1968) pointed out soon after Rough Rock's opening, American Indian people within the community had not failed to notice this key moment. Rough Rock had created the need for an entirely new term among Navajo people. Whereas before all types of schools had fallen under categories that translated to "Washington school" or "white man's school," there was "now a new type of school which I think has real significance: 'Dineh Beolta' (The People's school, the Navaho school)" (p. 2).

The example of tribal control at Rough Rock inspired reservation communities throughout the country to establish additional educational centers, largely focusing on an existing void in higher education and workforce development. By 1968, the OEO had approved a proposal to create Navajo Community College, and the tribe's approval of an all-Navajo Board of Regents represented an affirmation of American Indian authority at the first tribally controlled reservation college in the country (Nixon, 1968). By 1972, half a dozen TCUs had been established. The American Indian Higher Education Consortium (AIHEC) formed that same year as a support base and information-sharing group for these new and economically vulnerable institutions. Establishing AIHEC continued a process among Native people of sharing information and debating the best strategies for education and workforce development in particular communities.

Individual schools also began producing newsletters and other texts to achieve this aim. Navajo Community College, for example, produced texts that focused heavily on Navajo-specific issues such the contemporary relationships with the United States and the state of Arizona regarding possible sources of funding (Roessel, 1971). Through the *Sinte Gleska College News* (1978), faculty members at that college discussed ongoing efforts to develop curricula, encouraged students to enroll in Lakota-centered cultural programs, and published editorials on the benefits of education in challenging racial stereotypes.

For all the early TCUs, progress toward full control came in stages, and collaboration with outside institutions was necessary. Bismarck Junior College; Mary College; the Universities of South Dakota, Colorado, and Minnesota and other institutions offered initial extension programs on reservations in North and South Dakota (Stein, 1992). Navajos, too, had worked closely with Arizona State University, Northern Arizona University, and other area schools throughout the planning of Navajo Community College ("Navajo Junior College," 1968). And yet, the early mission statements and subsequent publications of TCUs contained explicit references to autonomous American Indian control, and they attempted to create "real alternative[s]" (One Feather, quoted in Stein, 1992, p. 41) as opposed to simply importing mainstream forms of education or workforce development. Still, the willing collaboration between tribal educators and outside institutions underscores the central vision of these early TCUs—that Native cultural identity was encouraged not as an end in and of itself, but as a crucial first step in a larger mission to build and maintain better-prepared community leaders and workforces. Whereas public schooling alone had seemingly failed to serve Native students in meaningful ways in terms of both cultural identification and the basic skills of workforce development, tribally controlled schools could now approach these seemingly disparate educational realms in tandem. In other words, the leaders of early TCUs recognized that workforce education on reservations might be best approached with an explicit recognition of the particular historical and cultural factors facing their students.

It is striking to see how closely the early TCUs' goals and mission statements align with the workforce education philosophies of recent authors such as Jacobs and Hawley (2009), who have emphasized the importance of "a sustainable livelihood" that is "consistent with the societal context" (p. 2543) of an individual's community. For example, the primary goals of Oglala Lakota College were "to develop teaching methods and course structure and contents fitting the learning psychology, job needs, and life styles of the Oglala Sioux" as a path to "solv[ing] the social, political, and economic problems plaguing the reservation" ("OSCC Survey," quoted in Stein, 1992, pp. 45–46). Both themes—cultural consistency and a path to a sustainable livelihood—existed side by side in the minds of the TCUs' founders, their instructors, and their students. Tribal colleges and universities became at once sites of tribal and American Indian identity as well as sites for attacking the problems that led to under-prepared workforces. In this way, they were also sites for working toward a notion of self-determination that Harris et al. (2011) have continued to endorse in the 21st century.

The overlapping and mutually beneficial goals of workforce education and self-determination were reflected early on in actions as well as in words. At Navajo Community College, for instance, programs such as Tribal Work Experience, Community Development and the Career Opportunities Program placed students of a variety of ages in direct contact with their Navajo communities as teachers' aides and other employees (Navajo Community College, 1972a). At the same time, the curriculum rooted students in their tribal and Native culture by requiring Navajo Studies, which emphasized the importance of clan systems and kinship networks as sources of strength and affirmations of identity. Inquiry Circles also provided counseling services to guide students through their coursework or simply offer help on "any question, problem, difficulty or conflict" they may have had (Navajo Community College, 1972b, p. 18). This approach permeated not just Navajo Community College but all of the TCUs. At Standing Rock Community College, the curriculum explicitly placed the goals of vocational and adult education side by side with the goal of increased appreciation for tribal culture, and other institutions mirrored this effort (Stein, 1992). In the course catalog of Sinte Gleska University, vocational or GED-oriented courses appeared alongside courses such as "Lakota music and dance," "Sioux history and culture," "Lakota thought and philosophy," "American Indian literature," and "Indian Education" ("Spring Semester," 1978).

This multifaceted approach embraced the general goals of workforce education at the same time that it sought to ground students in a context of tribal and American Indian identity that would prepare them for success in whatever context they chose (Benham, 1975). It also fostered connections between students and their families, communities, and cultural traditions in ways that educators and policymakers could not ignore. At Navajo Community College, for instance, enrollment not only increased by the hundreds within the first three years after founding, but retention approached 90 percent—a symbolic reversal of the nearly 90 percent dropout rate that had plagued Navajo students in off-reservation colleges (House, 1974; "Navajo College," 1969; Navajo Community College, 1972b). By the mid-1970s, the efforts of tribal colleges and universities were receiving vindication from accreditation agencies, and the schools were finally drawing greater support from federal lawmakers.

In the summer of 1976, the North Central Association of Secondary Schools and Colleges (NCA) awarded full accreditation to Navajo Community College ("NCC Granted," 1976). The NCA's committee noted the "clarity of philosophy and objectives" along with the "unity of the Board of Regents, faculty and staff, supportive of that philosophy" ("NCC Granted," 1976, p. 1) as key strengths at Navajo Community College. The NCA's approval of these principles marked a key endorsement of the expression of American Indian self-determination in education. Then, in early 1978, Sinte Gleska University President Lionel Bordeaux praised the "imminent" approval of the Tribally Controlled Community College Assistance Act. Bordeaux viewed "the funding of this bill [as] necessary to [the school's] survival" ("Message," 1978, p. 2), and saw great potential for the advancement of TCUs' efforts to enact self-determination and expand American Indian workforce education. Indeed, this vindication by agencies like the NCA, along with a permanent source of funding through the legislation of the 1970s, has helped spur the TCU movement for the past several decades.

ASSESSING THE LONG-TERM EDUCATIONAL AND ECONOMIC IMPACTS OF TCUS

Understanding the early intellectual bases of this movement better informs educators about how tribal colleges and universities operate today. In particular, this broad temporal framework shows that Native communities with TCUs have from the beginning operated with a holistic understanding of workforce education and have seen the basic tenets of self-determination as a key part of the effort to direct and improve that workforce education in meaningful ways. From the 1970s until the present day, there has been an explosion of tribal colleges and universities throughout the country. There are now 37 TCUs serving over 20,000 students in the United States, and they have displayed a remarkable degree of continuity with the goals and philosophies of the early movement toward tribal control in education (Higher Learning Commission [HLC], 2013).

Pavel, Inglebret, and Banks (2001) highlighted one main branch of this continuity by studying the mission statements and goals in publications by TCUs in the past couple of decades. At Bay Mills Community College in Michigan, for instance, the mission has been "to integrate traditional Native American values with vocational training and general education as a way of preparing students to assume responsible roles in their respective communities" (BMCC, 1994, p. 2, quoted in Pavel et al., 2001, p. 54). Similarly,

Little Priest Tribal College in Nebraska has worked to teach students to "interface within a diverse world" (LPTC, 1997, p. 6, quoted in Pavel et al., 2001, p. 55). More evidence of the same sentiment comes from Sisseton Wahpeton Community College in South Dakota, chartered in 1979 and accredited in 1990. Their guiding philosophy included the goal that students "participate with competence in both the Indian and the non-Indian worlds, and to appreciate the merits of both" (SWCC, 1994, p. 2, quoted in Pavel et al., 2001, p. 57). Even today, scholars of American Indian higher education continue to emphasize the importance of these same themes. For example, Cajete, Sachs, and Gagnier (2011) have argued that the most pressing issue in American Indian education remains the need to create a "contemporized, community-based education process that is founded upon traditional tribal values, orientations, and principles but that simultaneously utilizes the most appropriate concepts and technologies of modern education" (p. 323). These statements from several distinct voices and contexts all align with the original guiding principles of the tribal college movement—that the basic philosophy of self-determination in schooling can aid Native communities by balancing the protection of Native culture and identity with a dedication to practical workforce education.

In addition to the continued dedication to these principles, tribal colleges and universities have also demonstrated a significant and tangible impact on their communities over the course of the past several decades. While the presentation of hard data in this vein has been sporadic, it has also been encouraging. Katus (1980) presented the results of her own follow-up study on the first 68 students to graduate from Standing Rock Community College. Of the 64 respondents to her survey, 52 were employed while four others were continuing their schooling elsewhere—a striking contrast to the report of "nearly 60%" unemployment on the reservation as a whole (Katus, 1980, p. 4). These graduates also overwhelmingly maintained connections to their home community, with 98 percent of full-time working graduates employed on the reservation itself (Katus, 1980). A separate survey of Turtle Mountain Community College found an unemployment rate of just 13 percent among those who graduated during the 1980s, compared with a rate of 55 percent on the reservation as a whole (Boyer, 1997, as cited in AIHEC and The Institute for Higher Education Policy [IHEP], 1999). Researchers have also uncovered limited but encouraging results on dropout rates. In one case study from the early 1990s, American Indian students who attended Salish Kootenai College before transferring to the University of Montana fared markedly better in GPA and rate of graduation than those who went straight from high school (Zaglauer, 1993, as cited in AIHEC & IHEP, 1999). The periodic efforts to compile and display these encouraging results have continued into the 21st century, supported largely by the American Indian Higher Education Consortium (AIHEC & IHEP, 1999, 2000; His Horse Is Thunder, 2012).

While these results signal some of the positive impacts that tribal colleges and universities have made on workforce education and on quantitative markers such as employment and degree completion, critics still point to the many American Indian reservations that struggle with poverty and high unemployment. Even communities with TCUs do not quickly or easily escape these same problems (His Horse Is Thunder, 2012). This reality raises important questions regarding the role of TCUs and their ability to enact meaningful change. One recently published opinion piece (Burnett, 2013) by a former politician from a state with several TCUs illustrates how powerful and pervasive the negative rhetoric surrounding these schools can be. Burnett contrasted TCUs with "actual universities" (para. 18) and suggested that "spending on tribal colleges has proven to be a dubious investment" (para. 19). In contrast to the bulk of sources examined here in this chapter, Burnett also argued that the schools "give little weight to helping students increase their earnings or contribute to economic development" (para. 12). This negative appraisal of the goals and impacts of TCUs may be a minority opinion today, but it nevertheless represents an opinion that Native leaders and their advocates continue to grapple with. As Burnett and other prominent critics rely on data that emphasizes the frustrating persistence of low retention in schools and high poverty and social ills on reservations, it becomes ever more important for these communities to demonstrate the positive impact that does come from tribal control in higher education and workforce development.

Fortunately, recent research displays both qualitatively and quantitatively how beneficial TCUs have been and continue to be for Native people. As Pavel et al. (2001) have acknowledged, one of the most important qualitative results of TCUs is that they "have turned the balance of power" (p. 60) in favor of American Indian communities. With greater control in tribal colleges and universities, Native leaders can "create educational curricula that simultaneously allow them to build their community infrastructures and to promote participation in the larger . . . society of the United States" (p. 60). For example, Gonzalez (2012) noted that Little Big Horn College in Montana recently collaborated with the Australian-American Energy Company to offer programs for students to work on earning certificates or Associate degrees while also gaining skilled training geared toward company "positions paying upward of $100,000" (para. 39). Many TCUs also partner with non-reservation colleges and universities, combining to develop shared programs that address economic interests like tribal gaming or cultural interests like Indigenous studies and Native languages (Cajete et al., 2011). These partnerships have shown that American Indian workforce education can evolve according to the needs of Native communities through true collaboration with non-Native entities rather than depending solely on the basic labor demands of outside economic forces. These efforts also align with the broad goals of self-determination as defined by Harris et al. (2011)—to "revert to living well in [Native] communities while partnering with neighbors, the nation, and the world for mutual advancement" (p. vii).

Effective collaboration with nearby businesses and schools is part of the reason that TCUs have shown promising economic results in and around their communities. By surveying the needs of the local and regional economies, tribal colleges and universities have attempted to prepare workforces with skill sets as relevant and useful as possible. For example, Salish Kootenai College has provided extensive courses in forestry to match the industry needs of the surrounding region, while schools in heavily agricultural states have tailored courses toward agribusiness (AIHEC & IHEP, 2000). Graduates from TCUs thus not only attain employment at higher rates than non-graduates but often do so within the local economic systems of their home communities and regions. In one striking example of TCUs meeting local workforce needs, Oglala Lakota College's nursing program by the turn of the 21st century was providing about 50 percent of the nurses in the nearby Indian Health Service facility (AIHEC & IHEP, 2000). Without the college's directed effort to develop its nursing program, the hospital would be forced to hire non-Indian graduates with the requisite education. Tribal colleges and universities have also been shown to help communities broadly—not simply individuals. Reservations with TCUs have experienced faster-growing median incomes as well as reduced overall poverty rates for the reservation population (AIHEC & IHEP, 2000). Moreover, results indicate that there may be "a positive relationship between the number of years each Tribal College [has] been in existence and most of the income measures" (AIHEC & IHEP, 2000, p. 17). In general, then, the evidence of TCUs' impact on Native individuals and communities appears to contradict the pessimistic conclusions of outspoken critics like Burnett (2013).

As this section has illustrated, tribal colleges and universities today display a remarkable sense of continuity with the educational philosophies and practical workforce goals of the earliest TCUs. Beginning with a critique of the state of education for American Indians in the middle of the 20th century, Native leaders in education built a strong argument for the principles of self-determination as a path to building more meaningful relationships between educational institutions, students, and communities. Embracing a broad definition of workforce education, these leaders and their advocates took advantage of the opportunities of the 1960s and 1970s to found their own sites of higher education. At tribal colleges and universities, Native groups constructed forms of workforce education that directly involved students in serving their communities socially and economically, while also engaging them in a culturally relevant and supportive environment. The following section will describe how TCUs today work from a strong sense of continuity with their original goals and philosophies while continuing to innovate in order to address persistent challenges in American Indian education and workforce development.

FUTURE RESEARCH DIRECTIONS: BALANCING HISTORICAL CONTINUITY AND THE NEED FOR INNOVATION

Encouraging signs of commitment to long-term goals and philosophies have not slowed the effort for continual innovation and improvement at tribal colleges and universities. Educators and researchers at TCUs recognize not only the continuity with the past in terms of their missions but also the many particular challenges in American Indian education that persist as well. This section outlines some of the most recent attempts to address these challenges and introduces topics for further research.

One example of the benefit of the broad temporal framework used in this chapter is that, in highlighting some positive long-term trends, it also uncovers areas that require further study. For example, Brayboy et al. (2012) have acknowledged that the long-term progress made in American Indian education has not been spread evenly to all segments of the Native population. In particular, while all types of higher education degrees awarded to American Indian students increased from the 1970s through the 1990s, the notable exception was in PhDs awarded to men (Brayboy et al., 2012). Future research could focus on why Native women have experienced such dramatic progress in levels of education while progress among male students has been slower. Moreover, research that focuses on the motivations of different segments of the student population could aid Native communities in the broad goal of coordinating all aspects of workforce education, from childhood education through institutions offering advanced degrees and certificates.

A long-term framework for American Indian workforce education also aids in the understanding of the negative aspects of continuity with the past. For instance, one of the key efforts of tribal colleges and universities over the years has always been to improve student retention. Low retention rates in higher education have generally been a problem for American Indian students in mainstream American colleges. While attendance at TCUs has been shown to improve the retention of students who move on to non-reservation schools (AIHEC & IHEP, 1999; Cajete et al., 2011; HeavyRunner & DeCelles, 2002), tribal colleges and universities continue to address the retention issue at their own sites as well. Often this requires directly challenging or refining some of the traditionally accepted norms of American higher education. Fortunately, some research has recently shown the benefits of an approach that does not shy away from challenging old traditions to meet old trends.

HeavyRunner and DeCelles (2002) have explicitly addressed the issue of retention from multiple angles. On the one hand, they have examined the accepted norms at traditional non-reservation schools for characteristics that could cause high dropout rates. They have argued that if schools view dropping out as the result of "a lack of individual commitment or ability, these institutions fail to recognize the disconnect between the institutional values and student/family values; hence the real reasons for high attrition rates among disadvantaged students are never addressed" (p. 33). As an alternative, HeavyRunner and DeCelles have advocated the Family Education Model as one promising strategy to increase retention and graduation rates. This model seeks to include a student's extended family and community networks in the education process, building partnerships between the school, the student, and the student's home community in ways that foster greater numbers in retention and graduation (HeavyRunner & DeCelles, 2002; His Horse Is Thunder, 2012). In this model, the central emphasis is not the *time* of completion so much as the successful completion of the educational process in a way that keeps family support networks healthy and provides career opportunities for the student to support those family networks (His Horse Is Thunder, 2012). In the setting of a TCU, the Family Education Model seeks to take advantage of relatively small student populations as well as institutional flexibility to achieve the most relevant educational track possible for each individual. More recent work has validated the model's focus on the importance of family networks. For instance, Guillory and Wolverton (2008) reported that the Native American students in their own study listed 1) family relationships, 2) giving back to tribal communities, and 3) on-campus social support as the three most important positive factors affecting their retention in school. Not only that, but these students also reported that problems with family networks were the most important factor that could negatively affect their retention.

While Guillory and Wolverton (2008) focused on non-reservation schools, their results indicate the potential usefulness of the Family Education Model for tribal colleges and universities serving primarily Native students. However, the model's effective implementation relies on the intense dedication of multiple staff members, counselors, teachers, students, and family members. As His Horse Is Thunder (2012) has pointed out, the plan "includes participation in workshops, seminars, Learning Center assistance, and individual interventions" (p. 13) that require time and effort from a properly trained staff. Unfortunately, "these resource-challenged institutions often [already] ask their faculty and staff to serve in multiple roles, including instructor, advisor, and career counselor" (p. 14).

PROBLEMS WITH ATTAINING FUNDING FOR WORKFORCE EDUCATION MODELS IN TCUS

This observation hints at perhaps the most resilient continuity of all in the long-term context of tribal colleges and universities: underfunding. While TCUs search for innovative strategies to reach students and their communities in positive ways, the level of available funding has never matched these ambitions. This reality is the result of multiple factors. As noted by Ruth Roessel (1971) in the first years of the TCU movement, tribally controlled schools on reservations did not receive state or local funds. This aspect has not changed, leaving TCUs primarily dependent on federal funding

(Harvard Project on American Indian Economic Development, 2008). The federal funding authorized under the Tribally Controlled Community College Assistance Act (P.L. 95–471) currently provides for funding at a level of $8,000 per American Indian student (HLC, 2013, p. 9). However, "Congress actually funds TCUs far below the authorized amount. In fiscal year 2011, TCU operating funds amounted to $5,235 per full-time Indian student, with no funding for the non-Indian students that compose about 20% of all TCU students" (HLC, 2013, p. 9). As a comparison, "the only other minority-serving institution in the nation that receives its basic institutional operating funds from the federal government is Howard University. Congress funds Howard University at . . . approximately $19,000 per student" (His Horse Is Thunder, 2012, p. 9). Combined, these factors leave funding for tribal colleges and universities lagging behind the amount of money available for other comparable types of educational institutions. The current situation makes daily maintenance of TCUs difficult and hampers new research as well as the implementation of promising programs like the Family Education Model.

Recently, some members of Congress have worked to improve funding for TCUs while collaborating with the nationwide effort to fund workforce education through the Workforce Investment Act (P.L. 105–220) (AIHEC, 2014). The proposed Native Adult Education and Literacy Act would not require a new program or new funds, but would simply assign "2.3 percent of the funds appropriated annually for carrying out the Adult Education State Grant portion of Title II of the Workforce Investment Act . . . for competitive grants made directly to TCUs and Native Hawaiian Education Organizations (NHEOs)" (AIHEC, 2014). If approved, this Act could represent a modest but significant improvement in the federal commitment to TCUs, their daily efforts in American Indian workforce education, and their dedication to further research and innovation.

*****

One of the central purposes of this chapter has been to illuminate the larger historical context of tribal colleges and universities. This effort has been made in part to illustrate that contemporary TCUs explicitly align themselves with the fundamental goals of self-determination as a promising approach to a broad and holistic form of workforce education. The type of workforce education offered by TCUs stresses cultural relevance and the protection of Native identity while also attending to the practical needs of the local economy and the social conditions of the community.

Since the earliest years of the TCU movement, the advocates of these schools have fought to maintain their daily work, to find new and innovative ways to reach Native students and impact Native communities, and to garner greater support and funding. Even today, tribal colleges and universities face their share of critics, who rely on discouraging reports of American

Indian economic and social welfare to argue that TCUs are overfunded and ineffectual. Still, a variety of research efforts over the past several decades has shown that in a long-term framework, TCUs have made great strides toward expanding the educational and workforce opportunities for Native students while also effecting positive economic changes in their broader communities. Even more important, tribal colleges and universities continue to act as educational sites where the fundamental goals of American Indian self-determination allow Native students and communities to work toward their own notions of success.

As Brayboy et al. (2012) wrote, "Indigenous students and communities may not always be interested in pursuing or framing success in the same ways or for the same reasons as other students and communities" (p. 3). In other words, tribal communities will decide for themselves how closely they wish to align their communities with non-Native standards of educational and economic success. Do they want to mirror the educational and economic systems of mainstream America as closely as possible, or do they want to maintain a clear sense of separation from the mainstream, which can result in "government structures and policies that may discourage industry and private infrastructure investment," (His Horse Is Thunder, 2012, p. 20)? Where is the proper balance between these choices? These are difficult questions without a single answer, and the introduction of these questions does not suggest that tribal communities should or will be content or satisfied with their current educational and economic situations. The important factor is that Native communities themselves are empowered through a tradition of self-determination to manage workforce education on their own terms.

Tribal colleges and universities have been especially pivotal in this effort because of their prominence within their communities and their dedication to addressing immediate socioeconomic challenges on reservations. Advocates of self-determination in education have asserted that success means the ability of students and emerging workforces to rely on a foundation of positive individual and group identity to meet the challenges of whatever path they choose.

This argument has developed over the course of many years, and the existence of tribal colleges and universities has not ended it. The encouraging results mentioned in the previous sections of this chapter do not prove TCUs' status as a panacea for all American Indian communities. However, TCUs provide one promising arena from which the argument for self-determination in workforce education can be advanced and refined through continual innovation. With this in mind, it seems fitting to conclude with a succinct example of the powerful discourse that has surrounded tribal colleges and universities from their beginning: "As a young Navajo has expressed it, 'How do we change without destroying ourselves?' While self-determination does not answer this question, it allows Native Americans the freedom to wrestle with it" (Adams, 1974, p. 26).

REFERENCES

Ablon, J. (1962). The American Indian Chicago conference. *Journal of American Indian Education, 1*(2), 17–23.

Adams, D. (1974). A case study: Self-determination and Indian education. *Journal of American Indian Education, 13*(2), 21–27.

American Indian Higher Education Consortium. (2014). *Support for the Native Adult Education and Literacy Act of 2014.* Retrieved from http://www.aihec.org/resources/documents/FY15/3b_Native%20Adult%20Ed%20-Literacy_WIA_2-6-2014.pdf

American Indian Higher Education Consortium and the Institute for Higher Education Policy (AIHEC and IHEP). (1999). *Tribal colleges: An introduction.* Alexandria, VA: American Indian Higher Education Consortium.

American Indian Higher Education Consortium and the Institute for Higher Education Policy (AIHEC and IHEP). (2000). *Tribal college contributions to local economic development.* Alexandria, VA: American Indian Higher Education Consortium.

Benham, W. J. (1975). A philosophy of Indian education. *Journal of American Indian Education, 15*(1), 1–3.

Brayboy, B. M. J., Fann, A. J., Castagno, A. E., & Solyom, J. A. (2012). Postsecondary education for American Indian and Alaska Natives: Higher education for nation building and self-determination. ASHE Higher Education Report, 37(5). San Francisco, CA: Wiley Periodicals. doi:10.1002/aehe.3705

Burnett, T. (2013, June 9). *The tragedy of tribal colleges: Government-subsidized colleges for Native Americans spend lavishly but the results are poor.* The John William Pope Center for Higher Education Policy. Retrieved from http://www.popecenter.org/commentaries/article.html?id=2858#.U84JZ-NdXJD

Cajete, G. A., Sachs, S. M., & Gagnier, P. M. (2011). The spiral of renewal: Appropriate Indian education. In L. Harris, S. M. Sachs & B. Morris (Eds.), *Re-creating the circle: The renewal of American Indian self-determination* (pp. 317–378). Albuquerque, NM: University of New Mexico Press.

Charles, C. M. (1962). A tutoring-counseling program for Indian students at the University of New Mexico. *Journal of American Indian Education, 1*(3), 10–12.

Cobb, D. M. (2008). *Native activism in Cold War America: The struggle for sovereignty.* Lawrence, KS: University Press of Kansas.

DeJong, D. H. (1993). *Promises of the past: A history of Indian education in the United States.* Golden, CO: North American Press.

Forbes, J. D. (1966). An American Indian university: A proposal for survival. *Journal of American Indian Education, 5*(2), 1–7.

Gonzalez, J. (2012, April 4). Tribal colleges offer basic education to students "not prepared for college." *Chronicle of Higher Education, 58*(32), A25–A26.

Gray, K. C., & Herr, E. L. (1998). *Workforce education: The basics* (2nd ed.). Boston, MA: Allyn and Bacon.

Guillory, R. M., & Wolverton, M. (2008). It's about family: Native American student persistence in higher education. *Journal of Higher Education, 79*(1), 58–87.

Harris, L., Sachs, S. M., Morris, B., Hunt, D. E., Cajete, G. A., Broome, B., . . . Chaudhuri, J. (2011). Introduction and acknowledgements. In L. Harris, S. M. Sachs & B. Morris (Eds.), *Re-creating the circle: The renewal of American Indian self-determination* (pp. vii–xiv). Albuquerque, NM: University of New Mexico Press.

Harvard Project on American Indian Economic Development. (2008). *The state of Native nations: Conditions under U.S. policies of self-determination*. New York, NY: Oxford University Press.

HeavyRunner, I., & DeCelles, R. (2002). Family education model: Meeting the student retention challenge. *Journal of American Indian Education, 41*(2), 29–37.

Higher Learning Commission (HLC). (2013). *Distinctive and connected: Tribal colleges and universities and HLC accreditation—considerations for HLC peer reviewers*. Chicago, IL: Higher Learning Commission.

His Horse Is Thunder, D. (2012). *Building the foundation of success: Case studies of breaking through tribal colleges and universities*. Alexandria, VA: American Indian Higher Education Consortium.

House, L. L. (1974). *The historical development of Navajo Community College* (Unpublished doctoral dissertation). Arizona State University, Tempe, AZ.

Iverson, P. (Ed.). (2002). *"For our Navajo people: Diné letters, speeches & petitions, 1900–1960*. Albuquerque, NM: University of New Mexico Press.

Jacobs, R., & Hawley, J. (2009). Emergence of workforce development: Definition, conceptual boundaries, and implications. In R. MacLean & D. Wilson (Eds.), *International handbook of education for the changing world of work* (pp. 2537–2552). New York, NY: Springer.

Jobs for the Future. (n.d.). *Helping colleges advance low-skilled adults into careers*. Retrieved from http://www.jff.org/initiatives/breaking-through

Katus, J. (1980). *A follow-up study of Standing Rock Community College graduates* (Master's Thesis). Retrieved from ERIC Clearinghouse. (ED212320)

Kutsche, P. (1964). Cherokee high school dropouts. *Journal of American Indian Education, 3*(2), 22–30.

Message from the President. (1978, November). *Sinte Gleska College News*. Mission, SD: Sinte Gleska College.

Minton, C. E. (1961). The place of the Indian Youth Council in higher education. *Journal of American Indian Education, 1*(1), 29–32.

Navajo college opens on Monday. (1969, January 23). *Navajo Times*, p. 1.

Navajo Community College. (1972a). *Report to the Navajo Tribal Council for Navajo Community College*. Chinle, AZ: Navajo Community College.

Navajo Community College. (1972b). *The Navajo culture center: Purpose and plans: A shrine and living symbol for the Navajo*. Tsaile, AZ: Navajo Community College Press.

Navajo junior college will open at Many Farms in January, 1969. (1968, May 16). *Navajo Times*, pp. 1, 3.

NCC granted full accreditation. (1976, July 29). *Navajo Times*, p. A1.

Nixon, B. (1968, April 25). Navajos plan college on reservation. *Navajo Times*, p. 1.

Oglala Sioux educational survey. (1963, October). *Americans before Columbus, 1*(1), p. 9–10.

Pavel, D. M., Inglebret, E., & Banks, S. R. (2001). Tribal colleges and universities in an era of dynamic development. *Peabody Journal of Education, 76*(1), 50–72. doi:10.1207/S15327930PJE7601_04

Reno, T. R. (1967). A demonstration in Navaho education. *Journal of American Indian Education, 6*(3), 1–5.

Reyhner, J., & Eder, J. (2004). *American Indian education: A history*. Norman, OK: University of Oklahoma Press.

Roessel, R. A., Jr. (1968). The right to be wrong and the right to be right. *Journal of American Indian Education, 7*(2), 1–6.
Roessel, R. W. (Ed.). (1971). *Navajo studies at Navajo Community College*. Many Farms, AZ: Navajo Community College Press.
Shreve, B. G. (2011). *The National Indian Youth Council and the origins of native activism*. Norman, OK: University of Oklahoma Press.
Spring Semester Class Schedule. (1978, January). *Sinte Gleska College News*. Mission, SD: Sinte Gleska College.
Stein, W. J. (1992). *The tribally controlled colleges: Making good medicine*. New York, NY: Peter Lang.
Stein, W. J. (1999). Tribal colleges: 1968–1998. In K. G. Swisher & J. W. Tippeconnic III (Eds.), *Next steps: Research and practice to advance Indian education* (pp. 259–270). Charleston, WV: ERIC Clearinghouse.
Szasz, M. C. (1999). *Education and the American Indian: The road to self-determination since 1928* (3rd ed.). Albuquerque, NM: University of New Mexico Press.
Townsend, I. D. (1963). Reading achievement of eleventh and twelfth grade Indian students. *Journal of American Indian Education, 3*(1), 9–10.
Wesley, C. (1961). Indian education. *Journal of American Indian Education, 1*(1), 4–7.
Wilkinson, C. F. (2005). *Blood struggle: The rise of modern Indian nations*. New York, NY: W.W. Norton.

5 The Role of Tradition in Education
Economic Development and American Indian Higher Education

Amy Fann, Linda Sue Warner, and G. S. Briscoe

"Whoever controls the education of our children controls our future."

—Wilma Mankiller

Tribally articulated needs for higher education are complicated by tribes' unique status as sovereign nations and by tribal priorities for self-government, cultural preservation, and economic development—all of which have a long history of abusive experiences with formal education. Although many ethnic and social groups have strong neighborhood or community ties, unlike other groups, American Indians are dual citizens of both their tribal nations and the United States. Additionally, these tribal nations wish to remain distinct, sovereign peoples (Brayboy, 1999, 2005; Pevar, 2012; Wilkins & Stark, 2010).

Despite the increasing need for workforce development to support tribal nationhood, American Indian students still have the lowest higher education enrollment of any ethnic group. American Indian nations look cautiously to colleges and universities to prepare tribal citizens for participating in nation-building efforts that preserve the political and cultural self-determination of their communities (American Indian Higher Education Consortium, 2007; Champagne & Goldberg, 2005; Jennings, 2004), yet American Indians have the highest high school dropout rates, the lowest academic performance rates, and the lowest college admission and retention rates in the nation (Faircloth & Tippeconnic, 2010; Johnson, Strange, & Madden, 2010; Proudfit & Gregor, 2014; Proudfit & Warner, 2015; Thornton & Sanchez, 2010). After decades of national-, state-, and institutional-level initiatives to increase access to higher education for historically underrepresented students, the traditional college pipeline for American Indians is largely unaddressed by mainstream higher education. The exception is the growth and expansion of tribal colleges and universities (TCUs) and the recent addition of curricular changes caused through the establishment of Native American-Serving Non-Tribal Institutions (NASNTIs) designated by the United States Department of Education. As a result, little is known and even less is understood about the critical issues, conditions, and college transitions of American Indian students. This chapter describes current efforts in higher education's workforce development from the perspective of specific programs found in both TCUs and NASNTIs. We propose to review models of indigenous pedagogy (Native ways of knowing) and to reflect on the quality of content expertise and delivery that is expected by tribal nations before summarizing the results of Fann's study from 2009.

Native students' opportunities for higher education are influenced by a web of cumulative, complex, and interwoven factors, especially for rural students with limited proximity to higher education opportunities: socioeconomic status, culture, familial education level, knowledge about college, neighborhood and community resources, and geography. All of these factors are mediated or constrained by K-12 educational practices, personnel, and resources; post-secondary institution costs and admission requirements; and political policies based on the notion of who "merits" college education, including access to private resources (McDonough & Fann, 2007).

The political, historical, and contemporary experiences of Native Americans include a unique set of circumstances and dilemmas that Native students face as they negotiate their way through high school and make choices about higher education. This includes special consideration of the unique political status of tribes and tribal priorities for political and cultural self-determination. We propose that the circumstances and dilemmas are best addressed through the incorporation of Native ways of knowing. The success of this strategy is apparent in the growth and expansion of tribal colleges, but more recently it can be found in public institutions of higher education where Native ways of knowing is incorporated in the delivery of general education courses. Increasingly, efforts to use culture to connect students to the curriculum provide opportunities for educators to introduce Native ways of knowing to students throughout Indian Country. By examining the linkages between Native ways of knowing and specific examples of workforce education, we highlight successful strategies.

NATIVE WAYS OF KNOWING

Faculty in higher education continue to complain that students who enter, particularly minority students, are inadequately prepared. These faculty, whether in two-year institutions or research universities, are content experts. The only exceptions can be found in Schools of Education, where instructional learning strategies are taught to potential teachers. Research on faculty teaching methods assures us that content-prepared faculty teach using the methods their instructors used. These methods rarely if ever include pre-assessment of students' knowledge, skills, and abilities and rely instead on the age-old "stand and deliver" method found in education for decades. General education faculty development on teaching strategies can be found in the delivery of online coursework because these methods are radically different from those experienced by the instructor. Workforce development at both the high school and college level, whether in class or online in content delivery, is best accomplished through teaching methods that correlate with constructivist methodology. For American Indians/Alaska Natives, these methods are Native ways of knowing.

Institutions of higher education, those institutions responsible for preparing K-12 teachers so that they in turn can adequately prepare students to make the best choices for higher education, have in the past neglected or refused to incorporate traditional language or culture into the curriculum. Teachers of American Indian/Alaska Native students in public, tribal, or Bureau of Indian Education schools are often unprepared for the challenges of working with tribally diverse students. By the time these students are ready for higher education, they have fallen behind and may have to begin their higher education experience in remedial courses, even at the community college level. For workforce development to be successful, both high school and college faculty need to understand and incorporate Native ways of knowing.

There are over 500 distinct indigenous tribal communities in North America alone. Each indigenous community belongs to a specific language group and recognizes and practices cultural traditions in combinations that distinguish communities from each other, especially to insiders. Some indigenous communities share a language heritage or land base yet remain distinct in other characteristics. Kawagley and Barnhardt (1998) explain this process as recognizing generalization as indicative, but not definitive. The task in this process requires a balance of perspectives. Native ways of knowing, in contrast to Western education practices, is acquired and represented through the context of place, revolving around the needs of a community including the best efforts to actualize a holistic understanding of the community's environment. Native ways of knowing uses an indigenous research lens to study and interact in the world. Western educational practices dissect and disconnect knowledge, while Native ways of knowing presumes a holistic context. The primary difference between the two lies in the emphasis of Native ways of knowing on "knowing" as a verb and Western educational practices that emphasize the accumulation of "knowledge," a noun (Warner, 2006).

The 1960s were an era of exciting expansion into higher education with community colleges playing a major role. TCUs began to make their appearance within this timeframe. Though there is a visible separation between non-Indian community colleges and tribally controlled colleges, specifically self-determination through the incorporation of Native ways of knowing, their functions are more similar than different. Both strive to serve their communities as comprehensive institutions providing programs that respond to community and student needs (Stein, 1999).

TCUs have as part of their overall mission statements language that includes the promotion of economic well-being of their community. For example, the Blackfeet Community College's mission includes "meaningful employment" (Blackfeet Community College, 2015, para. 8), and Diné College's mission includes "preparation for further studies and employment in a multi-cultural and technological world" (Diné College, 2015, para. 1). The United Tribes Technical College's mission "provide(s) self-determination and economic development for all tribes" (United Tribes Technical College, 2015, para. 1). To accomplish this mission, TCUs rely on economic assessment studies to determine the needs of the community and to design specific training programs to reflect the job skills needed. Economic realities for many tribal communities, such as 60–80 percent unemployment, particularly seasonal unemployment, reflect the challenges that need to be addressed. Today there are 39 TCUs (AIHEC, 2015). Wherever possible, each college provides vocational and technical programs that help assure that students can find decent jobs in their communities upon completion of their studies (AIHEC, 2007; Boyer, 2008). TCUs have a 40-year history of addressing the needs of tribal peoples using culture and language, but in the past decade mainstream higher education institutions began to recognize the need to address the retention of their Native population as well.

The Native American-Serving Non-Tribal Institutions' Program was authorized by the Higher Education Opportunity Act of 2008, originally authorized by the College Cost Reduction and Access Act of 2007. Grants are available to public institutions to assist in the planning and development of strategies that will serve Native American and low-income individuals. Projects include the development of curriculum and academic instruction, and funds can be used to modify these to reflect Native ways of knowing. Currently there are 26 NASNTIs in the United States, maintaining a minimum of 10 percent enrollment of American Indian students.

TRIBAL TRADITION AND WORKFORCE DEVELOPMENT

Tribal nations need both skilled professional and technical expertise to sustain this sovereign status, yet Native students question the relevance of formal education since few post-secondary institutions offer culturally specific curricula such as tribal law, cultural resource management, tribal languages, or other courses of direct relevance to tribal development needs (Brayboy, 2005; Erdrich, 1997; Fann, Wilson, Teeter, Alvitre, & Champagne, 2003). In addition, formal education is characterized by some to be at odds with traditional tribal education, values, and teachings (Brayboy, 2005; Grande, 2004; Smith, 1999). Add to this a long history of coercive federal education practices, cultural discontinuity between tribal communities and public schools, and experiences of racism in schools as contributing factors to Native communities' alienation from mainstream education (Cleary & Peacock, 1998; Deyhle, 1995). All of these factors are cause for citizens of Native nations to weigh the potential loss of tribal identity and culture against the potential benefits of continued formal education as they prepare for and make decisions about higher education.

In development and economic research, there is generally a direct positive correlation between an increase in community members' post-secondary education and training and subsequent growth in economic development. Research on tribal economic development, however, has thus far shown that sustainable development in Indian County has not been dependent on human and education capital. Sustainable economic development in tribal nations only occurs when decisions about development and accountability for those decisions are held directly by the tribe and are culturally congruent with tribal values (Cornell & Jorgensen, 2007; Cornell, Kalt, Jorgensen, & Spilde, 2007; Cornel & Kalt, 1992, 1995, 2007). Because of this, tribal economic development research is not addressing the role or potential role of higher education in training a skilled Native workforce. That human capital has not played a significant role in successful tribal economic development is understandable given the scarcity of post-secondary education completion by American Indians working for their tribes.

Conversely, college access research has not been conceived for a Native nation-building approach, i.e., looking at higher education in the context of tribal sovereignty and economic development, except by tribal colleges. Ironically, successful tribal economic development has only increased the critical need for Native expertise within tribes in all manner of occupations, including attorneys, teachers, ecologists, health care professionals, and business and fiscal managers. Clement (2009) noted that "the growth of tribal colleges and universities over recent decades has been nearly as phenomenal—if far less heralded—than the growth of Indian casinos" (p. 49). He characterizes tribal colleges as "economic engines" (p. 50) whose origins included addressing the poor educational outcomes experienced by American Indians in mainstream colleges by recognition of the importance of Native ways of knowing to create economic engines to improve the living standards for individuals and communities across Indian Country. In addition, tribal colleges increase skill levels and foster employment in local economies (AIHEC, 2000) and represent a "vital component of the process of building a foundation for future growth on Indian reservations [by] strongly contributing to the economies of this nation's most disadvantaged areas" (His Horse is Thunder, Miller, & Anderson, 2013, p. 12).

Because tribal colleges are located on or near reservations, they often have an impact as employers, creating jobs in areas where a local boost in the economy is significant. Many tribal colleges' programs rely on data from local community economic needs to drive the curriculum. Some TCUs have their own businesses in both professional and technical fields. Southwestern Indian Polytechnic Institute (SIPI) in Albuquerque, NM, exemplifies the pace at which tribal colleges are adopting new technologies. In 1993, the Institute had less than eight computers on its entire campus. Through several grants and funding sources, the institute tied all of its campus buildings together by fiber optic cable to enable Internet access, putting computer labs in every academic building and all the residence halls. Today, SIPI has a robust technology infrastructure with more than 200 computers—a 1:4 ratio of computers to students, all of which are networked and connected to the Internet. Through distance learning, SIPI provides classes and training opportunities to reservations throughout the Southwest. SIPI recently opened a state-of-the-art science and technology building, which houses an engineering program in which students are working on robotics projects in collaboration with partners such as NASA's Jet Propulsion Lab (Billy & Kuslikis, 2009). Programs such as these respond to the needs of local tribal economies.

Tribal colleges continue to reflect the workforce needs of local communities through the development and delivery of post-secondary curricula that incorporate Native ways of knowing while addressing workforce needs. A summary of the awards available to tribal college students is reflected in the following degree types/numbers available:

- Associate of Arts/200
- Associate of Science/140
- Certificate/212
- Diploma/8
- Associate of Applied Science/150
- Bachelor of Arts/20
- Bachelor of Science/4
- Bachelor of Applied Science 1
- Associate of Technical Arts/3
- Master of Arts/2
- Master of Education/1

The majority of the degrees available in tribal colleges and universities are at the two-year level, and 68 percent of the available degrees reflect an emphasis on meeting current community workforce needs. This emphasis can also be seen in the two-year public NASNTIs' delivery of coursework and degree availability. An example of the gear-up for NASNTIs can be seen in the development of three online degrees at Northeastern Oklahoma A&M College, where tribal input was sought in the development of Associate degrees in Early Childhood Education, Hospitality Management, and Criminal Justice. Each of these degrees is embedded with Native ways of knowing throughout the curriculum, including the general education courses linked to Associate degrees.

ONE CAMPUS, MANY NATIONS

The designation of NASNTIs by the U.S. Department of Education moved Native ways of knowing from the boundaries of tribal colleges into state-supported institutions. Northeastern Oklahoma A&M College (NEO), a two-year public college in Oklahoma, integrated Native ways of knowing into the curriculum as part of two federally funded grant projects—Title III, Part A, and Title III, Part F. The integration of Native ways of knowing is exemplified by the motto, "One Campus, Many Nations" because NEO is located in Miami, OK, home to nine federally recognized tribal governments. NEO developed a model to embed Native ways of knowing into existing and newly developed courses. At NEO, Native ways of knowing is defined as place-based or constructivist delivery to achieve course objectives and indicators of success. As NEO is a NASNTI, educators emphasized constructivist learning processes that encourage authentic exchanges, instructive demonstrations, and the opportunity to focus on real-life applications. A model was created to guide curriculum development that links Native ways of knowing and the "place" where students live and learn embedded in the rich history of NEO, the local American Indian tribes, and the communities in which students live (Warner & Fahnestock, 2013).

NEO maintains ties to the nine tribes who maintain tribal headquarters in Ottawa County. The college is built on land originally allotted to the Ottawa tribe. Currently 26 percent of the enrollment at NEO is American Indian, one of the largest in this country for a state-supported institution. NEO was founded as the Miami School of Mines in 1919 to meet the needs of a large mining community in northeast Oklahoma, southeast Kansas, and southwest Missouri. Through the years, the mission of the college changed to meet the needs of a broad spectrum of students. Today, the college serves as a comprehensive residential college, providing a range of student activities and intercollegiate sports.

The NORSE model emerged as the working framework to embed Native ways of knowing and place-based education in the NEO curriculum. In this model, NORSE is defined as follows:

Native Opportunities: Placed-based expectations
Retention: Forward movement
Success: Degree completion
Education: Lifelong learning.

Native opportunities or place-based expectations anchor the curriculum in northeast Oklahoma and emphasize the link to multi-tribal histories and heritage. Additionally, it affirms the "place" the student is in personally and respects the norms of each of the places the student is engaged in while pursuing a post-secondary degree. This definition of "place" also includes expectations for gender and age.

Retention, the second component of the NORSE model, is defined as forward movement. Retention at NEO is the timely matriculation of students to completion of a degree or certificate. Success at NEO is defined as degree completion in alignment with the national initiative, Complete College America. Strategies for retention and success go hand in hand. For students to reach their ultimate goals of degree or certificate completion, students matriculate through their academic programs in a timely manner. The emphasis on place in the curriculum and classroom supports both retention and completion.

Education is defined as lifelong learning in this model. Lifelong learning (education) assigns an emphasis on the creation of learners who have the opportunity to freely shape their individual life choices by responsible action. Instructors have begun to develop and link the artifacts of the curriculum to the NORSE framework. The process for moving mainstream curriculum to reflect Native ways of knowing included professional development and curricular redesign. The correlation between Native ways of knowing and constructivist teaching is high, and instructors are able to align assignments and assessments through reflection. For example, the course syllabi for the new online courses reflect the indicators of NORSE. Specific learning objects, which reflect NORSE as a framework, have been developed and are online for all instructors to use.

The individual course objectives reflect Native ways of knowing and include place-based education. The faculty teaching these courses developed course assessment strategies to determine the overall performance of students in relation to the objectives. Further assessment is being conducted at the college level. Faculty and staff are given an opportunity to provide feedback about Native ways of knowing, place-based education, and the use of the NORSE model in achieving the goals and promoting student retention and success. Native ways of knowing provides an opportunity for the administration and faculty to discuss the needs of NEO as a NASNTI to ensure that all students benefit from the programs and opportunities available.

One example of how Native ways of knowing and placed-based education can be found in the integration of the NORSE framework is a general education science class. Portions of Ottawa County were heavily mined for lead and zinc during the first half of the 20th century. The chat removed from the mines has a heavy lead content, and the water runoff from the mines carries minerals that are dangerous to the environment, creating a significant health hazard. Efforts to mitigate the distribution of minerals and their effects are ongoing. The local American Indian tribes are at the forefront of this effort because this impacts their "place."

An NEO faculty member who teaches a science course embedded with the NORSE framework incorporated learning activities that used local water, plants, and soil as a live science laboratory. She also incorporated the Native approaches to reducing the risk associated with the contamination into the curriculum. These place-based learning activities promoted students understanding of where they lived and the ways they can contribute to improving the environment of this "place."

While this example illustrates a clearly distinguishable learning experience in Native ways of knowing and place-based education, the principles can be applied to all fields of study. One only has to look at the rich history, culture, heritage, and needs of the community in which one lives to identify strategies for integrating Native ways of knowing and placed-based education for the common good of its people. The road to embedding Native ways of knowing into an institution's curriculum begins with understanding the institution, its purpose, and its values. At NEO, these elements provided the foundation for developing the NORSE framework, which faculty and students could relate to as they transitioned to a constructivist perspective for curriculum development and classroom learning through Native ways of knowing and place-based education.

Regional two-year institutions were established to provide cost-effective opportunities for higher education throughout the nation. The growth of the junior and community college movement and the integral purpose they continue to serve reflects each state's commitment to education for the common good. These institutions reflect a regional economic perspective, and they contribute to the intellectual growth of the community. For NASNTIs, this contribution to the local community fosters partnerships with tribes. Tribal economic development strategies reflect a commitment to local tribal members, and the merging of these resources with higher education institutions is important in a climate of declining resources. The various tribal commitments to NEO range from student scholarship support to partnerships in federal grant proposals. NEO also supports the tribes with specific language course delivery on campus. The incorporation of Native ways of knowing in the new online curriculum provides an opportunity for a significant partnership with local tribes as the institution acknowledges tribal philosophy for teaching and learning in a mainstream venue. NEO serves as a national model for the use of Native ways of knowing for NASNTIs as they continue to serve multi-tribal students in higher education. The framework and examples developed for use at NEO are a direct reflection of the Native ways of knowing as a philosophy for teaching and learning.

ACCESS AND RETENTION

This chapter describes a multi-year study on American Indian college access within the context of Native nations' sovereignty as well as social and economic development. Tribally developed and operated programs, services, and support for higher education were also studied.

American Indian students from reservation communities may share many similar experiences with other first-generation, rural, and historically underrepresented students with regard to schooling and access to college. Fann (2005) interviewed American Indian junior and senior high school students from California reservation communities about their experiences navigating the pathway to college. Access to college was considered in a context that included students' families, tribes, school experiences, and life in a rural reservation community. Although all students in the study had aspirations for college, few students knew about or had taken the requisite coursework for university eligibility, and even fewer knew about or had taken the

SAT. Students' opportunities to learn were often constrained by the limited resources of rural high schools and geographic isolation from post-secondary institutions. Most students indicated that they would attend a community college by default, seeing this as their only option for higher education.

It is difficult to adequately convey students' sense of connectedness to family, tribe, and homeland. Students had to make tough decisions about going away to college because this meant leaving the sustaining power of highly interdependent, extended families living in a tribal community and foregoing significant cultural, tribal language, and religious practices to attend post-secondary institutions where they expected to find few students like themselves.

The political, historical, and contemporary experiences of Native Americans include a unique set of circumstances and dilemmas that Native students face as they negotiate their way through high school and make choices about college. This includes special consideration of the unique political status of tribes and tribal priorities for political and cultural self-determination. Federally recognized American Indian tribes are sovereign, self-governing entities maintaining a government-to-government relationship with both the federal and state governments. Knowledge of the political relationship between Native nations and the federal government is essential to understanding tribal struggles to exercise sovereignty. Tribal sovereignty is the bedrock which all research on American Indian education as well as economic and social development should emphasize (Brayboy, 2005; Champagne & Goldberg, 2005; Cornel & Kalt, 1992, 2007). Parallel to tribal priorities for maintaining political sovereignty is nation-building, best described as the development of tribal government, including the economic and social infrastructure that supports sovereignty.

Despite the increasing need for Native professionals, some Native students question the relevance of a college education since few post-secondary institutions offer culturally specific curricula such as tribal law, cultural resource management, tribal languages, or other courses of direct relevance to tribal development needs (Brayboy, 2005; Fann et al., 2003,). A university degree does not automatically confer social status in tribal communities as it does in mainstream society; some scholars believe formal education may actually be at odds with traditional tribal education, values, and teachings (Brayboy, 2005; Grande, 2004; Smith, 1999).

Fann's (2005) study explored college access within American Indian communities in the context of the perceived role of higher education as a vehicle for strengthening tribes' sovereignty and nation-building efforts and within the context of tribally developed and operated programs, services, and support for higher education. There are more than 152 tribes in California, including 110 federally recognized tribes with reservation lands primarily in rural areas. California Indians survive after multiple waves of genocide, slavery, and forcible removal to reservations along with geographic confinement within their boundaries (Forbes, 1993; Trafzer & Hyer, 1999; Wilson, 2000). Colonization has taken a heavy toll on California Indigenous ecology, cultures, and languages; more than 90 percent of California Indigenous languages are at risk of disappearing within the next generation (Hinton, 2003). Goldberg and Champagne (1996) found that California Indians have higher rates of poverty, lower incomes, slightly less education, less post-secondary education, and higher rates of unemployment than reservation Indians in other states, and these combined indices of adverse socio-economic conditions put California reservation Indians among the most economically deprived groups in the nation. There are still tribes in the state where more than 85 percent of tribal citizens live below the national poverty level, and tribes in remote areas of the state are still without electricity or telephone service (Glionna, 2001).

Fann's study (2005) includes taking stock of what tribes report as their goals for higher education; tribal perceptions of obstacles to, and sources of tension around, college-going; and the state of the art in tribal support for post-secondary transitions. To that end, the following questions were addressed:

1) What role does higher education play in tribal sovereignty as well as economic and social development?
    a) What are intrinsic individual *and* community-based economic and/or social motivations for pursuing higher education or not pursuing higher education?
    b) Has higher education benefited tribal efforts in language revitalization, cultural preservation, business, law, government, etc., and if so, how?
    c) What gaps, if any, are there in the ability of public colleges and universities to offer education and training relevant to tribal development?
    d) How are tribes reckoning with formal Western higher education in a way that compliments traditional tribal education and tribal citizenship?
2) What are tribal policies and practices for getting students into college?
3) What services and programs are needed to support students' post-secondary transitions?

Tribal Critical Race Theory (TribalCrit) is an emerging theoretical framework developed principally by Brayboy (2005) that specifically addresses the educational experiences of Indigenous people. With interdisciplinary roots in critical race theory, anthropology, law, political science, education, and American Indian studies, contemporary educational issues for Indigenous students are seen as resulting from and connected to hundreds of years of abusive relationships between mainstream educational institutions and American Indian communities. TribalCrit has unique explanatory power because it addresses the complicated relationship between American Indians and the federal government and the liminal position of American Indians as both racial and legal/political groups and individuals (Brayboy, 2005).

Centered on the narratives of tribal citizens, TribalCrit provides a framework for conducting research and analyzing data that privileges Indigenous ways of knowing and struggles for the exercise of tribal sovereignty. For Indigenous communities, colleges and universities represent spaces of both forced assimilation and possibility. TribalCrit is a uniquely well-suited lens for exploring higher education access issues and needs of Indigenous communities with the purpose of creating change in the education system and developing relevant strategies that support Native students' transitions into and through college.

Fann's (2005) study provided a broad overview of the existing higher educational issues and initiatives across California Native nations through telephone interviews with tribal education representatives. Smith (1999) draws on Harding's distinction between method and methodology: "A research methodology is a theory and analysis of how research should proceed ... and a research method is a technique for gathering evidence" (p. 143). Methodology is important because it is framed by the questions being asked and determines the research process. The qualitative nature of this study is based on the assumption that the naturalistic technique of listening to stories of people's experiences (Lincoln & Guba, 1985) is more compatible with "traditional Indian ways of knowing" (Crazy Bull, 1997, p. 24). No discussion on research involving Indigenous people can begin without acknowledging that research in these communities has resulted in centuries of violation, disrespect, and subjectivism (Brayboy & Deyhle, 2000; Champagne & Goldberg, 2005; Crazy Bull, 1997; Deloria, 1992; Hermes, 1998; Mihesuah, 1998; Smith, 2000). In sum, most Native Americans feel that they have been unbearably researched (Champagne & Golderg, 2005; Deloria, 1992).

Data analysis was conducted by reading transcripts and identifying an initial set of codes or "things that go together" (LeCompte, 2000, p. 152) using the theoretical framework (TribalCrit) as an initial lens and organizational tool. Fann used peer review as a "lens for establishing credibility from persons external to the study" (Creswell & Miller, 2000, p. 129). A peer review can also corroborate the validity of data interpretations by someone familiar with the research, data, or the phenomenon explored (Creswell, 2012; Creswell & Miller, 2000; Isaac & Michael, 1995; Lincoln & Guba, 1985).

STATUS OF TRIBAL HIGHER EDUCATION PROGRAMMING IN CALIFORNIA

Telephone interviews with 43 tribal education representatives were conducted to explore the range and complexity of tribal higher education programs/services and contexts. Given the geographic dispersion of tribes across the state, in-person interviews were not possible. Therefore, one-on-one telephone interviews were conducted using a semi-structured protocol designed to elicit in-depth information from participants about tribal higher education issues and initiatives. Interviews typically lasted one hour, and copious hand notes were taken and transcribed.

The size of the tribal enrollment or citizenship within the tribes whose representatives Fann spoke with varies from over 5,000 to fewer than 50 members. Likewise, the size of their reservation, Rancheria, colony, or trust land is equally varied. Most tribes are situated in semi-rural to exceedingly remote and rural areas. Out of 43 sovereign tribal entities, more than 20 different tribal groups are represented.

Given the scope of historical, cultural, political, and economic conditions and contexts among tribes and experiences between tribal individuals and mainstream education institutions, there is a wide range of higher education program development. As a way to visualize the diversity of California tribal government headquarters, picture buildings that range from modern, multi-story buildings with dozens and dozens of offices and classrooms, a museum or cultural center, a library, a computer lab, large meeting rooms, and myriad other amenities to a doublewide trailer or portable unit that houses the tribal government, staff, and services.

Not surprisingly, the range of departments and staff vary tremendously. Some tribes have all manner of departments from health, education, cultural resource management, business, finance, human resources, tribal court, and tribal police and fire departments while other tribes have a staff of fewer than a dozen, which may include a handful of elected tribal council members. Some tribal education departments are formally articulated within tribal codes (laws) and have well-funded programs with a large staff. Most tribes have more of an "education office" run by one or two staff people who are responsible for everything from the Head Start programming to college counseling. In the smallest and least funded tribes, there are no formal education programs, and any Bureau of Indian Affairs (BIA) or other education funds are managed by a general tribal administrator who may also serve in other positions.

CULTURE IN WORKFORCE EDUCATION

The range of tribal higher education services and programs varies in the extreme. The recent emphasis on workforce education in Indian Country has seen the development and deployment of major federal initiatives from a wide range of agencies and administrations (East-West Gateway Coordinating Council, n.d.). The breadth and scope of federally funded initiatives in the areas of workforce planning and program implementation allow tribes to be innovative and proactive in accessing federal resources. These programs and resources, however, change frequently and are subject to political and fiscal realities that are difficult to predict. The economic and market reforms throughout Indian Country still lag behind mainstream American culture, producing infrastructure deficiencies that starkly contrast with our understanding of tribal communities prior to contact (Miller, 2012). Miller (2012) believes that his study of the past, primarily the study of what was held communally and what was held in private ownership, can be "prescriptive" for the future of economic development (p. vii). Miller's analysis relies on Native ways of knowing by providing a clear link to the historical accounts where rich traditions and complicated histories are at the heart of self-determination, with evidence that contemporary tribal communities are restoring economic stability. For example, the Chickasaw Nation of Oklahoma's mission and vision for workforce development highlight a "grow our own" approach to increase employment retention and effect greater involvement in their culture. (The Chickasaw Nation, 2015, para. 3).

Workforce development on tribal lands includes various ventures that range from hospitality to health care. Each of these ventures requires infrastructure and market opportunity. This requires a trained, knowledgeable workforce; formal education and workplace learning are complementary in maintaining and enhancing a productive workforce. To create infrastructure within tribes, tribal leadership and educators should work collaboratively to foster place-based learning opportunities that reflect the tribe's culture, i.e., Native ways of knowing. This collaboration requires a call to arms if tribes are to produce the warriors they need for entrepreneurial stewardship. The evidence for the historical importance of Native ways of knowing includes reframing Miller's (2012) economic imperatives to reinforce this pedagogy by incorporating its policies and practices of reform in workforce preparation. This imperative requires tribes to seize the opportunities and meet the new challenges of the mainstream science and technology revolution that relies on a knowledge economy. The imperative also requires that tribes create and use their own intellectual property and proprietary product lines to enhance original innovation through co-innovation or re-innovation with mainstream economies. Using contemporary methods does not require assimilation or absorption; it requires introducing Native ways of knowing to a larger audience.

THE ROLE OF HIGHER EDUCATION IN TRIBAL SOVEREIGNTY

When asked how higher education could support tribal sovereignty, participants described how important it was for tribal members to have some level of post-secondary education so that they could assume management positions within the tribe and lamented that senior management positions were often filled by non-tribal members, ultimately limiting or removing decision-making power from tribal members. Tribal control over decisions relevant to tribal economic, social, and cultural development is paramount to the exercise of tribal sovereignty and sustainable nation-building.

> Higher education supports tribal sovereignty through training because we need more professional managers . . . sovereignty issues are dealt

> with in these positions and those with tribal ties are in the best position to make sure that tribal sovereignty is protected.
>
> We need tribal members to fill professional level positions. A lot of upper level decisions are being made by Non-Tribal members. Currently we do not have enough tribal members with higher education to help take over these duties.
>
> When you have tribal members who make decisions for the tribe, this supports sovereignty.

Participants described the need for tribal leaders to possess a good education. In most cases, the only qualification for running for tribal council is being 18 years of age or older. Out of 43 interviews, only three participants indicated that their tribal Chairman, the highest level of tribal leadership, had a graduate degree. In some cases, participants shared that none of their council members had a college degree and may not have completed high school. Yet, the responsibilities of a tribal council member are akin to any high-level government position and require the synthesis of high volumes of technical, legal, and policy information; meetings with local, state, and federal government; and negotiation, leadership, and communication skills.

> In tribal government, we need council members who are educated. There is such a multitude of issues council members deal with, legal issues, fishing and water issues, education issues, this requires the commensurate education and understanding of business.
>
> When you put someone on tribal council, you have thrown them into a whirlwind of politics . . . They need to meet with legislature at the state and federal level and they may be placed on something like the Board of Rural Health and I can go on.
>
> As Chairman, my priority is having more people get skills for governance. Very few youth will be ready to take on leadership and they need to be prepared to take over governance roles for the tribe. Also, we need more tribal members to be part of business agreements so we don't get cheated. I'm looking 20 years down the road. I'd rather see my own people with a degree come back and run our business than outsiders. Then I can go on into the next world in peace.

Related to this, participants described the need for college-level courses in federal Indian law and tribal sovereignty, business management, and related coursework in all manner of subjects. Also needed was curriculum that addressed the realities of tribal nations and nation building.

SEVEN GENERATIONS

Tribes have indicated that a healthy, educated workforce is essential to preparing their members to assume all manner of leadership and managerial positions such that tribes can rely on the capacity of their own citizens and not outside agents. The factors that influence educational attainment are not same for all individuals and communities, and for solutions to be sustainable, programs need to be desired, shaped, and controlled by the local people (Jennings, 2004). When tribes control economic development, economic development is more likely to be sustainable (Cornel & Kalt, 1992, 2007). When tribes control education, American Indian students do better (Tippeconnic, 1999, 2000). When tribes take control of higher education programs and services, their students will be more likely to gain access to and succeed in college. However, tribes' abilities to control higher education support is mediated by a complex set of factors.

Especially promising is the connection between students' participation in tribal culture and academic achievement, leading to motivation and support for college-going. There is a growing body of research in Indian education that demonstrates the positive connection between students' tribal culture and academic success (see for example, Castagno & Brayboy, 2008). Cultural integrity, for example, speaking or learning one's tribal language, and participating in tribal religious ceremonies should be fostered as part of a holistic effort to support college-going, encouraging students to believe that they will not have to choose between being American Indian and being a college student.

Even though the majority of American Indian high school students attend public schools en route to mainstream post-secondary institutions outside of tribal control, tribes can and do play an active role in the process and can continue to work with policymakers, schools, and post-secondary institutions to develop tribally relevant ways to support Native students' transition from tribal communities to higher education communities and back again. Successful tribal higher education programs make college preparation and planning a process and not an event. Successful programs are embedded within existing educational programs and services that help develop early awareness and preparation for college.

*****

"The battle of Indian children will be won in the classroom.... The students of today are our warriors of tomorrow."

(Mankiller, 2001, p. i)

We began this discussion with a quote from Wilma Mankiller, late Principal Chief of the Western Band of the Cherokee Nation, and we conclude with a quote attributed to her. Chief Mankiller was well known for her work in education, believing, we think, that economic self-sufficiency and tribal sovereignty were well served by an educated tribal membership. She oriented her strategies and efforts toward increasing opportunities for building capacity within her nation through education, particularly education that included Native ways of knowing.

REFERENCES

American Indian Higher Education Consortium. (2000). *Tribal college contributions to local economic development*. Retrieved from ERIC database. (ED456946)

American Indian Higher Education Consortium. (2007). *The benefits of higher education for Native people and communities*. Retrieved from http://www.aihec.org/our-stories/docs/reports/ThePathOfManyJourneys.pdf

American Indian Higher Education Consortium. (2015). *Tribal colleges: Educating, engaging, innovating, sustaining*. Retrieved from http://www.aihec.org

Billy, C. L., & Kuslikis, A. (2009). Technology at the TCUs. In L. Warner & G. Gipp (Eds.), *Tradition and culture in the millennium: Tribal colleges and universities* (pp. 201–208). Charlotte, NC: Information Age Publishing.

Blackfeet Community College. (2015). *Mission*. Retrieved from http://bfcc.edu/about.php

Boyer, P. (2008). *Tribal college and university profiles: New directions in math and science*. Pablo, MT: Salish Kootenai College Press.

Brayboy, B. M. (1999). *Climbing the ivy: Examining the experiences of academically successful Native American Indian students in two Ivy League universities* (Unpublished doctoral dissertation). University of Pennsylvania, Philadelphia, PA.

Brayboy, B. M., & Deyhle, D. (2000). Insider-outsider: Researchers in American Indian communities. *Theory into Practice, 39*(3), 163–169.

Brayboy, B. M. J. (2005). Toward a tribal critical race theory in education. *The Urban Review, 37*, 425–446.

Castagno, A. E., & Brayboy, B. M. J. (2008). Culturally responsive schooling for Indigenous youth: A review of the literature. *Review of Educational Research, 78*, 941–993.

Champagne, D., & Goldberg, C. E. (2005). Changing the subject: Individual versus collective interests in Indian Country research. *Wicazo Sa Review, 20*(1), 49–69.

The Chickasaw Nation. (2015). *School to work program*. Retrieved from https://www.chickasaw.net/services/school-to-work-program.aspx

Cleary, L. M., & Peacock, T. D. (1998). *Collected wisdom: American Indian education*. Needham Heights, MA: Allyn & Bacon.

Clement, D. (2009). Growth by degrees. In L. Warner & G. Gipp (Eds.), *Tradition and culture in the millennium: Tribal colleges and universities* (pp. 49–60). Charlotte, NC: Information Age Publishing.

College Cost Reduction and Access Act of 2007. HEA, Title II, Part F. Section 371 (2008).

Cornell, S., & Jorgensen, M. (2007). *The nature and components of economic development in Indian Country*. Washington, DC: National Congress of American Indians Policy research Center. Retrieved from http://citeseerx.ist.psu.edu/viewdoc/download?doi=10.1.1.173.661&rep=rep1&type=pdf

Cornell, S., & Kalt, J. P. (1995). Where does economic development really come from? Constitutional rule among the contemporary Sioux and Apache. *Economic Inquiry, 33*, 402–426.

Cornell, S., & Kalt, J. P. (2007). Two approaches to the development of Native nations: One works, the other doesn't. In M. Jorgensen (Ed.), *Rebuilding Native nations: Strategies for governance and development* (pp. 3–32). Tucson, AZ: University of Arizona Press.

Cornell, S. E., & Kalt, J. P. (Eds.). (1992). *What can tribes do? Strategies and institutions in American Indian economic development.* Los Angeles, CA: American Indian Studies Center, University of California, Los Angeles.

Cornell, S. E., Kalt, J. P., Jorgensen, M., & Spilde, K. A. (2007). *Seizing the future: Why some Native nations do and others don't.* Native Nations Institute, Udall Center for Studies in Public Policy. Tucson, AZ: University of Arizona.

Crazy Bull, C. C. (1997). Advice for the non-Native researcher. *Tribal College,* 9(1), 24.

Creswell, J. W. (2012). *Qualitative inquiry and research design: Choosing among five approaches* (3rd ed.). Los Angeles, CA: Sage.

Creswell, J. W., & Miller, D. L. (2000). Determining validity in qualitative inquiry. *Theory into practice,* 39(3), 124–130.

Deloria, V., Jr. (1992). The evolution of federal Indian policy making. In V. Deloria Jr. (Ed.), *American Indian policy in the twentieth century* (pp. 239–256). Norman, OK: University of Oklahoma Press.

Deyhle, D. (1995). Navajo youth and Anglo racism: Cultural integrity and resistance. *Harvard Educational Review,* 65, 403–445.

Diné College. (2015). *Mission.* Retrieved from http://www.dinecollege.edu/about/about.php

East-West Gateway Coordinating Council. (n.d.). *Federal funding streams for workforce development planning and programming.* St. Louis, MO: Author. Retrieved from http://www.doleta.gov/usworkforce/communityaudits/docs/Files%20for%20CA%20Website/MO-St%20Louis/MO-St%20Louis-Product-Federal%20Funding%20Streams%20Directory.pdf

Erdrich, L. (1997). Introduction. In C. Larimore (Ed.), *First person, first peoples: Native American college graduates tell their life stories* (pp. 1–22). Ithaca, NY: Cornell University Press.

Faircloth, S. C., & Tippeconnic, J. W., III. (2010). *The dropout/graduation crisis among American Indian and Alaska Native students.* Retrieved from https://escholarship.org/uc/item/4ps2m2rf

Fann, A. (2005). *Forgotten students: American Indian high school student narratives on college access.* (Unpublished doctoral dissertation). University of California, Los Angeles, CA.

Fann, A. (2009, April). *Higher education and nation building.* Paper presented at the American Education Research Association Annual Meeting, San Diego, CA.

Fann, A., Wilson, D., Teeter, W., Alvitre, C., & Champagne, D. (2003, November). *Tribal partnership in higher education: Bridging academic and cultural scholarship.* Paper presented at the Annual Meeting of the Association for the Study of Higher Education, Sacramento, CA.

Forbes, J. D. (1993). *Native Americans of California and Nevada.* Happy Camp, CA: Naturegraph Publishers.

Glionna, J. M. (2001, July 22). Isolated tribe struggles without phones, power. *The Los Angeles Times,* p. A-1.

Goldberg-Ambrose, C., Champagne, D., & Cleaves, W. T. (1996). *A second century of dishonor: Federal inequities and California tribes.* Los Angeles, CA: UCLA American Indian Studies Center for the Advisory Council on California Indian Policy.

Grande, S. (2004). *Red pedagogy: Native American social and political thought.* New York, NY: Rowman & Littlefield.

Hermes, M. (1998). Research methods as a situated response: Towards a First Nations' methodology. *International Journal of Qualitative Studies in Education*, 11(1), 155–168.

Higher Education Opportunity Act of 2008. HEA, Title III, Part A, Section 319 (2008).

Hinton, L. (2003). Language revitalization. *Annual Review of Applied Linguistics*, 23, 44–57.

His Horse is Thunder, D., Anderson, N., & Miller, D. G. (2013). *Building the foundation for success: Case studies of breaking through tribal colleges and universities*. Arlington, VA: American Indian Higher Education Consortium.

Isaac, S., & Michael, W. (1995). *Handbook in research and evaluation: A collection of principles, methods, and strategies useful in the planning, design, and evaluation of studies in education and the behavioral sciences*. San Diego, CA: Edits Publishing.

Jennings, M. (2004). *Alaska Native political leadership and higher education: One university, two universes* (Vol. 9). Walnut Creek, CA: Rowman Altamira.

Johnson, J., Strange, M., & Madden, K. (2010). *The rural dropout problem: An invisible achievement gap*. Washington, DC: Rural School and Community Trust.

Kawagley, A. O., & Barnhardt, R. (1998). *Education indigenous to place: Western science meets Native reality*. Fairbanks, AK: University of Alaska Press.

LeCompte, M. D. (2000). Analyzing qualitative data. *Theory into Practice*, 39(3), 146–154.

Lincoln, Y. S., & Guba, E. G. (1985). *Naturalistic inquiry*. Newbury Park, CA: Sage Publications.

Mankiller, W. (2001). Introduction. In L. S. Warner (Ed.), *Won in the classroom: Guide to the selection of culturally appropriate classroom materials* (p. i). Milwaukee, WI: Indian Community School.

McDonough, P. M., & Fann, A. J. (2007). The study of inequality. In P. Gumport (Ed.), *Sociology of higher education* (pp. 53–92). Baltimore, MD: Johns Hopkins University Press.

Mihesuah, D. A. (1998). American Indian identities: Issues of individual choices and development. *American Indian Culture and Research Journal*, 22(2), 193–226.

Miller, R. J. (2012). *Reservation" capitalism": Economic development in Indian Country*. San Bernardino, CA: ABC-CLIO.

Pevar, S. (2012). *The rights of Indians and tribes* (4th ed.). New York, NY: Oxford University Press.

Proudfit, J., & Gregor, T. (2014). *The state of American Indian and Alaska Native education in California*. San Marcos, CA: The California Indian Culture and Sovereignty Center.

Proudfit, J., & Warner, L. S. (2015). *California tribal college feasibility study*. San Marcos, CA: Naqmayam Communications.

Smith, G. H. (2000). Protecting and respecting indigenous knowledge. In M. Battiste (Ed.), *Reclaiming Indigenous voice and vision* (pp. 209–224). Vancouver, BC: University of British Columbia Press.

Smith, L. T. (1999). *Decolonizing methodologies: Research and indigenous peoples*. London, UK: Zed Books.

Stein, W. J. (1992). *Tribally controlled colleges*. New York, NY: Peter Lang.

Stein, W. J. (1999). Tribal colleges: 1968–1998. In K. G. Swisher & J. W. Tippeconnic III (Eds.), *Next steps: Research and practice to advance Indian education* (pp. 359–370). Charleston, WV: ERIC.

Thornton, B., & Sanchez, J. E. (2010). Promoting resiliency among Native American students to prevent dropouts. *Education, 131*, 455–465.

Tippeconnic, J. W., III. (1999). *Tribal control of American Indian education: Observations since the 1960s with implications for the future.* Retrieved from http://files.eric.ed.gov/fulltext/ED427904.pdf

Tippeconnic, J. W., III. (2000). Reflecting on the past: Some important aspects of Indian education to consider as we look toward the future. *Journal of American Indian Education, 39*(2), 39–48.

Trafzer, C. E., & Hyer, J. R. (Eds.). (1999). *Exterminate them: Written accounts of the murder, rape, and enslavement of Native Americans during the California gold rush.* East Lansing, MI: Michigan State University Press.

United Tribes Technical College. (2015). *Mission.* Retrieved from http://www.uttc.edu/about/mission

Warner, L. S. (2006). Native ways of knowing: Let me count the ways. *Canadian Journal of Native Education, 29*(2), 149–164.

Warner, L. S., & Fahnestock, B. (2013). *Native ways of knowing for the common good.* Manuscript submitted for publication.

Wilkins, D. E., & Stark, H. K. (2010). *American Indian politics and the American political system.* New York, NY: Rowman & Littlefield Publishers.

Wilson, J. (2000). *The earth shall weep: A history of Native America.* New York, NY: Grove Press.

6 Educating the Educators
Making Workforce Education Successful Through Understanding and Respect for Indigenous Cultures

Delilah F. O'Haynes

Since the inception of Indian reservations, the education of American Indians has failed (Adams, 1997; Provenzo & McCloskey, 1981) in many respects because it has been approached as a missionary effort or government mandate rather than a respectful collaborative endeavor. Because so many efforts to help Indians have harbored ulterior motives, "including the government's 'futile and destructive efforts to annihilate Indian cultures'" (Edwards, 2012, para. 3), any attempt to approach a workforce education plan for American Indians must involve the re-education of any non-Indian policymakers, counselors, instructors, and/or corporate trainers involved in such a plan—if it hopes to succeed. This directive includes those workforce education programs already under way.

Furthermore, Americans' beliefs about Indians have been steeped in "skewed" Indian history (Wingo, 2011, para. 1) and Hollywood-produced stereotypes of Indian culture to the point that without a sincere effort on the part of non-Indian educators to venerate American Indians' concepts of their history and culture, the prejudice created by past failures will prevail. Without question, such a program must have proper funding and assurance of actual job/career opportunities if its originators hope to make a dent in the unemployment situation on reservations and among urban Indians; moreover, its organization and execution must be driven by Indian initiative to be successful. Therefore, in order to construct a viable workforce educational design for American Indians, educators must take several steps toward understanding and respecting Indian culture—along with providing assurance of the program's benefits—before the education process begins.

PRIORITY ONE—INDIAN SELF-DETERMINATION

Before the planning stage for a project of educating the educators, Indian tribes involved as well as any participating Indians living off reservations must set the tone, the goal, and the parameters of said plan, depending on the individual needs of each group. Designers must not rely solely on non-Indian scholars, educators, or corporate/governmental executives to draw up such a plan; rather, they must first involve Indian tribes in a dialogue concerning future needs and goals.

Until ratification of U.S. Public Law 95–638, the Indian Self-Determination and Education Assistance Act (1975) and its amendments of 1988, the United States government told Indians what they needed, how they should think, and what they should do according to white society. European education—along with European dress, religion, and identity—was forced upon Indians from the inception of Indian reservations. "Treaty provisions frequently include early efforts to educate Indian people in the American system of learning" ("Native American Education," 2003, para. 1). The Snyder Act of 1921, the Indian Reorganization Act of 1934, and the Indian New Deal all stressed "American" education with the idea that Indians needed the benevolent aid of government; funding education became "a major form of federal assistance to the tribal nations and American Indians" ("Native American Education," 2003, para. 1). For reference, D. W. Adams' book, *Education for Extinction: American Indians and the Boarding School Experience 1875–1928* (1997), offers a thorough understanding of the heinous methods used to assimilate Indians through the use of education. Lomawaima (2013) states:

> The US possessed powerful reasons to maintain Indian individuals as wards and tribes as domestic dependent nations, even after 1924 blanket citizenship . . . Maintaining American Indians as wards, in circumstances that denied or destroyed economic development, served to legitimate US belief in its just inheritance of lands and freedom from Native peoples. The necessary existence of Indians as "Indians"— marked by selectively maintained cultural differences, economic incapacity, and communal property—reminded the world of the settler colony's assumed rights to nationhood and territory. (para. 5)

The worst entity created by the United States government to care for Indians is the Bureau of Indian Affairs, which Edwards (2012) calls "America's first 'welfare state'" (para. 19). Edwards states that this "inefficient, mismanaged, and . . . corrupt . . . bureaucracy . . . became the" principal power on reservations (para. 19, 22), providing not only staples and health care but also imposing white civilization on Indian culture with white education, government, laws, and work—handing out "farm implements to Indian tribes" (para. 20). It should, therefore, be easy to understand why any educational workforce vision concerning American Indians that begins in the minds of non-Indians, even if it purports to be for the good of Indians, may collapse. The Obama administration's efforts to revamp the Bureau of Indian Education (BIE) in order to better handle American Indian education is an example of an ill-fated proposal; many Indian tribes oppose "the plan as an infringement on their sovereignty and a one-size-fits-all approach that will fail to improve student achievement in Indian Country" (Maxwell, 2014, para. 1).

One historic document that speaks to the way Indians feel about being in charge of their own lives, government, and labor conditions is a conversation recorded in 1934 between Senator Thomas of Oklahoma and a Menominee Indian named Ralph Fredenberg concerning the Indian Reorganization Act passed that same year (also called the Wheeler-Howard Bill). In this conversation, Mr. Fredenberg tells Senator Thomas this:

> The self-government title, I understand, will give us the authority to organize and to submit a charter. . . . [W]e felt that something would be done [under the last administration], some proposal would be offered that would answer this thing that everybody recognizes as a need of the Indians—the right to govern their own lives and work out their own destiny.
>
> (Moquin & Van Doren, 1973, p. 312)

Surely, this need for self-assertion and self-governance embodies the United States' constitution and bill of rights, which offer to fulfill this need for every United States citizen. Studies done through the University of Arizona and Harvard University conclude the following about Indian self-determination:

> [F]ederal promotion of tribal self-government under formal policies known as "self-determination" is turning out to be, after a century or more of failed efforts to improve the lives of the U.S. indigenous people, the only strategy that has worked. In so doing, the strategy is improving the well-being of its poorest and, arguably, historically most oppressed and disempowered people.
>
> (Cornell & Kalt, 2010, p. 13–14)

Education and work ventures that have started in the minds of Indians, such as the American Indian College Fund, have flourished. Such ventures that have started with a dialogue between cultures yet continued with a preconceived notion of what is best for Indians despite the input of the Indians have failed—and might always fail. If past disappointments are any predictor, the dominant population may blame the Indians in the event of such a breakdown. White America has pushed aside the failure of its government and its citizens to honor historic agreements with Indians; indeed, white America has largely forgotten Indians altogether. Therefore, before corporate and/or government leaders sit down with any tribal council or Indian group to discuss a workforce education plan for Indians, those leaders need a review of this nation's historical alliances with the American Indians with a recap of the reasons for their collapse. These leaders can be certain that the Indians to whom they present their plan have not forgotten.

Early in American history, founders set forth official government documents that should have established peace and goodwill among settlers and the first Americans. Shortly after America was formed as a nation, a clause was placed into the U.S. Constitution that guaranteed Indian tribes the rights of sovereignty. Article 1, Section 8 designates three sovereign units within the United States: the federal government, state governments, and Indian tribes. In other words, Indian tribes were to have the same power to govern themselves as the states. Shortly thereafter, the Northwest Ordinance of 1787 promised Indian nations the rights of liberty and property, strictly stating that Indian lands would never be seized. Later, the Indian Trade and Intercourse Act of 1790 reiterated the sovereignty of Indian tribes by regulating commerce among races and affording protection for Indian properties (Olson-Raymer, 2001). Congress later ratified 371 Indian treaties; these treaties were often signed "under military threat and/or subterfuge" (Cornell & Kalt, 2010, p. 2). Most, if not all, of these treaties were then broken by the United States government. According to the report of the U.S. Commission on Civil Rights (2003):

> A series of Supreme Court cases in the 1830s established the analytical framework upon which Indian law is based today. *Cherokee Nation v. Georgia* determined that tribes are not foreign nations but rather "domestic dependent nations." This decision forms the basis of what is now known as the trust relationship between tribes and the federal government and the consequent fiduciary responsibilities of the United States. (pp. 12–13)

This report by the U.S. Commission on Civil Rights is a must-read for all those involved in any venture with American Indians. Finally, in 1871, Congress seized all rights and power afforded the Indians by the Constitution. American Indians have every reason to be skeptical of any proposition brought to them by non-Indians (Olson-Raymer, 2001).

Only when Indians regained some rights to govern themselves under the 1975 Indian Self-Determination and Education Assistance Act did tribes begin to show, in the 1980s, some meaningful progress toward "a widespread and systematic restructuring of tribal governments and their relations with the federal government" (Cornell & Kalt, 2010, p. 10). This restructuring allowed tribes to write their own constitutions, collect their own taxes, and create their own rules for schools and law enforcement in a period of unprecedented tribal actions known as the "nation-building" movement.

Consequently, for an American Indian workforce program to succeed, its blueprint must be Indian-inspired and promoted. In order to create a strong economic base for their families, not a stronger white corporate economic base, Indian leaders as well as Indians living off the reservations must be convinced that it is for the good of their own communities to become educated for work in or out of Indian culture. If Indians perceive that companies are looking for cheap workforce labor to replace jobs that whites feel are beneath them or that they are being offered education or training without sufficient prospects for resulting jobs, negotiations might close; furthermore, if those Indians do not feel respect from negotiators, the program will be in jeopardy from the beginning.

One successful cooperative American Indian educational venture for study is the American Indian Opportunities Industrialization Center in Minneapolis. This program was started by area citizens to help urban Indians adjust, but it is now almost totally run by Indians themselves. Rather than helping Indians find jobs, this center's mission concentrates on providing a broad education toward better employment opportunities and continuing financial improvement. Any plan for a general workforce education program for Indians would do well to copy this center's approach, which uses Indian self-determination to foster and continue its success.

PRIORITY TWO—HISTORICAL KNOWLEDGE

The best way that policymakers, counselors, instructors, and corporate or government trainers involved in such an effort can show necessary respect for Indian culture is by demonstrating to Indian leaders that they thoroughly understand the history of relations between the Europeans and Indian tribes and the true nature of Indian cultures—not Hollywood stereotypes. In other words, organizers and managers must go back to school themselves—the second most important step in such an educational process, which should commence even before negotiations start.

Along with learning the history of the United States government's disloyalty concerning Indian rights, originators of any Indian workforce program must also re-learn the history of the European "invasion" of America, not only from the Indians' point of view but also from the perspective of non-Indian scholars who now concede that the Indian version of the conquering of the Americas is the more historically true version. The following suggestions of readings and films are not exhaustive but will offer such leaders a beginning reference point from which to understand the Indian point of view concerning historical tribal interaction with the dominant American culture, especially where workforce education is concerned. A detailed list of these recommended sources follows the references at the end of this chapter.

Many people in the dominant culture are vaguely aware that the Indians were treated unfairly; however, they have no concept of the real reason for the initial takeover of South America, still assuming that there were few if any aborigines on the continent when Columbus sailed. Americans who read Columbus' (2009) "Letter to Ferdinand and Isabella" for the first time are often shocked to find that Columbus and subsequent voyagers to the new land were in search of gold and other resources beyond what they had hoped to trade for in India. Thinking he was in India, Columbus wrote, "I contend that these [gold] mines of the Aurea [Malay Peninsula] are identical with those of [the country of] Veragua [in Central America]" (quoted in del Castillo, 2009, p. 818). Americans are also shocked to learn that Columbus used native slaves to plant the first crop of sugarcane at Hispaniola, where he set up a colony in order to ship resources to Spain. On his return to the colony with "seventeen ships, 1200 men, sugarcane plants, and much livestock" (McDonnell, n.d., para. 3), he found the men—whom he had left there during his voyage home—quarreling with the natives. Columbus then captured hundreds of natives on several islands, killing many and sending the rest to Spain to be sold into slavery. Remaining island natives were used as slaves until such time that they could pay for their freedom with gold. Although Spain's rulers denounced such treatment of Indians, they "kept a loophole open for Spanish colonizers to legally enslave any Indians taken in so-called 'just-wars'—which colonists characterized as any violence they conducted against resisting natives" (McDonnell, n.d., para. 3).

Thus began the working relationship between American Indians and Europeans; from the start, native inhabitants were seen as chattel to be worked as slaves or sold into slavery. Traditional history justifies this treatment of the first Americans by describing them as little more than naked, primitive beasts. However, the reverse was true in most instances. Some documents depict American Indians as more civilized and cultured than Europeans, and some parts of the Americas were comparable to some European cities. In fact, the great city of Tenochtitlan and surrounding cities are described by one of Cortés's soldiers as "wonderful sights." Published 48 years following the writer's death, *The True History of the Conquest of New Spain* describes the approach to Montezuma's great city:

> [O]n one side, on the land, there were great cities, and in the lake ever so many more, and the lake itself was crowded with canoes, and in the Causeway were many bridges at intervals, and in front of us stood the great City of Mexico.... When we arrived where another small causeway branches off (leading to Coyo- acan, which is another city) where there were some buildings like towers, which are their oratories, many more chieftains and Caciques approached clad in very rich mantles, the brilliant liveries of one chieftain differing from those of another, and the causeways were crowded with them.
>
> (del Castillo, 2009, p. 828)

Readers of this account will more fully understand the reason Cortés took this great city in 1519 and the reason Emperor Montezuma was subsequently killed. Gifts from Montezuma to Cortés included "a wheel like a sun, as big as a cartwheel, with many sorts of pictures on it, the whole of fine gold ... worth more than ten thousand dollars"; a second, larger wheel "made of silver of great brilliancy in imitation of the moon with other figures shown on it"; and also a "helmet full of fine grains of gold ... worth three thousand dollars." The author comments on these treasures: "This gold in the helmet was worth more to us than if it had contained twenty thousand dollars, because it showed us that there were gold mines there" (del Castillo, 2009, pp. 824–825).

After learning of these accounts, can anyone doubt the reason American Indians have mistrusted Europeans from the beginning and the reason a workforce training program proposed by whites must have the cooperation and inspiration of Indians themselves or be suspect as yet another attempt to use American Indians for purposes of slavery and robbery? In Indian Country, time is irrelevant; it is not a healer of wounds or an agent of amnesia.

Two useful documentaries, *America Before Columbus* (2006), a National Geographic endeavor, and *Conquest of America* (2005), an A&E series, could be used to help program originators and educators further understand the above concepts. *America Before Columbus* shows the ways American lands were managed by intelligent and capable tribes of people, and it also shows the condition of European countries and lands at the time of Columbus—depleted of resources. It leaves viewers with an overall picture of the desperate state of affairs on the European continent, conditions that led leaders to lie to their people about the vast and empty (albeit for a few savages) continent Columbus had *discovered* (emphasis added). *Conquest of America* traces the footsteps of five conquerors who came to America after Cortés in search of gold and other resources: Bering, Menéndez, Coronado, Hudson, and Ribault. Although these accounts are at times overly dramatized, they leave no doubt as to the purpose of the "conquest" or the detestable treatment of Indian peoples, even those who were hired as guides and who were generally hospitable until treated poorly by Europeans.

After reading about Emperor Montezuma's generosity toward the newcomers, workforce designers and educators will profit from reading about other Indians' viewpoints concerning the Europeans as the latter proceeded to occupy the entire continent. At least two historical memoirs tell of the coming of the whites from early childhood recollections: *Life Among the Piutes* (sic) (1883) by Sarah Winnemucca Hopkins and *Black Elk Speaks*, as told through John G. Neihardt (1932). Sarah Winnemucca's grandfather had anxiously awaited the coming of his "white brothers" (Hopkins, 1994, p. 5), hoping to be friends with them. By the time the Oglala, Black Elk's people, learned of the coming immigrants, however, "everyone was saying that the Wasichus [whites] were coming and that they were going to take our country and rub us all out and that we would have to die fighting" (Neihardt, 1961, p. 8). These books, among others, show the progressive threat posed by the immigrants and the transition for the Indians, who at first welcomed the newcomers but later realized the changes would not be good for their own people. Most settlers who came later—at the urging of the United States government for the taking of Indian lands—were unaware of what had been done to Indian tribes before their arrival. For non-Indian Americans who learned about Indians from Hollywood picture shows, these memoirs are essential reading toward a true understanding of Indian history, especially for those proposing an Indian workforce program.

In most of those Hollywood western productions, Indians were called "red devils" and "heathen savages," meaning un-Christian, beastly, and uncontrolled. Just like Columbus's letter to his king and queen, these movies promoted the doctrine of "manifest destiny," i.e., Christians were destined by God to inherit the earth, to take it and its resources by force. These movies leave the impression that since the Indians did not convert to Christianity when told to do so, it was perfectly acceptable to wipe them out and take their lands. However, some of the above readings will instruct those willing to learn about the true nature of the Europeans' efforts to proselytize Indian tribes.

One historic document illustrates not only the continued arrogance of the conquerors concerning religion but also the underlying intention of these Europeans in using religion as an excuse to gain the intended prize: land, gold, and other resources. Most speeches made by American Indian chiefs are eloquent because many tribes considered being an orator a greater accomplishment than being a warrior, but one chief's speeches show that Indians of the 1800s understood the motives of white immigrants—the speeches of Red Jacket (1973). His speech of 1805 in answer to Missionary Cram of the Boston Missionary Society in particular exemplifies this leader's intelligence and mastery of argumentative persuasion. Before the speech, Missionary Cram had told the Seneca Indians that their worship of the Great Spirit was wrong and that they were in need of religious education from the whites. In his speech, Red Jacket reminds Cram that the Indians have not sought to take away the white man's religion as the whites do the Indians. He then makes note of one of the reasons for the white man's church services—to gather money. Finally, he offers Cram a proposition:

> Brother, we are told that you have been preaching to the white people in this place. These people are our neighbors. We are acquainted with them. We will wait a little while, and see what effect your preaching has upon them. If we find it does them good, makes them honest and less disposed to cheat Indians, we will then consider again of what you have said.
>
> (Moquin & Van Doren, 1973, p. 33)

This speech, along with many other speeches, letters, testimonials, and official statements about the Indians, can be found in *Great Documents in American Indian History* (Moquin & Van Doren, 1973). It is also included in *American Indian Literature: an Anthology*, edited by Alan R. Velie (1991), another text recommended for further study for those involved in any venture with the first Americans.

American Indians have not forgotten the white conquerors' arrogance and greed and are still wary of proposals from the dominant culture on this account. Another work that clearly illuminates the treachery perpetrated by the dominant culture is the documentary *The Trail of Tears Cherokee Legacy* (2006). Many Americans are aware of the forced removal of the Cherokee from several southern states to Oklahoma. However, most are not aware that five tribes—Creek, Cherokee, Chickasaw, Choctaw, and Seminole—were divested of their property and rights under what is called the "Removal Treaty" so that whites could have the land that belonged to these tribes and all the resources therein, especially gold. Perhaps the injustices done to the Cherokee are remembered most because they had already almost completely assimilated into the white culture, including the white religion and white farming methods; furthermore, one-fourth of those Cherokee who were marched across the country perished as a result of the government's cruelty. For a contemporary perspective on this subject, the book *Mankiller: A Chief and Her People* by Chief Wilma Mankiller (1999) is recommended. Another book, *The Cherokee Perspective*, edited by French and Hornbuckle (1981), is worth reading. If one seeks a more intimate view of the hardships experienced by the Indians on this forced march, the novel *Pushing the Bear* by Diane Glancy (1998) will offer such insight.

Finally, Helen Hunt Jackson's book, *A Century of Dishonor*, originally published in 1881, has been made available again by several presses. Instead of educating Congress and the public, as Jackson had hoped, this book drew much reproach after its debut. Today, since the book chronicles whites' discriminations toward seven tribes, it holds important historical lessons for those who need to understand Indians' lingering distrust of European Americans.

The lesson taught to all Indians by the forced march westward was this: Whether they cooperate or not, whether they assimilate or not, whether they accept the white man's religion or not, they will still be cheated and pushed off their land by whites' greed. Those who wish to devise a workforce education plan for American Indians must understand that this lesson has never been forgotten by the Indians.

This lesson has not been forgotten partly because of the lingering prejudice against Indians. Much of this prejudice remains among white families who lost loved ones during what are known as The Indian Wars. Because American Indians chose to fight for their lands, they are still stereotyped and punished, largely because Hollywood glorified the United States' Cavalry and vilified the Indians. The most famous battle against Indians, of course, was led by General George Armstrong Custer, who was foolish enough to attack an enormous caravan of Indian tribes camped near the Little Bighorn. Of the Indians' viewpoint on these wars, only a modicum was ever told, but one book in particular stands out as an Indian testimonial concerning Custer's war against the Indians: *Lakota Noon: The Indian Narrative of Custer's Defeat* (1997), edited by Gregory F. Michno. Some Indian accounts of the battle at Little Bighorn also appear in *Great Documents in American Indian History* (Moquin & Van Doren, 1973).

Many written and oral testimonials of battles between whites and Indians are included among the documents in Moquin and Van Doren's (1973) collection. One, written by a Cheyenne Indian, is entitled, "Eyewitness Report of the Sand Creek Massacre, November 28, 1864." Although a five-part documentary done by Mill Creek Entertainment in 2010, *The Great Indian Wars: 1540–1890* describes this massacre as a "battle," Two Moon[s]'s account makes clear the fact that Colonel Chivington and Major Anthony "undertook a deliberate, surprise massacre of the encampment, [of] about 700 people [of] the Cheyenne and Arapahos [who had] stopped fighting and set up camps to await peace negotiations ... of whom 500 were women and children" (as quoted in Moquin & Van Doren, 1973, p. 191). This Indian eyewitness account follows:

> I saw that Black Kettle [one of the chiefs] had a large American flag up on a long Lodgepole (sic) as a signal to the troop that the camp was friendly. Part of the warriors were running out toward the pony herds and the rest of the people were rushing about the camp in great fear. All the time Black Kettle kept calling out not to be frightened; that the camp was under protection and there was no danger. Then suddenly the troops opened fire on this mass of men women, and children, and all began to scatter and run.
> (as quoted in Moquin & Van Doren, 1973, p. 192)

Also recommended are the film *Bury My Heart at Wounded Knee* (2007), directed by Yves Simoneau, and the Report of the Commissioner of Indian Affairs for 1891, Volume 1, which detail the Indians' viewpoint with eyewitness accounts of the Wounded Knee massacre. These resources help clarify American Indians' mistrust of the dominant culture, a factor that must be considered when constructing a workforce education plan for American Indians.

PRIORITY THREE—CULTURAL RECONCILIATION

Along with American Indian resolve to achieve self-determination and Euro-Americans' lack of true knowledge concerning the history of Indian/white relations, another hindrance to a viable workforce educational design for American Indians stems from the above-mentioned antagonism between Indian cultures and the dominant society. Indians living within the reservation system especially feel this antagonism since they are partially isolated from mainstream American society. Two authors explain the strain of this situation in the following terms:

> The United States has a long history of advocating policies of both extermination and assimilation of Native peoples. This historical context provides an important backdrop for understanding issues of trust/

mistrust and the impact of acculturation on Native Americans who often find they have to reconcile [two] cultures.

(Garrett & Pichette, 2000, para. 1)

Animosity directed against whites—created by past attempts at genocide and current conditions of Indian poverty on and off reservations—sustains a long-maintained rivalry. In fact, the number one problem facing American Indians who leave the reservation to work in the "enemy camp" is the anxiety of dealing with their own evolving identities—described as a fragmented personality—and learning to become successful in the dominant society without losing their indigenous culture and feeling as if they have betrayed their own people. In addition, the federal government's designation of American Indians as "citizens-but-wards" added another dimension to Indians' feelings of dual existence (Lomawaima, 2013, para. 2). Those Indians recruited for any proposed educational plan must be made to feel that they can maintain their culture within the workforce without prejudice.

Therefore, a third component to a successful workforce educational program for American Indians is reassurance that traditional Indian culture can be sustained. Educators must encourage Indian students involved in any program to celebrate their own culture, even while working outside that culture; to do so, those educators must know and respect the tribal culture within which their students live, including their religions, customs, rituals, and languages. In addition, prejudices and remedies for prejudices must be explored so that Indians may reconcile their own cultural identities with their adopted identities within the dominant culture.

The search for true "identity" among Indians is a common problem whether they live on or off the reservation, partly because of their cultural differences, partly because of their isolation, and partly because of their "ward" status in the eyes of the U.S government. This complication for any workforce program—"citizen-but-ward status"—is explained by Lomawaima (2013):

> [C]onceptions of citizen-but-ward and sovereign-but-domestic dependent served the agendas of settler colonial entitlement and federal plenary power. [For the last century] citizenship co-existed with wardship (sic) for Indians; with Jim Crow laws and denial of the vote for blacks; and with gross inequities in domestic and work settings for women. Citizenship was promised as a cure for the pathological ambiguities of ward status, but the promise was a lie. All the ambiguities attendant to wardship have persisted to the present day precisely because they have been so useful to federal powers, and occasionally to Native people and nations as well. (para. 21)

This status exacerbates the already crushing isolation of reservation life. Several prominent American Indian authors who have addressed the problem of altered identity experienced by American Indians include but are not limited to Sherman Alexie, Louise Erdrich, N. Scott Momaday, and Leslie Marmon Silko.

The most important of the works by these authors—for the purpose of understanding the identity crisis felt by reservation and urban Indians—is the film *The Business of Fancy Dancing* (2003), written and directed by Sherman Alexie. In this film, the theme of the split-personality syndrome experienced by many Indians who leave the reservation is embodied in the character of Seymour who, having immersed himself in the white culture, returns to the reservation for a funeral. Throughout his visit, his new white persona is juxtaposed against the persona of his once-best friend, Aristotle, who returned to reservation life after a failed attempt to make it in the white world. Seymour's personality is further split by his homosexuality, used by Alexie to heighten and exaggerate this character's divided sense of self, which on the reservation is readily perceived as Indians' tendency toward a divergence of loyalties. After his visit, Seymour literally sees himself split into two people, one who leaves to return to the white world and one who stays behind on the reservation. This film graphically shows the problem of split loyalties prevalent among Indians who work or live off the reservation; its message is an essential lesson for those constructing a workforce education program for American Indians.

Louise Erdrich has written several novels that at some point deal with American Indians' cultural identity crisis. Her most famous book, *Love Medicine*, deals with the theme of identity through the character of Lipsha, a young boy in the Ojibwa tribe who has healing gifts like his forefathers. A suggested collection of essays to accompany this novel is Louise Erdrich's *Love Medicine: A Casebook* (Wong, 2000). Erdrich's later novels examine identity more closely than her early novels. *The Last Report on the Miracles at Little No Horse* uses a priest, Father Damien Modeste, to illustrate the frustration of a dual identity as Father Damien is actually a woman in man's clothing. In addition to reconciling two personalities, the priest very artfully blends Catholicism with Ojibwe tribal beliefs and customs, demonstrating the way Indians must accustom themselves to two different cultures. *The Antelope Wife* best exemplifies the theme of cultural identity through many stories of displaced Ojibwe family members from the 19th century until contemporary times. However, Erdrich blends Ojibwe myth with her characters' stories in a postmodern method that can leave all but graduate-level English majors grasping for meaning. Therefore, a suggested lecture to accompany this novel is delivered by Mary Magoulick (2000), folklorist and professor of English & Interdisciplinary Studies at Georgia College; "Women Weaving the World, Louise Erdrich's *The Antelope Wife* as Myth" is available online for download.

The last two authors mentioned above, Momaday and Silko, have written novels about American Indian war veterans who feel alienated from both worlds once they return from military service. N. Scott Momaday's (1966) first novel, *House Made of Dawn*, won a Pulitzer Prize, perhaps because it was one of the first Indian novels to deal with alienation within two worlds so accurately. A young Indian named Abel returns to America to live with his grandfather after World War II, a war that brought many Indians off reservations for the first time. After living with many white soldiers, Abel is alone in both his grandfather's world and in that of whites because of his own inability to communicate in either the old Indian ways or the ways of those outside the reservation. Leslie Marmon Silko's novel *Ceremony* also follows a young Indian boy, Tayo, as he returns from the Asian theater of WWII, having been a prisoner of war. Like Abel, Tayo must adjust to being back on the reservation after war, and also like Abel, Tayo finds his connection to home not in people but in the old ways of his people.

Additional recommendations toward helping reservation Indians reconcile the two cultures toward a workforce education plan involve further study and a review of an already-successful program. The book, *Issues in Native American Cultural Identity* (1995), edited by Michael K. Green, offers in-depth discussions on this topic. Also, educators involved in any program for American Indians should take a look at The Tribal Learning Community and Educational Exchange program at UCLA, of which DeAnna M. Rivera is director. This program is a higher education initiative connected to UCLA's School of Law and seems to offer Indian students a way to negotiate both cultures. In a recent article, the director explains:

> Our youth, my students, are faced with mixed signals about the kind of intellectuals they should aspire to be: Native intellectuals or academic intellectuals. They get caught in "us-them" dichotomies. . . . The . . . program at UCLA is designed to address this us-them barrier . . . by allowing productivity in [the] barrier-like space.
>
> (Rivera, 2013, pp. 88–89)

Any workforce education plan for American Indians must also help participants address "us-them" dichotomies if it hopes to succeed in reconciling the two cultures.

PRIORITY FOUR—RESERVATION REALITY

A fourth and final step in the process of educating educators who hope to construct a viable workforce educational design for American Indigenous people involves learning the reality of Indian life and culture. Falsehoods that exist in white America concerning the lifestyles and value systems of American Indians must be dispelled. These white assumptions about Indians include—but are not limited to—the following: indigenous peoples are adequately cared for by the U.S. government; those not cared for by our government are rich due to casinos; and all Indians are worthless drunks.

Statistics from the latest U.S. Census Bureau dissipate the first of these fabrications:

> More than one-quarter of the American Indian and Alaska Native Population is living in poverty, a rate that is more than double that of the general population and one that is even greater for certain tribal groups (e.g., approaching 40%). . . . 27% of American Indian and Alaska Native families and children live in poverty, whereas 32% of those with children younger than 5 years do—rates that are again more than double those of the general population and again are even higher in certain tribal communities (e.g., 66%).
>
> (Sarche & Spicer, 2008, p. 126)

While tribal governments and programs receive U.S. government assistance, individual Indians receive assistance on an individual, case-by-case basis just like all other needy Americans. They must apply and be eligible for assistance. Poor education and lack of job opportunities contribute to the overall outlook of poverty. Unemployment on reservations can be as high as 35 percent (Sarche & Spicer, 2008, p. 127). Other data conveys the following:

> American Indians residing in Indian Country remain the poorest group in America . . . Income per American Indian household on reservations in 2000 . . . was [at the last census] $24,249, compared to $41,994 for the average U.S. household. Not surprisingly, accompanying Indian poverty have been concomitant indicators of social stress—high rates of suicide, ill health, poor housing, crime, school dropouts, and the like.
>
> (Cornell & Kalt, 2010, p. 5)

Conditions on many reservations have improved since the previous census, but not because of casino gambling—the second falsehood: "Notwithstanding the much publicized growth and success of the casino gaming enterprises owned by many tribal governments, gaming incomes have been concentrated in a relatively small number of tribes near major metropolitan patron populations" (Cornell & Kalt, 2010, p. 5). However, these researchers attribute the rapid growth to the fact that American Indian incomes have increased more rapidly than American incomes as a whole over the last two decades (p. 7). This welcomed change can be attributed neither to government funding nor to absorption of Indians into the dominant culture but rather to the system of self-determination allowed by the 1975 passing of the Indian Self-Determination and Education Assistance Act (U.S. Public Law 95–638) (p. 10). This positive outcome reinforces the need for any Indian workforce education plan to be determined by the Indians themselves.

Finally, concerning Indians' alleged propensity to drink heavily, a study completed in 2010 concludes that "cumulative and point-in-time measures of neighborhood poverty are important predictors of alcohol consumption"

(Cerdá, Diez-Roux, Tchetgen, Gordon-Larsen, & Kiefe, 2010, Abstract, para. 4). Therefore, as economic conditions on reservations improve due to Indians' own self-determined workforce education and progress, we should see a correlative decrease in alcoholism and, in turn, a decrease in related problems such as violence, teen suicide, and some health issues. A close look at current conditions for American Indigenous people can facilitate understanding concerning the mindset among them and the resulting problems—alcohol and drug addiction, domestic violence, chronic disease, and teen suicide.

Here again, American Indian writers can open up the world of Indian culture to those who wish to study and comprehend the third-world-like conditions on many reservations in hopes of constructing a workforce education plan that will work best for Indians as well as the dominant culture. The most prominent author to open the eyes of whites concerning these conditions is once again Sherman Alexie, who grew up on the Spokane Indian Reservation in Washington State. Although some of Alexie's profile of reservation conditions is said to be exaggerated, his writings and films remain some of the most accessible work through which non-Indians can gain a perspective of the reservation mindset. Three of Alexie's works are recommended for this study, including *Reservation Blues* (2005), his first complete novel; *Smoke Signals* (1998), his first film; and *The Absolutely True Diary of a Part-Time Indian* (2007), his first attempt at young adult fiction.

Reservation Blues has been criticized heavily for its exaggeration of Indian conditions. However, its genre is magical realism, wherein the fantastic interrupts reality. In addition, Alexie most often uses comedic irony in his writing, sometimes playing on the exaggerated stereotypes imposed upon Indians by whites. In this novel, themes become motifs, such as the hunger that is first mentioned in the song at the beginning of the book. Hunger as a contemporary condition on the reservation might be slightly exaggerated in the book; however, hunger is a condition with which American Indians are well acquainted, especially hunger as a forced condition brought about by war with whites. Hunger can also be symbolic of different types of need or longing. Another theme of the book is the elusiveness of Indian culture; if Alexie represented Indian culture realistically in the book, the meaning of this theme—that even Indians do not understand Indians—would be lost. Along with poverty and lack of understanding, the novel clearly shows the lack of choice on the reservation. Lack of choice brings about a hungry heart in most humans. Those who plan a workforce educational construct for Indians must weave "individual choice" into the plan if it is to be successful.

Alexie again works with Indian stereotypes and reality on reservations in his film *Smoke Signals*, which was adapted from his book of stories entitled *The Lone Ranger and Tonto Fist Fight in Heaven* (1993) and was the first film to have been written, produced, directed, and performed by American Indians. The two Indian youths in the movie, Victor and Thomas, loosely represent the stereotypical warrior and visionary medicine man who take the typical "hero's journey" toward enlightenment when they have reached manhood. Through their childhood remembrances, however, viewers get a clear picture of life on the reservation, especially poverty and alcoholism, along with the lack of choices that young Indians face, an important lesson for those planning an Indian workforce program

This tremendously popular Indian author portrays reservation life best in his young adult novel, *The Absolutely True Diary of a Part-Time Indian* (2007), which is both loved by critics and hated by parents and censorious educators. It won a National Book Award, yet it is banned in some school districts because of its language, sexual suggestions, and candid emotion. Somewhat autobiographical, the book is more accessible than others, perhaps because it shows reservation life through the eyes of a young boy, Arnold Spirit, who is bullied by his classmates to the point that he leaves the reservation to attend a white school. This book shows not only the poverty and alcoholism that Alexie saw on his reservation but also the identity crisis that many young reservation inhabitants face. Each Indian child confronts a dilemma—stay on the reservation and conform to peers' limiting expectations, or leave the reservation and be hated by those who feel their culture has been betrayed. Any workforce education plan for Indians must address this dilemma.

Supplementary resources that convey hardships faced by youth on Indian reservations are the book *Growing up Native American* (1993) and the movie *Skins* (2002). *Growing up Native American* offers essays and story snippets from prominent American Indian writers and a foreword that discusses cultural identity. *Skins*, directed by Chris Eyre, who also directed *Smoke Signals*, shows the realities of poverty and alcoholism on the most deprived reservation in America, Pine Ridge Reservation, which is in reality the poorest place in America. A new documentary, *Pine Ridge* (2013), shows the stark reality Indian youth face on this impoverished reservation, "where Americans with native blood live a life in the middle—and yet outside—of American society." This rare film "explores what shapes the lives and dreams of today's Native American youth, whose future is uncertain and . . . resembles their traditional way of life less and less" (*Pine Ridge*, 2013). A quick glimpse of the despair on this reservation can be seen on the YouTube video *Pine Ridge Movie 2011*. Films and books such as those mentioned here can open up the confusing world where Indian youth live for the purposes of constructing an Indian workforce education plan that fits the needs of these youth and offers them a brighter future which includes both their traditional way of living and a fulfilling career—if the plan is carefully laid with these goals in mind from the outset.

A prominent reason for Indian despair, which stems from and perpetuates poverty, which in turn perpetuates alcoholism, domestic violence, and teen suicide among Indians—is a lack of adequate educational opportunities and a lack of jobs. Any workforce education program proposed to Indians, especially those living on the poorest reservations such as Pine Ridge and

Rosebud, will be futile unless jobs that require such education or training are provided in the area—with easy access (i.e., transportation). Because private-sector jobs are scarce, many reservation Indians rely on public-sector jobs, which can be unstable due to their dependence on limited funding like grants; when funding for such jobs is gone, the Indians who rely on these jobs are unemployed ("Native American Employment," 2013, para. 1). An article published in *Discovering Multicultural America* reveals that American Indians have a growing need for more and better educational opportunities at the same time that the job market has been shrinking. Researchers predict that if both education and job opportunities are not "addressed, American Indians' traditional role as the nation's poorest of the poor will continue indefinitely into the future" (Gale Research, 1996, para. 6).

An additional hindrance to any workforce educational program is the Indians' lack of basic education, especially on the poorest reservations. The above-mentioned article offers the following insight:

> After generations of living at the margins of the U.S. economy, it should be no surprise that American Indians face some of the greatest economic hardships known in American society ... Without the resources to compete successfully in a modern urban labor market, American Indians have few prospects for success. The marginal areas where many American Indians live often lack the resources required to succeed in the labor market. Lack of education is often a serious impediment to Indians who seek work. On the other hand, it is difficult to encourage American Indian youth to pursue an education when the lack of employment opportunities offers little incentive to stay in school. (para. 4)

Sarche and Spicer (2008) narrow their focus to poverty among American Indians and Alaska Natives in their report concerning differences in education and job opportunities among Indigenous peoples:

> Overall, there are fewer individuals within the American Indian and Alaska Native population who possess a high school diploma or GED (71% versus 80%) or a bachelor's degree (11.5% versus 24.4%). Such educational discrepancies appear early, with American Indian and Alaska Native children's math and reading skills progressively behind those of their white peers as early as kindergarten to fourth grade, as well as other challenges persisting throughout the school years, including higher dropout rates and grade retention. (para. 1)

Along with lack of employment opportunities, the high dropout rates could also be attributed to lack of funding for Native schools. The U.S. Commission on Civil Rights (2003) has this to say:

> Native American students are not afforded educational opportunities equal to other American students. They routinely face deteriorating

school facilities, underpaid teachers, weak curricula, discriminatory treatment, outdated learning tools, and cultural isolation . . . [They score] lower than any other racial/ethnic group in basic levels of reading, math, and history . . . [and] are more likely to drop out. (p. 8)

Part of the problem, of course, is the fact that standardized testing has, in the past, been designed according to the dominant society's standards, making Indians' cultural isolation more devastating. Moreover, federally funded subprograms were cut drastically between 1998 and 2003, and although grant-funded vocational and technical programs were afforded an increase during those years, they faced drastic cuts in 2004 (U.S. Commission on Civil Rights, 2003). The Obama administration's answer to the poor performance of BIE-run Indian schools involves updating these schools through a reorganization of the BIE, including more effective funding, to bring up standards and test scores (Maxwell, 2014). However, educational standards would still be set by the dominant society. Bryan V. Brewer, chairman of the Oglala Sioux tribe in Pine Ridge, South Dakota, states, "It's time for us to decide what our children will learn and how they will learn it because [BIE] has been a failure so far" (quoted in Maxwell, 2014, para. 7). Here again, education has failed the Indigenous people because government continues to ignore its own "self-determination" standard for first Americans—a wake-up call for all those involved in building a better American Indian workforce education design.

Summing up the educational deficiencies and poverty experienced by American Indians and the subsequent low chances for employment, Sarche and Spicer (2008) conclude as follows:

> American Indian and Alaska Native people have lower labor force participation rates than those of the general population, whereas family unemployment rates range from 14.4% overall to as high as 35% in some reservation communities. The poverty and unemployment observed in American Indian and Alaska Native communities is related to broader economic development challenges in American Indian and Alaska Native communities, including geographic isolation and the availability of largely low-wage jobs. (p. 126)

Furthermore, those who design or attempt to continue a workforce education program for American Indians should be aware that some Indian programs exist to promote higher education of American Indians rather than to provide alternative workforce training. Both the Harvard Project, a research project and educational program initiated and administered by Harvard University, and the Native Nations Institute of the University of Arizona advocate higher education for American Indians rather than vocational or other training. These programs of study have provided ample research evidence to show that Indian nations progress more successfully when they take charge of their own Indian-based governments and businesses. The Native Nations Institute concluded, "Native political leaders make their nations more attractive to the Native citizen with a college degree" and that "successful Native nations share three essential characteristics: 1) They assert the Nation's powers of self-rule; 2) they build strong institutions of self-government to backup those powers; and 3) they root their development efforts and institutions in Native culture" (Taylor, 2008, para. 2).

Most definitely, more opportunities for higher education should be afforded to American Indians; however, a push for every American Indian to possess a college degree is unrealistic, just as Obama's notion that all Americans should have a college degree is unrealistic. Not all persons desire, nor can they afford or achieve, a college degree, and a focus on higher education alone is detrimental to any nation's workforce goals. It takes many types of education and training to make up a diverse workforce; therefore, any workforce education plan for American Indians should include all forms of education and training available to the population at large per job opportunities for those living within the boundaries of proposed programs.

*****

Despite the many hindrances to workforce education plans for American Indians, such efforts are desperately needed. Many of the impediments to such an endeavor have developed because past educational plans have been ill conceived and poorly executed. If originators of a workforce education plan for Indigenous people feel that the steps suggested here imply a long and laborious undertaking, they are correct. However, government officials, policymakers, grant writers, and corporate officials who might find this prospect daunting should first stop and consider the unproductive time that has passed for American Indians under the control of European conquerors—more than 500 years. For those wishing to upgrade the education and skills of Indigenous peoples and help them become productive members of the American workforce while honoring their cultural identity, the above steps are essential.

A workforce education program for American Indians must be devoted to preserving and improving the life circumstances of many tribal nations rather than securing a cheap labor force and/or prematurely ending government assistance. Therefore, a first step must always be a dialogue with the tribes or groups of Indians to be involved, which means a friendly and respectful collaboration with prospective students. The best education happens when the instructor is face to face with the pupil, and in this case, the instructor must first become the pupil. Sharing a meal along with an open dialogue is the best way to break down prejudices. The 2014 proposal to reorganize the BIE is a good example of the wrong way to go about establishing programs for Indigenous people; the proposal was drafted and released by the Obama administration before the President visited the tribes to sell said proposal (Maxwell, 2014, para. 2). Without a sincere effort on the part of planners and educators from the very beginning, a non-Indian's vision of Indian education will not be welcomed.

During such a dialogue, all those involved, from the top down, must sincerely convince tribal members and urban Indians that their own educational process has gotten under way—that they have studied and are studying the true history of American Indians, the true nature and goals of past government relations with the first American landowners, and the true living conditions of American Indians, both on and off reservations. If first Americans perceive that their educators have not made an earnest effort to unlearn old stereotypes forced on them by Hollywood, by prejudices enhanced by the government's desire for gold and land, and by falsehoods produced by inadequate programs and media hype, no negotiations will ensue.

First and foremost, says the research of the Harvard Project, the American Indians involved in any such program must retain power over the outcome for the program to be successful. Effective Indian programs, according to the conclusions drawn from this project, "assert the power [of American Indians] to make core decisions about resources, policy, and institutions." The absence of such power over their own destinies was the driving force toward poverty for American Indians. "The research is clear," declare the investigators who reported the findings of this project. "Outsiders perform poorly when managing Native resources, designing Native policy, and creating Native governing institutions—no matter how well-meaning or competent they may be" (Taylor, 2008, para. 3).

Therefore, for any idea of a workforce education plan for American Indians to be effective, the aforementioned steps are crucial. Such a program must look toward preserving and improving the life circumstances of individual Indians and tribal nations, not securing a cheap labor force and/or ending government assistance. Planners must honor indigenous peoples by allowing them to help determine the program's plan from the outset. Additionally, all involved must seek to understand Indian history and Indian culture. If American Indians are willing to help plan, organize, and participate in such a program, the plan must be undertaken with adequate funding, heroic diligence, and as much time as is needed to make it successful.

REFERENCES

Adams, D. (1997). *Education for extinction: American Indians and the boarding school experience 1875–1928.* Lawrence, KS: University Press of Kansas.

Cerdá, M., Diez-Roux, A., Tchetgen, E., Gordon-Larsen, P., & Kiefe, C. (2010). The relationship between neighborhood poverty and alcohol use: Estimation by marginal structural models. *Epidemiology, 4,* 482–489. doi:10.1097/EDE.0b013e3181e13539

Columbus, C. (2009). Letter to Ferdinand and Isabella. In D. Damrosch & D. L. Pike (Eds.), *The Longman anthology of world literature* (2nd ed., Vol. C, pp. 815–821). New York, NY: Pearson/Longman.

Cornell, S., & Kalt, J. P. (2010). *American Indian self-determination: The political economy of a successful policy.* Retrieved from https://research.hks.harvard.edu/publications/getFile.aspx?Id=610.pdf

del Castillo, B. D. (2009). The true history of the conquest of New Spain. In D. Damrosch & D. L. Pike (Eds.), *The Longman anthology of world literature* (2nd ed., Vol. C, pp. 822–841). New York, NY: Pearson/Longman.

Eborn, A. (Director). (2013). *Pine Ridge* [Motion picture]. United States: Torchfilms.

Edwards, C. (2012). *Indian lands, Indian subsidies, and the Bureau of Indian Affairs.* Retrieved from http://www.cato.org/people/chris-edwards

Gale Research, Inc. (1996). *DISCovering multicultural America: African Americans, Hispanic Americans, Asian Americans, Native Americans.* Detroit, MI: Author.

Garrett, M. T., & Pichette, E. F. (2000). Red as an apple: Native American acculturation and counseling with or without reservation. *Journal of Counseling & Development, 78,* 3–13. doi:10.1002/j.1556-6676.2000.tb02554.x

Hopkins, S. W. (1994). *Life Among the Piutes: Their wrongs and claims.* Reno, NV: University of Nevada Press.

Lomawaima, K. T. (2013). The mutuality of citizenship and sovereignty: The society of American Indians and the battle to inherit America. *The American Indian Quarterly, 37*(3). Retrieved from http://www.nebraskapress.unl.edu/

Maxwell, L. (2014). Plan to reshape Indian education stirs opposition. *Education Week.* Retrieved from http://www.edweek.org/ew/articles/2014/07/09/36indian.h33.html

McDonnell, M. (n.d.). *The "conquest" of the Americas: The Aztecs.* Retrieved from http://www.anzasa.arts.usyd.edu.au/ahas/conquest_overview.html

Moquin, W., & Van Doren, C. (1973). *Great documents in American Indian history.* New York, NY: Da Capo Press.

Neihardt, J. G. (1961). *Black Elk speaks: Being the life story of a holy man of the Oglala Sioux.* Lincoln, NE: University of Nebraska Press.

Olson-Raymer, G. (2001). *Narrative historical overview.* Retrieved from http://www.americanindiantah.com/history/nar_19thcenturyrelations.html

Provenzo, E. F., Jr., & McCloskey, G. N. (1981). Catholic and federal Indian education in the late 19th century: Opposed colonial models. *Journal of American Indian Education, 21*(1). Retrieved from http://jaie.asu.edu/v21/V21S1opp.html

Red Jacket. (1973). Speech in response to missionary efforts, 1805. In M. Wayne & C. Van Doren (Eds.), *Great documents in American Indian history* (pp. 31–33). New York, NY: Da Capo Press.

Rivera, D. M. (2013). Tribal learning community & educational exchange: Examining the space between the "us-them" binary. *American Indian Culture and Research Journal, 37*(3), 87–94. doi:0161–6463.

Sarche, M., & Spicer, P. (2008). Poverty and health disparities for American Indian and Alaska Native children: Current knowledge and future prospects. *Annals of the New York Academy of Sciences, 1136,* 126–136.

Taylor, J. (2008). *Determinants of development success in the Native nations of the United States.* Retrieved from http://nni.arizona.edu/resources/inpp/determinants_of_development_success_english.pdf

U.S. Commission on Civil Rights. (2003). *A quiet crisis: Federal funding and unmet needs in Indian country.* Retrieved from http://www.USCCr.gov/pubs/na0703/na0204.pdf

Wingo, R. (2011). *Through the lens of civilization: Using photos as history.* Retrieved from http://history.unl.edu/podcasts/digprojects.aspx

RECOMMENDED RESOURCES

Alexie, S. (1995). *Reservation blues.* New York, NY: Grove Press.

Alexie, S. (Director). (2002). *The business of fancy dancing* [Motion picture]. United States: Miramax Films.

Alexie, S. (2007). *The absolutely true diary of a part-time Indian.* New York, NY: Little, Brown.

Alexie, S. (Producer) & Eyre, C. (Director). (1998). *Smoke signals* [Motion picture]. United States: Miramax Films.

Alexie, S. (Producer) & Eyre, C. (Director). (2002). *Skins* [Motion picture]. United States: Miramax Films.

Commissioner of Indian Affairs. (1891). *Report of the Commissioner of Indian Affairs for 1891, Vol. 1.* Retrieved from http://digicoll.library.wisc.edu/cgi-bin/History/History-idx?id=History.AnnRep91p1

Erdrich, L. (1993). *Love medicine.* New York, NY: Harper Perennial.

Erdrich, L. (1999). *The antelope wife.* New York, NY: Harper Perennial.

Erdrich, L. (2009). *The last report on the miracles at Little No Horse.* New York, NY: Harper Perennial.

Glancy, D. (1998). *Pushing the bear.* New York, NY: Harcourt Brace & Company.

Green, M. K. (1995). *Issues in Native American cultural identity.* New York, NY: Peter Lang.

Hornbuckle, J., & French, L. (Eds.). (1981). *The Cherokee perspective.* Boone, NC: Appalachian Consortium Press.

Jackson, H. H. (1995). *A century of dishonor.* Norman, OK: University of Oklahoma Press. (Original work published in 1881)

Kersken, U. (Producer). (2009). *America before Columbus* [Documentary]. United States: National Geographic.

Magoulick, M. (2000). *Women weaving the world, Louise Erdrich's the antelope wife as myth.* Retrieved from http://www.faculty.de.gcsu.edu/~mmagouli/cv2000.htm

Mankiller, W. (1999). *Mankiller: A chief and her people.* New York, NY: St. Martin's Griffin.

Michno, G. (Ed.). (1997). *Lakota noon: The Indian narrative of Custer's defeat.* Missoula, MT: Mountain Press.

Momaday, N. S. (1966). *House made of dawn.* New York, NY: HarperCollins.

Richie, C., & Heape, S. (Directors). (2006). *The trail of tears Cherokee legacy* [Documentary]. United States: Rich-Heape Films.

Riley, P. (Ed.). (1993). *Growing up Native.* New York, NY: Avon Books.

Silko, L. M. (1977). *Ceremony.* New York, NY: Penguin Books.

Simoneau, Y. (Director). (2007). *Bury my heart at wounded knee* [TV movie]. United States: HBO Films.

U.S. Commission on Civil Rights. (2003). *A quiet crisis: Federal funding and unmet needs in Indian country*. Retrieved from http://www.usccr.gov/pubs/na0703/na0204.pdf

Velie, A. (Ed.). (1991). *American Indian literature: An anthology*. Norman, OK: University of Oklahoma Press.

Wolfinger, L. (Producer). (2005). *Conquest of America* [Documentary]. United States: The History Channel.

Wong, H. D. S. (2000). *Love Medicine: A casebook*. New York, NY: Oxford University Press.

7 Career Development Counseling for American Indian Students

Carsten Schmidtke

Toneva Stamphill, a member of the Choctaw Nation, was a first-year student in the Information Technologies program at a technical college in the central United States. When this author spoke with Toneva, she expressed a desire to earn her degree to provide a better life for her children, a son aged three and a daughter aged two. She further described herself as a quiet person who spent more time observing than talking and added that she felt it was her responsibility to study and to learn and not to expect her professors to spoon-feed her every bit of information. At the same time, she admitted that childcare obligations often made studying difficult and that she had been experiencing anxiety attacks and fatigue although she had not seen a doctor for her symptoms. During a classroom observation, Toneva exhibited little involvement in the project work her small group was engaged in and later confided that her fondest experience had been those times when the group was off-task, discussing private matters.

Shortly after our conversation, Toneva dropped out of the Information Technologies program. Her case came to mind when I began to think about the effects of career development and counseling for American Indian students. Had Toneva received any guidance? Did she know how challenging a college education could be? Had she been given all the facts about a career in information technologies? Was her withdrawal from the program a sign that information technologies was the wrong career for her? Was the career guidance she received appropriate for American Indians? Would she have remained in the program if the guidance had been different? Were there any services the university could have provided to help Toneva complete her education? These questions can no longer be answered as Toneva has moved without leaving her new address, but they suggest that maybe counselors and advisors ought to take a closer look at how they provide career development for American Indian students.

As a result, the question of what career guidance counselors must do to ensure that they provide culturally sensitive and appropriate career development counseling for American Indian high school students seeking to enter the workforce or trying to decide on a college major comes to mind. This chapter explores what the relevant literature has to say about how career guidance counselors can provide services to American Indian students by taking into account the two most important factors of the career development process, career maturity and salience. Kerka (1998) asserted that for all minority students, career development activities hinged on career maturity and salience. Career maturity was defined "readiness to make appropriate career decisions" (p. 1), but this readiness was influenced by real and perceived barriers as well as a lack of career-related information and guidance. Salience was the importance people attached to the various roles they played in their lives, including work and career, and ethnic identity in combination with the degree of acculturation might have a significant effect on people's career development patterns. Juntunen et al. (2001) lamented that misconceptions about the counseling needs of American Indian students still prevailed because the research on this topic had been limited, so it made sense to conceive this chapter as an overview of the literature to determine what kind of information was actually available to counselors about the barriers American Indian students faced and the solutions that were available.

Career counselors can help students make sense of the career and life choices they are faced with only if they have a thorough understanding of how their students' cultural backgrounds affect career maturity and salience. If career counselors can lead their students to greater career maturity, i.e., provide them with the knowledge and skills they need to make informed career decisions by themselves, they also help them develop salience, and students who have a clear concept of the role of a career in their lives can make better choices for themselves and for their communities.

SITUATION FOR AMERICAN INDIANS

Although American Indians are counted among the minority groups in American society, their situation is often quite different from that of other minority groups. In fact, it has been suggested that American Indians should not be considered a minority in the first place since treaty rights make them members of sovereign tribal nations (Newcomb, 2013). Tribes acting on their sovereignty, however, often face resentment in areas such as privileges for small businesses (Yang, 2006), hunting and fishing rights (Johnson, 2015), and, of course, gaming (Fletcher, 2007).

There is no such thing as a global American Indian culture. American Indians exhibit substantial between-group diversity in areas such as language (200 to 250 languages are still actively spoken), material culture, subsistence, customs, and spirituality. Within tribes or bands, diversity can also be significant. Johnson, Swartz, and Martin (1995) mentioned five cultural orientations or levels of assimilation (traditional, transitional, marginal, assimilated, and bicultural) that each describe how people relate to their tribal cultures. All American Indians fall somewhere within this continuum, and their cultural orientation is further complicated by whether they live in an urban area, in a rural area, or on a reservation. Counselors who fail to understand the interaction of these factors are likely to recommend careers that do not suit students' interests, needs, and talents well. As students dissatisfied with their college majors often drop out and some adults dissatisfied with their careers prefer unemployment over working in a job they despise, uninformed counselors may well be contributing to the problem of under-education and underemployment among American Indians instead of helping to solve it.

Schools often show a lack of concern and support for American Indian students attempting to retain their cultural identity in that they do not value and respect American Indian cultures, and instead of providing culturally appropriate support, they expect students to give up or suppress their cultures to be academically successful. This sacrifice is too great for many students to make, who will then resist by dropping out (Huffman, 2001; Klasky, 2013; Wentzlaff & Brewer, 1996). Instead of more integration, it has been argued, American Indian students need more empowerment (Yang, Byers, & Fenton, 2006).

Peavy (1998) stated unequivocally that American Indians should not be looked at in terms of multiculturalism because they did not immigrate to America, and their attempts to retain their cultural identity has less to do with themselves than with the struggle to ensure the survival of their cultures. Most career counseling for minorities, Peavy noted, had an assimilationist undertow in that it tried to prepare students for "full membership in the North American dominant society" (p. 1). American Indians, however, have no interest in such membership, and career choice has to be one aspect of their desire and their right to keep their tribal culture distinct and even separate from mainstream culture.

Finally, American Indians have some of the lowest overall high school graduation rates in the United States. Only 35 percent of American Indians over 25 have finished high school (Freeman & Fox, 2005), and of those American Indian students finishing high school, between 33 percent and 64 percent enrolled in college (Hoover & Jacobs, 1992; Kirkness & Barnhardt, 1991; Tierney, 1993, 1995). American Indians thus are the least likely of all minority groups to enroll in college (DeVoe, Darling-Churchill, & Snyder, 2008; Pewewardy & Frey, 2004), and when they do, they are more likely than other ethnic groups to choose two-year colleges (Aud et al., 2011; Cole & Denzine, 2002; Tierney, 1993) and to have the highest dropout rates (DeVoe et al., 2008; James, 2001).

Johnson et al. (1995) added that on the ten most populous reservations, graduation rates had remained below 50 percent, and such a lack of educational achievement naturally put severe limitations on students' career choices. All these differences from other minority groups, Martin (1995) and Peavy (1998) asserted, had to be noted so that career guidance counselors could help American Indian students manage the challenge of remaining culturally distinct without becoming part of the dominant North American society, however multicultural it may be, while simultaneously acquiring the ability to interact with and function in this society if needed.

BARRIERS TO EFFECTIVE CAREER DEVELOPMENT

Most American Indians are likely to encounter career problems and will face a number of barriers to career development that are unique to them, tend to arise simultaneously, and overlap in scope (Vega, 2012). Other minority students and white students usually have to deal with such barriers to a lesser degree or not at all (Juntunen & Cline, 2010). Wentling and Waight (2000) divided such barriers into four categories: school-related, work-related, societal related, and individual-related.

School-Related Barriers

The mainstay of career development counseling is career development theories, theoretical approaches to career development that are designed to take into account both students' career maturity and their concept of salience. Their purpose is to help students build a foundation of knowledge and insight that ultimately leads to an appropriate career choice. Although these theories can be used for anyone seeking career counseling anywhere, high school and college guidance counselors were trained to use them and tend to rely on them, and it therefore made sense to include them under this heading.

Gray and Herr (1998) divided career development theories into five types: trait-and-factor theory, decision theory, situational or sociological approaches, personality approaches, and developmental theory. Trait-and-factor theory is based on the belief that individuals have certain interests or talents that have to be compared to the requirements for certain occupations until a perfect match is found. Decision theory operates under the assumption that individuals have different choices of career paths, and the best way to help them discover the best path is to explore the advantages and disadvantages of each one. Situational or sociological theories acknowledge that people's environments both provide and limit the career choices someone can make, and they seek to help people realize which factors bear upon their career choices. Personality approaches believe that people's career choices are driven by a need for gratification developed in early childhood, which means childhood issues have to be explored. Developmental theories, finally, assert that people's occupational preferences and needs change as they enter different stages of their lives (and because of this, they are also called life-stage or life-span theories). A career chosen by an adolescent, therefore, has to be able to adapt to changing needs and desires later in life.

The literature was unanimous in its verdict that these career development theories in their current form have at best limited applicability and are generally unsuitable for and irrelevant to minorities in general and American

Indians in particular (Alliman-Brissett & Turner, 2005; Juntunen & Cline, 2010). Sources especially contended that all models were developed with middle-aged white males as participants and as a result had limited generalizability to the situation of minorities (Kerka, 1998; Leong & Serafica, 2001; Smith, 1983). Kerka (1998) and Leong and Serafica (2001) detailed some of these objections. The major objection is that these theories use unclear definitions of the concepts of race, ethnicity, and minority and also fail to include the interaction of social class with these concepts, all of which have an effect on career maturity. Trait-and-factor theories are accused of being insensitive to the life experiences of minorities because stereotyping, racism, and discrimination have a major impact on the skills, knowledge, and interests people have cultivated. Developmental theories ignore the fact that ethnicity and minority identity affect people's needs at different life stages, especially if they perceive their opportunities to be limited. In addition, the effects of discrimination make planning for needs at different life stages next to impossible (Smith, 1983). Situational or sociological approaches fail to consider the political, economic, and cultural contexts of individuals trying to negotiate two cultures. However, Kerka and Leong and Serafica did not advocate abandoning these theories altogether. Instead, they recommended that they be modified to include factors that are germane to career decisions for minorities.

The second major school-related barrier is counselor attitudes and training. Counselors often lack the skills to interpret career assessment results in a culturally appropriate manner, which can lead to irrelevant guidance and the recommendation of career choices and pathways that do not align with true student interests and needs (Flynn, Duncan, & Evenson, 2013; Juntunen & Cline, 2010). An additional problem often arises when counselors treat all American Indians the same and assume they all have similar needs, ignoring differences between tribes and cultures or the different needs of urban or reservation residents (Flynn et al., 2013).

Along with a lack of understanding on the part of counselors often came ignorance among teachers, administrators, and staff members, which Peavy (1998) had already mentioned in the context of American Indian students' attempts to preserve their cultures. One problem was ethnocentrism and stereotyping in the curriculum. Teachers have grown up with stereotypes about ethnicity, culture, and race, and textbooks still assign professional white-collar careers (physicians, managers, lawyers, politicians, etc.) predominantly to white people and show American Indians only in traditional cultural contexts. This situation is exacerbated by the frequent lack of teachers who might serve as role models and sources of information and encouragement for students (Esters & Bowen, 2003; Leong & Serafica, 2001). Connected to this situation are low expectations of American Indian students, which Swisher and Deyhle (1988) attributed to a lack of understanding of American Indian social norms. For example, reserved behavior that is appropriate at home is seen as an indication of low aptitude in the classroom.

Other barriers concern access to programs based on the location of the school. Many schools on reservations or in remote rural areas do not offer career and technical education (CTE) because there are no teachers or the schools cannot afford to build the needed facilities and purchase equipment. The location of many schools also makes work-based learning (WBL) impossible. WBL encompasses a range of activities where students spend part of their education on the job in area businesses and then engage in connecting activities at school that explore the relationship between classroom and on-the-job learning. However, the lack of employers within a reasonable distance, especially near reservations, effectively shuts many American Indian students out of WBL (Martin, 1991). If WBL is possible, overworked teachers often are unable to communicate with businesses to find out about workplace demands or to supervise students in WBL programs (Wentling & Waight, 2000). Another access problem is the lack of appropriate career development materials (Smith, 1983). Leong and Serafica in 2001 still mentioned the absence of current job information, showing that little had changed, and even today, computers with Internet access may not be available. If information is available, students are often overwhelmed by the number of choices and confused by the terminology used in career development.

All these school-related barriers have serious effects. The difficulty of obtaining clear and understandable information makes many students suspicious of the true intent of career guidance counseling and reluctant to participate in counseling sessions (Juntunen & Cline, 2010; Leong & Serafica, 2001; Wentling & Waight, 2000). Students who do not seek career guidance or have the opportunity to participate in WBL have much lower levels of career maturity and a weaker concept of career salience (Johnson et al., 1995).

Work-Related Barriers

The most frequently mentioned work-related barrier is the absence of a truly open labor market (Smith, 1983). Career choices especially for rural or reservation students are limited, and many of the non-Indian employers in the vicinity often harbor deep prejudices against American Indian employees because they do not understand their values, beliefs, and behaviors. The result is that many American Indians do not have equal access to job training, employment, raises, and promotions (Kerka, 2003). This situation leads to a high unemployment rate, and people who do not work also have no opportunity to set up job networks in case they should lose their jobs. Thus, a vicious cycle is created (Wentling & Waight, 2000). This first problem then feeds into the second one, a lack of knowledge. The absence of WBL in school and the dearth of employment opportunities lead many young people to have a poor understanding of the requirements of the workplace and of basic employability skills, making them even less employable. Limited exposure to jobs outside the community and the limited number of American Indian role models further convince young people that they are not welcome in many companies and that their career choices have been severely curtailed by the dominant society, leading to diminished career maturity and salience (Flynn et al., 2013; Johnson et al., 1995; Leong & Serafica, 2001; Wentling & Waight, 2000).

Societal-Related Barriers

Martin (1991) asserted that external pressures play a significant role in the barriers American Indian students face. The most obvious societal barriers are racism and prejudice. Many employers have negative attitudes toward American Indian cultures or American Indian students and are often unwilling to hire them into career track positions if they are willing to hire them at all (Leong & Serafica, 2001). Other external pressures come from the students' immediate environment, usually in the form of lack of support or even open hostility or ridicule (Juntunen et al., 2001; Leong & Serafica, 2001). First, unemployed peers exert considerable pressure on individuals, equating a wish for steady employment and a possible desire to move away from the community with disloyalty to friends and community (Wentling & Waight, 2000). Families often react by showing no interest in the career development plans of their children, sending an indirect but powerful message that family is to come before career and that choosing a career would be seen as turning one's back on one's family. Other families speak out openly against any career choice that would take individuals away from home and not involve or benefit the family (Juntunen et al., 2001). In community-oriented American Indian cultures, the groups students belong to has a profound effect on salience (Kerka, 1998, 2003).

A second problem lies in the fact that many counselors ignore the social and economic conditions of many American Indian students and their effects on career maturity (Juntunen et al., 2001; Kerka, 2003; Leong & Serafica, 2001; Marshall et al., 2011; Smith, 1983). Supporting the family under often-challenging conditions comes first, and especially those students whose families do not know where their next meal will come from or who deal with health and other issues have not given much thought to career development. Their major objective is to find not a career but gainful employment that can pay the bills, buy food, and support family members (Kerka, 1998; Marshall et al., 2011; Martin, 1991). A lack of appreciation for putting family first often fuels mistrust in counselors and reluctance to participate actively in counseling, resulting in the recommendation of unsuitable career paths.

Individual-Related Barriers

The most important individual-related barrier is certainly limited self-efficacy (Wentling & Waight, 2000). As a result of some of the school- and work-related barriers, many American Indian students have a limited vocational identity, meaning that their awareness of what is required of them in the workplace is underdeveloped and that they cannot properly assess their own skills, knowledge, and aptitude (Herring, 1990; Johnson et al., 1995; Leong & Serafica, 2001). Persistent career myths among the student population are one of the consequences of this lack of career maturity. Herring (1990) described career myths as unrealistic beliefs about career development. Some of the symptoms are a lack in specific knowledge of what workplaces require of employees, an exaggeration of one's own career plans, magnification or minimization of problems in choosing a career, a tendency to pay attention only to extreme experiences at work or in interactions with others, and a personalization of any negative experiences one might have on or off the job.

Limited self-efficacy is also related to an individual's worldview. Some American Indian students, especially those who have grown up on reservations, tend to be quite ethnocentric. For many, traditional beliefs take precedence over choosing a career, and once they have chosen one, they often have difficulty dealing with values different from those of their communities (Johnson et al., 1995; Kerka, 2003; Leong & Serafica, 2001; Smith, 1983; Turner & Lapan, 2003). Contact with mainstream culture then leads to anxiety followed by an identity crisis and subsequently a preoccupation with finding one's place in life, which supersedes any considerations of doing well in one's chosen career (Herring, 1990). Kerka (1998) explained that the extent to which people have accepted the dominant culture affects salience and can lead to diminished career maturity, which in extreme cases means that students exclude themselves from careers that are actually very much open to them.

Another barrier is to be found in the relationship between the student and his or her community. Self-efficacy and career decisions are often based on community need rather than individual interest, and the future career is placed in the context of how to be the best possible community member. Students wanting to support their communities thus often fail to seek help from a counselor, who is seen as an agent of the dominant society that wishes to install mainstream values (Juntunen & Cline, 2010).

Residence preferences create barriers as well. Many American Indian students are loath to move to a neighboring community or, worse yet, off the reservation or out of state, and this naturally limits their career choices (Juntunen et al., 2001; Martin, 1991). A final barrier in this category is limited finances. Because many families live in poverty, students cannot afford to move away from home to attend post-secondary institutions, and even if they can secure some financial aid, expenses like rent, food, and transportation often remain prohibitively expensive (Cohn, 1997).

As a result of all of these above barriers, a situation arises where students are interested mainly in commonly chosen careers and do not consider new careers paths that are clearly open to them. Although the interest in something tried and true may be more realistic than the dreams of others, it also results in a disproportionate interest in careers requiring two-year degrees and steers students away from many of the options higher education has to offer them (Turner & Lapan, 2003).

Discussion

It is a tall order for counselors to keep in mind all these barriers when they try to help American Indian students choose an appropriate career. Dealing with so many individual variables and the frequent overlap of barriers can easily overwhelm and frustrate even the most dedicated and experienced counselor. Therefore, researchers have also focused on a number of solutions that counselors can use to help their students overcome real and perceived barriers.

SOLUTIONS FOR EFFECTIVE CAREER DEVELOPMENT

Which initiatives are most likely to develop career maturity and salience? This is the question that according to Kerka (1998) drives all solutions as these two factors are at the core of all minority students' ability to make a suitable career choice. Herring (1990) underscored that American Indian students have unique needs and need specific counseling strategies, but he did not proffer any such strategies other than very general ones. Martin (1995) further asserted that these solutions cannot just parallel the barriers, i.e., dividing solutions into the same categories as barriers will not suffice. To be able to help students overcome school-related barriers, for example, counselors also have to look at societal and individual barriers. Therefore, Martin recommended that the solutions be subdivided into training, acculturation, culture, community, family, and individual.

Training Solutions

This type of solution is the easiest to define but possibly the hardest one to implement. Peavy (1998) explained that two changes have to be made: (1) more American Indian counselors have to be trained and hired, and (2) non-Indian counselors have to receive better training in American Indian language, culture, history, and psychology. This is a challenging proposition at best. Peavy did not discuss how tribes can go about encouraging more of their members to pursue counseling degrees and whether non-Indian counselors would be willing to relocate to remote areas where they will likely be viewed with suspicion, especially if they need more training than their college classmates in the first place and are possibly facing lower pay and less job security than elsewhere. Peavy's suggestion certainly has merit, but meanwhile, real counselors are counseling real students, and they need help in recognizing and preventing bias to counsel their students in a culturally sensitive manner (Herring, 1990).

As a result, Juntunen and Cline (2010) recommended that counselors working with American Indian students receive professional development to conduct culturally appropriate assessments of students' career knowledge, including salience and maturity; barriers students face; available or expected family and community support; and the resources students can reasonably devote to career planning and development. Alliman-Brissett and Turner (2005), along with Flynn et al. (2013), made a number of specific recommendations as to what counselors can do even without specific cultural training to work successfully with American Indian students, e.g., provide images of American Indians in various careers, have professionally successful American Indians come into schools and talk with students, provide service learning and job shadowing opportunities, practice career-related activities such as job interviews, involve parents and families in the career development process, and continue to provide services for school dropouts.

Acculturation Solutions

Acculturation in a nutshell means that when the members of two or more cultures are in long-term close contact, they eventually exhibit changes in language, behavior, social organization, values, etc., inspired by the other culture, both at the macro-cultural and the individual level (Rudmin, 2009). For American Indians, Tierney (1993) suggested that the level or degree of such acculturation had been associated with student success. Using college students as an example, Schiller and Gaseoma (1993) concurred with Tierney (1993) that academic success among American Indians was closely tied to the appropriate level of acculturation, and their research showed that not the assimilated student but the one who was able to function in both Indian and mainstream cultural contexts (i.e., the bicultural student) was most likely to persist and be successful. In fact, they stated that extreme behaviors (complete rejection of one culture and complete immersion in the other) were always detrimental and that the ability to follow both American Indian and mainstream cultural patterns seemed to make students more empowered and ready to overcome the challenges of college life and of choosing a career.

One factor of acculturation that is often forgotten is language proficiency. Americans usually hear about how American Indian languages are threatened with extinction, but many do not know that in some areas, especially on reservations, children still grow up speaking mainly their tribal languages and may have limited English proficiency. Counselors, therefore, would be well advised to assess Indian students' language proficiency first and not to expect everyone to be fluent in English. After such an assessment, counselors should simplify questions and vocabulary if needed and consider English proficiency when looking at career options (Martin, 1995).

Counselors had to be aware of the different levels of acculturation because of their influence on interpreting the answers provided by students (Subich, 1996). "Traditional" individuals were those who spoke their tribal languages and observed traditional customs while rejecting the dominant culture. "Transitional" meant that people spoke English and their tribal language. They were critical of some aspects of their tribal culture but did not fully embrace the dominant culture. When people had difficulty accepting the heritage of either their tribe or of the dominant culture, they were considered "marginal" and experienced the largest identity crisis. "Assimilated" individuals accepted and had been accepted by the dominant culture, and "bicultural" individuals were those who accepted and respected both traditions and could move easily between them (Johnson et al., 1995). Leong and Serafica (2001) listed occupational segregation, mobility, salience, aspirations and expectations, and interest among the decisions in the career development process that were influenced by the individual level of acculturation. Knowing the level of acculturation of students will be very helpful in preventing misunderstandings about career maturity and salience, enable counselors to determine which counseling strategies might be effective and culturally appropriate, and give them a better sense of how to interpret student responses to their questions.

Once counselors are aware of a student's level of acculturation and acknowledge that students from traditional communities might not be traditional themselves or that students from urban areas might not be assimilated, they can then begin discussing the importance of school in an appropriate fashion. Impressing upon students the need to continue and complete their schooling to fulfill their career goals and convincing dropouts to return to school can be done successfully only if counselors are aware of how acculturation affects salience and maturity so that they do not push too hard or choose arguments that the student might not be open to (Marshall et al., 2011).

Culture Solutions

Cultural identity is a major factor in assessing the needs and responses of American Indian students (Leong & Serafica, 2001). Knowing about and respecting their students' cultures is invaluable to counselors who want to understand salience and career goals in their cultural context. Counselors have to take cultural differences into account by using cultural accommodation, avoiding cultural bias, and learning about their students' cultures, cultural orientations, and social contexts (Alliman-Brissett & Turner, 2005; Herring, 1990; Leong & Serafica, 2001; Martin, 1995). If counselors are able to recognize each student's worldview and understand how American Indian history in general and individual tribal histories, societies, and ways of thinking in particular shape individual perceptions, they can then understand students' values and expectations for career development (Herring, 1990; McDaniels & Gysbers, 1992; Vega, 2012).

One way to reach this level of understanding, Juntunen and Cline (2010) and Peavy (1998) recommended, is to use storytelling, a traditional

American Indian form of instruction, as a counseling tool. Framing needs and desires as stories helps students see how their career plans are connected to the social and economic conditions of their communities and families and also presents them with a way to explore the issue of how to remain culturally distinct under constant pressure by the dominant society to assimilate more. A supplementary approach suggested by Juntunen and Cline (2010) was to foster trust through learning about collectivist societies and to appreciate collectivist values that are important for American Indians.

Once they have made an effort to recognize, respect, and understand the cultural and social uniqueness of American Indian students, counselors can begin to develop a culturally relevant model of assessment. Such a task would first of all acknowledge that current career development theories are inappropriate for American Indians and then fill in what is missing (Leong & Serafica, 2001). McDaniels and Gysbers (1992) suggested that one way for counselors to fill the gaps was to look at counseling techniques that had been successful in the past, and Herring (1990) proposed that school districts, universities, employer associations, and others make available or even write new materials that are free of bias against American Indians. Romantic images that all American Indians are noble savages with chiseled physiques and Indian princesses in tight-fitting buckskin dresses who live in tipis and ride long-maned stallions are as damaging to effective counseling as ideas that American Indians are inferior to white people in intellectual ability and fine motor skills and therefore should be steered into less demanding occupations. Leong and Serafica (2001) used the term *cultural specificity*, which means that only materials and techniques specific to and truly representative of the culture of each student can successfully develop career maturity and clarify salience. For American Indians, specificity means taking a look at how students are connected to their cultures, how they find social and emotional balance, how they see their roles and responsibilities in their families and their communities, how they want to use their capabilities and skills, and how they make meaning of their lives (McCormick & Amundson, 1997).

In order to provide more culturally appropriate career counseling, Juntunen and Cline (2010) suggested the *cultural formulation approach*. This approach requires counselors to pay attention to the following factors:

1) Cultural identity, which involves factors such as gender, social class, religion, and level of acculturation; a tribe's specific history; the degree to which a tribe or its members have been stereotyped; and relationships with family, friends, and other community members.
2) Cultural explanations for career choices, e.g., a desire to give back to the community, the dilemma of real or perceived personal resources, or the fear of discrimination when leaving a familiar setting.
3) Culturally influenced personal environmental factors, such as awareness of which people in a student's life are or are likely to be supportive

(or unsupportive, as it were). In addition, how much is a student willing to sacrifice for occupational and career gains if faced with a lack of support?
4) Cultural factors that influence how students relate to their counselors. The relationship with the counselor can be impeded by cultural misunderstandings, different communication styles, the level of knowledge about tribal traditions, and the assumptions a counselor might have about what American Indians are like or what they need.
5) The influence of culture on assessment strategies. An overall assessment of career desires and needs must include the above elements if the counselor is to be successful in helping identify a career and a career development path that harmonizes with personal values and goals.

A related suggestion was made by Young, Marshall, and Valach (2007), who contended that salience can be addressed only when culturally sensitive career development theories are being employed. Absent such theories as discussed above, counselors will be required to develop their own based on the needs and contexts of each particular culture and tribe. This development consists of a five-step process:

1) Counselors familiarize themselves not only with the cultures of their students but also with the concept of culture in the first place. The result of this engagement, it is hoped, is that culture comes to be understood as dynamic rather than static.
2) Counselors assume a social constructionist stance and explore how individuals create meaning in their cultural contexts and move from meaning to goals and actions.
3) Students' narratives are seen not as an assessment tool but as part of the meaning-making process to help them understand how their life stories influence their decision-making. The second phase of this process is showing students how their career allows them to have meaningful interaction with their culture and their community.
4) After these initial steps, "naïve observation" (p. 10), that is, observations not filtered through a particular theoretical lens, is being conducted to lead to counselor reflexivity on their understanding of the student's culture.
5) Finally, counselors use contextual action theory to understand that student actions are always part of interrelated processes of setting and trying to reach goals.

What Young, Marshall, and Valach hope for is that at the end of this process, counselors understand that student actions are always the result of the complex interaction of relationships, cultural contexts, and the construction of meaning. Having reached this awareness then allows counselors to guide their students through the process of career development rather than simply identify cultural differences among American Indians and the difficulties that may arise from these differences. Instead of recommending that their students take certain actions, counselors allow them to embark on a journey during which they form goals based on their specific contexts, devise actions to reach those goals, and then repeat these steps. Doing so builds a career path that culminates in a situation where career and culture interact and mutually reinforce each other.

Community Solutions

To be able to help students explore those aspects of their lives mentioned by McCormick and Amundson (1997) (see above), counselors have to be familiar with the communities they work in, be that a reservation town or an urban neighborhood, and be ready to help not only their students but also the communities their students live in (Vega, 2012). Counselors are encouraged to conduct community outreach by simply walking around the area, talking to people, looking at the surroundings, analyzing the economic and social context of the community, and working with local organizations (Martin, 1995; McDaniels & Gysbers, 1992; Vega, 2012). This outreach can enable counselors to develop an understanding of which careers may be relevant for communities, how career success can be a way to contribute to the community, how work can be shared with others to become a community-building experience, and how and where individuals can fit into roles as productive community members. Understanding the importance of work for students as opposed to the importance of community membership is an important component of understanding salience (Juntunen & Cline, 2010; Juntunen et al., 2001; Martin, 1995).

A final variable to be considered by counselors is whether students wish to live in their home communities or away from home. Because of the collectivist nature of most American Indian societies, there is usually a high price to pay for leaving home. Once they leave, many young people are later unable to return to become respected and contributing community members (Juntunen et al., 2001). Counselors must take community reactions to leaving home into account to understand salience and to recommend appropriate career paths.

Family Solutions

Family is paramount to many American Indians. They will usually put family obligations before work or other obligations and at times even risk job loss to attend family events or help a relative in need. It is no wonder then that family influence on career decisions is significant (Flynn et al., 2013) and that student confidence in the ability to be successful in a chosen career is highly correlated with family support (Turner & Lapan, 2003). To guide students successfully to a suitable career choice, families should be involved in career counseling (Flynn et al., 2013). In fact, career choice should be linked to family survival to the extent that career counseling becomes a joint conversation with students' families in which families go through career development exercises and together choose the career path that serves the family and the student best (Marshall et al., 2011)

Counselors have to assess the family as much as the student. First of all, counselors must understand the student's family structure through including the family in the career development process, even to the point of group counseling sessions with multiple family members present (Juntunen et al., 2001; Martin, 1995). Counselors also have to assess to which degree families influence or even decide an individual's career choice and which role they anticipate for their children in the future. This type of assessment includes a look at which occupations are common in families, which career paths parents have in mind for their children, and whether there will be support if a student desires to break with family tradition (Martin, 1995). It might even be necessary to look at careers where the work can be shared with family members. Salience to many American Indians means that work can benefit the family and the community directly and can even be performed jointly. If it cannot fulfill these functions, it is often not worth the effort (Juntunen et al., 2001).

Individual Solutions

The first advice to give counselors when looking at solutions for the individual is quite straightforward: Never waiver from being encouraging and supportive. Students need to know that counselors always have their needs and their best interest in mind (Flynn et al., 2013). To develop and sustain such an attitude, Flynn et al. recommended that social cognitive career theory be employed, meaning that the actions of others play an important role in the choices an individual will make in the future. They recommended that counselors discuss how students feel about pay and environment related to career; how the opinions of peers, family members, and community members might make a difference; and how the student thinks about matters of finding meaning, satisfaction, and empowerment in work. Part of that process will have to be a clarification of values, especially with regard to how the career choice is linked to supporting and caring for others.

The second suggestion is probably the most uncomfortable one. Many counselors of European-American background are nervous about bringing up the subject of racism, fearing that they might inadvertently say something offensive or that a student might lash out at them about past injustices. However, effective counseling cannot happen if the elephant of racism is always in the room, so counselors have to address this issue openly and take the time to truly listen to their students. They have to acknowledge that racism, prejudice, and discrimination are a reality and that they are probably going to play a role in the student's career development process (Cohn, 1997; Martin, 1995). Once students realize that counselors are willing to consider their lives in a holistic fashion and treat them as partners, they in turn will be more willing to become partners rather than just consumers in the career development process (Subich, 1996).

To understand students' career maturity and salience, counselors have to assess their socioeconomic status first, including the current social and legal status of students and their communities or tribes as well as unique historical events that make the tribes what they are today (Johnson et al., 1995). Next, internal factors related to career opportunities have to be explored. What do the students perceive to be career barriers? Do the students adhere to any career myths? How much academic and technical knowledge and skills do the students possess? (Wentling & Waight, 2000)

Once this information is available, counselors can then move to a discussion of career options. First, they should find out which level of access students have had to occupational information and then provide materials that go beyond this level. In its simplest forms, this means giving students brochures about certain occupations or providing computer access so that students can search for career information online. However, a counselor can do much more. If students have a limited view of which occupations might be available or suffer from career myths, counselors can expose students to non-traditional career paths they might never have considered by showing them information on such careers or, better yet, finding role models from non-traditional careers (Johnson et al., 1995; Smith, 1983).

After students have been given better access to occupational information, salience must be addressed by showing them how choosing the right career can be an asset to them, their families, and their communities. Students will also understand what their values are and which occupations can best help them realize these values. At the same time, career maturity also has to be developed. Students have to determine where their strengths and weaknesses lie so that they can make an informed choice about how much education they still need to be able to follow the career path they have chosen (Martin, 1991).

To accomplish these tasks, Alliman-Brissett and Turner (2005) recommended what is called the *Two Feathers Curriculum*. In this approach to career counseling and development, counselors try to broaden a student's view of career options and paths. After the cultural baseline has been established, counselors help students find information on and explore careers they had not considered, look beyond a limited number of common career choices, openly discuss barriers and help students understand that those can be overcome, find those people in the student's social network that will be supportive of their career choice, make the case for how educational achievement is linked to career success, and help students set goals and make decisions.

RECOMMENDATIONS AND CONCLUSION

This review of pertinent research in the field of career development for American Indian students shows that much work remains to be done to help students with issues of career maturity and salience. Barriers exist at the school, work, community, and individual levels, and inadequate counselor training combined with inappropriate theoretical career development models makes it difficult to give American Indian students the culturally sensitive career development counseling they deserve. Several solutions were suggested, ranging from hiring more American Indians counselors and training counselors better to looking at acculturation, learning about a student's culture and community, including the family in the counseling process, and modifying career development theories.

Having background knowledge of students' cultures and communities is undoubtedly necessary for counselors to deliver culturally appropriate career services. The real question, however, rests in how this training is to be delivered. Adding additional college courses in American Indian culture and language is certainly an option but may be unworkable because (1) such courses lengthen a student's program of study, (2) students may not yet be sure if they want to work in an area with many American Indian students, and (3) no university program could possibly address all the cultural differences among American Indian tribes. A reasonable alternative may be to require all counseling students to complete at least one foundation course in American Indian cultures if their universities determine that they are likely to encounter American Indian students on the job. The knowledge from this course may then be expanded through professional development once counselors have found jobs in school districts with large American Indian student populations. Tribes, communities, and school districts can cooperate to develop culture- and community-specific training that helps counselors develop more understanding of and sensitivity toward their students' needs. Such an undertaking will require money, but if all involved entities contribute time and resources and help in the search for outside funding, the cost for each party can likely be contained.

Overall, what this author has noticed is that two themes have woven their way through the discussion of barriers and solutions: communication and open-mindedness. Counselors just by their very nature should always be open-minded to their students' cultures, personal backgrounds, and idiosyncrasies, and although it may not meet the standard of cultural specificity, taking an interest in and being willing to learn in conjunction with the student can go a long way in providing sensitive and useful counseling. The second theme, communication, speaks for itself (no pun intended). Many misunderstandings can be avoided by simply keeping the lines of communication open. Even if counselors are not always quite certain about students' needs and the connection of those needs to culture or ethnicity, listening goes a long way. To most people, it is not talking to others but being heard by others that is important, and any counselor who can make his or her students feel important will be able to elicit the type of information needed to understand salience and career maturity from the student's perspective.

Future plans of training more American Indian counselors and providing more culture-specific training for others are well advised, but having an open mind and a willingness to listen and learn should not be underestimated in providing culturally appropriate and useful services to American Indian students seeking a career that is right for them, their families, and their communities.

REFERENCES

Alliman-Brissett, A. E., & Turner, S. L. (2005). Supporting the career aspirations of American Indian youth. *Cura Reporter*, *35*(2), 20–24.

Aud, S., Hussar, W., Kena, G., Bianco, K., Frohlich, L., Kemp, J., &Tahan, K. (2011). *The condition of education 2011* (NCES 2011–033). Washington, DC: National Center for Education Statistics.

Cohn, J. (1997). The effects of racial and ethnic discrimination on the career development of minority persons. In H. S. Farmer and Associates (Eds.), *Diversity & women's career development: From adolescence to adulthood* (pp. 161–171). Thousand Oaks, CA: Sage.

Cole, J. S., & Denzine, G. M. (2002). Comparing the academic engagement of American Indian and white college students. *Journal of American Indian Education*, *41*(1), 19–34.

DeVoe, J. F., Darling-Churchill, K. E., & Snyder, T. D. (2008). *Status and trends in the Education of American Indians and Alaska Natives: 2008* (NCES 2008–08). Washington, DC: National Center for Education Statistics.

Esters, L. T., & Bowen, B. E. (2003). Race and ethnicity equity issues. In M. L. Scott (Ed.), *Equity issues in career and technical education* (pp. 27–34). (Information Series No. 390). Columbus, OH: Center on Education and Training for Employment, College of Education, The Ohio State University.

Fletcher, M. L. M. (2007). Bringing balance to Indian gaming. *Harvard Journal on Legislation*, *44*, 39–95.

Flynn, S. V., Duncan, K. J., & Evenson, L. L. (2013). An emergent phenomenon of American Indian secondary students' career development process. *The Career Development Quarterly*, *61*, 124–140.

Freeman, C., & Fox, M. A. (2005). *Status and trends in the education of American Indians and Alaska Natives* (Report No. NCES 2005–108). Washington, DC: US Department of Education, National Center for Education Statistics.

Gray, K. C., & Herr, E. L. (1998). *Workforce education: The basics*. Needham Heights, MA: Allyn & Bacon.

Herring, R. D. (1990). Attacking career myths among Native Americans: Implications for counseling. *School Counselor*, *38*(1), 13–18.

Hoover, J. J., & Jacobs, C. C. (1992). A survey of American Indian college students: Perceptions toward their study skills/college life. *Journal of American Indian Education*, *32*(1), 21–29.

Huffman, T. E. (2001). Resistance theory and the transculturation hypothesis as explanations of college attrition and persistence among culturally traditional American Indian students. *Journal of American Indian Education, 40*(3), 1–23.

James, K. (2001). There are doorways in these huts: An empirical study of educational programs, Native Canadian student needs, and institutional effectiveness in British Columbia and Ontario, Canada. *Journal of American Indian Education, 40*(3), 24–37.

Johnson, E. M. (2015, April 29). *Washington state tribe's whale hunting request triggers new backlash.* Reuters. Retrieved from http://www.reuters.com/article/2015/04/29/us-usa-whales-washington-idUSKBN0NK21W20150429

Johnson, M. J., Swartz, J. L., & Martin, W. E., Jr. (1995). Applications of psychological theories for career development with Native Americans. In F. T. L. Leong (Ed.), *Career development and vocational behavior of racial and ethnic minorities* (pp. 103–133). Mahwah, NJ: Erlbaum.

Juntunen, C. L., Barraclough, D. J., Broneck, C. L., Seibel, G. A., Winrow, S. A., & Morin, P. M. (2001). American Indian perspectives on the career journey. *Journal of Counseling Psychology, 48,* 274–285.

Juntunen, C. L., & Cline, K. (2010). Culture and self in career development: Working with American Indians. *Journal of Career Development, 37*(1), 391–410.

Kerka, S. (1998). *Career development and gender, race, and class* (Report No. EDO-CE-98-199). Columbus, OH: ERIC Clearinghouse on Adult, Career, and Vocational Education. (ERIC Document Reproduction No. ED421641)

Kerka, S. (2003). *Career development of diverse populations.* (Report No. EDO-CE-03-249). Columbus, OH: ERIC Clearinghouse on Adult, Career, and Vocational Education. (ERIC Document Reproduction No. ED482536)

Kirkness, V. J., & Barnhardt, R. (1991). First Nations and higher education: The four Rs—respect, relevance, reciprocity, responsibility. *Journal of American Indian Education, 30*(3). Retrieved from http://jaie.asu.edu/v30/V30S3fir.htm

Klasky, P. M. (2013). Making it real: An engaged approach for Native American students in higher education. *American Indian Culture and Research Journal, 37*(3), 97–106.

Leong, F. T. L., & Serafica, F. C. (2001). Cross-cultural perspectives on Super's career development theory: Career maturity and cultural accommodation. In F. T. L. Leong & A. Barak (Eds.), *Contemporary models in vocational psychology: A volume in honor of Samuel H. Osipow* (pp. 167–205). Mahwah, NJ: Erlbaum.

Marshall, S. K., Young, R. A., Stevens, A., Spence, W., Deyell, S., Easterbrook, A., & Brokenleg, M. (2011). Adolescent career development in urban-residing aboriginal families in Canada. *The Career Development Quarterly, 59,* 539–558.

Martin, W. E., Jr. (1991). Career development and American Indians living on reservations: Cross-cultural factors to consider. *Career Development Quarterly, 39,* 273–284.

Martin, W. E., Jr. (1995). Career development assessment and intervention strategies with American Indians. In F. T. L. Leong (Ed.), *Career development and vocational behavior of racial and ethnic minorities* (pp. 227–248). Mahwah, NJ: Erlbaum.

McCormick, R. M., & Amundson, N. E. (1997). A career-life planning model for First Nations people. *Journal of Employment Counseling, 34,* 171–179.

McDaniels, C., & Gysbers, N. C. (1992). *Counseling for career development: Theories, resources, and practice.* San Francisco, CA: Jossey-Bass.

Newcomb, S. (2013, October 14). Don't treat Indian nations as a minority group. *Indian Country Today Media Network*. Retrieved from http://indiancountrytoday medianetwork.com/2013/10/14/dont-let-tribes-be-turned-just-another-minority

Peavy, R. V. (1998). *Career counseling with Native clients: Understanding the context* (Report No. EDO-CG-95-45). Greensboro, NC: ERIC Clearinghouse on Counseling and Student Services. (ERIC Document Reproduction No. ED399485)

Pewewardy, C., & Frey, B. (2004). American Indian students' perceptions of racial climate, multicultural support services, and ethnic fraud at a predominantly white university. *Journal of American Indian Education*, 43(1), 32–60.

Rudmin, F. W. (2009). Catalogue of acculturation constructs: Descriptions of 126 Taxonomies, 1918–2003. *Online readings in psychology and culture*, 8(1). Retrieved from http://scholarworks.gvsu.edu/cgi/viewcontent.cgi?article=1074&context=orpc

Schiller, P., & Gaseoma, L. (1993). Analysis of self-reported strategies for successful adjustment to higher education by bicultural Native American students. In Y. I. Song & E. C. Kim (Eds.), *American mosaic: Selected readings on America's multicultural heritage* (pp. 44–54). Englewood Cliffs, NJ: Prentice Hall.

Smith, E. J. (1983). Issues in racial minorities' career behavior. In W. B. Walsh & S. H. Osipow (Eds.), *Handbook of vocational psychology: Vol 1. Foundations* (pp. 185–218). Hillsdale, NJ: Erlbaum.

Subich, L. M. (1996). Addressing diversity in the process of career assessment. In M. L. Savickas & W. B. Walsh (Eds.), *Handbook of career counseling theory and practice* (pp. 277–287). Palo Alto, CA: Davies-Black.

Swisher, K., & Deyhle, D. (1988). Adapting instruction to culture. In J. Reyhner (Ed.), *Teaching American Indian students* (2nd ed., pp. 81–95). Norman, OK: University of Oklahoma Press.

Tierney, W. G. (1993). The college experience of Native Americans: A critical analysis. In L. Weis & M. Fine (Eds.), *Beyond silenced voices: Class, race, and gender in United States schools* (pp. 309–323). New York, NY: SUNY Press.

Tierney, W. G. (1995). Addressing failure: Factors affecting Native American college student retention. *Journal of Navajo Education*, 13(1), 3–7.

Turner, S. L., & Lapan, R. T. (2003). Native American adolescent career development. *Journal of Career Development*, 30(2), 159–172.

Vega, T. D. (2012). Voices from the circle: Career planning strategies for serving low-income, urban native Americans. *Career Planning and Adult Development Journal*, 28(1), 88–98.

Wentling, R. M., & Waight, C. (2000). *Initiatives that assist and barriers that hinder the successful transition of minority youth into the workplace*. Berkeley, CA: National Center for Research in Vocational Education.

Wentzlaff, T. L., & Brewer, A. (1996). Native American students define factors for success. *Tribal College*, 7(4), 40–44.

Yang, J. J. (2006). Small business, rising giant: Policies and costs of Section 8(a) contracting preferences for Alaska Native Corporations. *Alaska Law Review*, 23, 315–363.

Yang, R. K., Byers, S. R., & Fenton, B. (2006). American Indian/Alaska Native students' use of a university support office. *Journal of American Indian Education*, 46(1), 35–48.

Young, R. A., Marshall, S. K., & Valach, L. (2007). Making career theories more culturally sensitive: Implications for counseling. *The Career Development Quarterly*, 56(1), 4–18.

8 Young Native Men's Work Experiences

J. K. Payden Spowart and E. Anne Marshall

Employment success and educational attainment are major issues for young Native people throughout North America. In the United States, the unemployment rate for 16-to-24-year-old Native American males is 17 percent—5 percent higher than that of the general population in the same age range (U.S. Census Bureau, 2013). The picture in Canada is similar—in the 15-to-24-year-old category, unemployment rates are higher for Natives, and the rate of unemployment for those living on reserve (23 percent) is almost double compared to that for those living off-reserve (12 percent) (Statistics Canada, 2011). Native men also face increased hardships in the workforce. This population is underrepresented in vocational and educational psychology research, and there is limited understanding of the issues that relate to their career and educational development (Juntunen et al., 2001; Turner et al., 2006). Hoffmann, Jackson, and Smith (2005) urge researchers to explore the career and educational development of Native American males. In recent years, there is a growing body of literature that highlights strengths and successes as well as the many challenges that Native Americans experience related to employment and educational attainment (Coverdale, 2012; Merrill, Bruce, & Marlin, 2010).

This chapter focuses on the work experiences of young Native men. We begin with our theoretical framework outlining relational and social constructionist approaches to employment and education. We present some current demographics related to education and employment in the United States and Canada. We discuss the education and workforce experiences and transitions of young Native people with a focus on challenges, barriers, and expectations. Following this, we present findings from a research project, Walking in Multiple Worlds, and discuss relevant implications for education, knowledge, and employment-related practice. The chapter concludes with suggestions for future research and culturally relevant career development.

THEORETICAL FRAMEWORK—RELATIONAL AND SOCIAL CONSTRUCTIONIST THEORIES

Relational perspectives serve as a meta-framework and are particularly relevant in collectivist Native American contexts because they focus on the impact of connection (Blustein, Schultheiss, & Flum, 2004; Schultheiss,

2007). Relationships are a central human function; interpersonal and intrapersonal struggles reflect natural human strivings for connection, affirmation, support, attachment, and mattering (Schultheiss, 2007). Relationships are needed at all points in an individual's life, and through building and maintaining positive connections, a sense of well-being and safety is achieved (Jordan, 2008). Blustein (2011) noted that people learn about themselves and the world around them through relationships and that there is a sizable overlap between relationships, work, and education. Individuals are rooted in family, social, and cultural relational contexts; understanding these contexts is necessary for learning about how plans for work are created and implemented (Schultheiss, 2007). Schultheiss puts forward four tenets for understanding career development from a relational perspective:

1) The influence of the family as critical to understanding the complexities of vocational development;
2) The psychological experience of work as embedded within relational contexts (e.g., social, familial, and cultural);
3) The interface of work and family life;
4) Relational discourse as a challenge to the cultural script of individualism. (p. 192)

Blustein and colleagues (2004) argued that looking at the connection between interpersonal relationships and the career and work world is necessary for understanding individual and community career concerns. A relational perspective of careers provides a framework for understanding how people comprehend, construct, and act in response to the contemporary working landscape. Getting closer to individuals' experiences as they reflect on their work and careers provides a deeper understanding of the connection between relationships and work. Blustein and colleagues maintained that the goal of a relational perspective of career "would be to construct generative discourses that challenge existing traditions of knowledge and suggest new possibilities for practice and policy. In effect, these novel perspectives present an opportunity to dignify the lived experiences of people as they engage in the activities and tasks of their lives" (p. 435).

Relational theory understands work and education as inherently relational acts that are embedded in external and internal relational contexts. It helps explain how people come to understand, choose, and plan their work and educational directions. Blustein (2011) maintained, "[C]onceptualizing working as a relational act underscores that each decision, experience, and interaction with the working world is understood, influenced, and shaped by relationships" (p. 1).

Relational theory allows for exploration of the intertwined nature of experiences related to work and education life domains (Schultheiss, Watts, Sterland, & O'Neill, 2011). Native American ways of being stress the importance on community and connectedness; thus, this framework provides understanding of the aspects and intricacies that are relevant in their work-life transitions.

Consistent with an overarching relational framework, a social constructionist contextual framework is also relevant. The underlying premise of social constructionism is that reality is created and maintained through cultural, socioeconomic, and socio-political contexts (Gergen, 1999; Whiston & Rahdjya, 2005). Blustein et al. (2004) list four key assumptions:

1) Challenging the idea that all knowledge is unbiased and objective and questioning positivism and conventional empiricism;
2) Acknowledging both the historical and cultural basis of knowledge and traditions;
3) Creating knowledge through interpersonal relationships and interactions;
4) Accepting that socially constructed views of the world will vary and lead to patterns of actions and to new possibilities of discourse and action.

Social constructionists maintain that reality is co-constructed through language in both social and cultural settings and that multiple perspectives exist, each influenced by culture, history, and context. This perspective is noted to be particularly useful for understanding career development. Whiston and Rahdjya (2005) stated that qualitative career assessment is often focused on social processes and the influence of historical and cultural contexts. Adding to this, Blustein, Kenna, Murphy, DeVoy, and DeWine (2005) maintained that social constructionism is highly useful for understanding career and education. Further, Blustein and colleagues observed this:

> Social constructionist research seeks to establish a more empathic and closer connection to participants and gain a deeper understanding of their experiences through first-hand accounts, conversation analysis, discourse analysis, interviews, and narratives . . . these inquiry tools help researchers to not only gain a more complex and realistic understanding of their participants' lives but also offer a means to join with participants as they construct meaning . . . 'joining with' offers a more equitable and empowering relationship between researchers and participants, while also stressing the importance of participants' active engagement in the process. (p. 356)

A social constructionist framework allows the researcher to embrace both the societal and cultural components of people and their stories. Acknowledging that multiple truths exist and that knowledge is co-constructed between people through their interactions and relationships is also consistent with Native American ways of relating.

THE PSYCHOLOGY OF WORKING

Blustein, Kenna, Gill, and DeVoy (2008) stated that the field of career counseling lacked the means to adequately explore the lives of those who were oppressed and the lives of those who had to work to survive. In contrast to many popular career development theories, the psychology of working perspective (Blustein, 2006) specifically addresses the need within the field of career counseling to look at and support those who have been typically left out of the research due to marginalization, racism, and other forms of social oppression—this is appropriate for Native populations.

Blustein and colleagues (2008) defined three human needs that can be satisfied through working: survival and power, social connection, and self-determination. Using this lens, the first function of work is to provide people with the resources for survival and power—people are able to meet their basic survival needs with the funds acquired from working and gain social power and resources such as status, prestige, and privilege. The second function of work is to provide people with a way to connect to others—work serves as a place to build interpersonal relationships and give an organized means of people relating to their social contexts. The third function of work is to support and facilitate the need for self-determination by providing people with the opportunity to have extrinsically motivated actions become internalized as part of personal values, behaviours, and goals. Working includes a diverse range of actions and experiences; for example, choice and preference are central themes in work for some, while for others, work is only a necessity for survival.

EMPLOYMENT AND EDUCATION DEMOGRAPHICS

Historic and current demographics in the United States and Canada indicate that Native people have higher unemployment rates and lower employment rates and levels of educational attainment than non-Native people (Statistics Canada, 2011; U.S. Census Bureau, 2013). Although the underlying factors are complex and interrelated, researchers and scholars have cited the effects of colonization and residential or boarding schools, lack of training opportunities, inadequate schooling (particularly on reserves), community expectations, parenting, substance abuse, and discrimination (Juntunen et al., 2001; Merrill et al., 2010). Moreover, the economic crisis in 2008 led to decreased employment levels, increased unemployment levels, and a wider gap in these rates between non-Aboriginal and Aboriginal people.

According to 2012 United States statistics (U.S. Census Bureau, 2013), in the 16 and older age range, the employment rate for Native Americans is 49.6 percent while for non-Native Americans, it is 57.5 percent. Additionally, in the 16–24-year age range, the unemployment rate for Native American males is 16.4 percent compared with 12.1 percent for Native American females and 11 percent for the general population. When considering educational attainment, 21.2 percent of Native Americans had not completed high school compared to 13.6 percent for the general population, and 8.9 percent had completed a Bachelor's degree compared with 18.2 percent in the general population. Additionally, Native men were almost three times less likely to have a Bachelor's degree or higher compared with the general population, whereas Native women were two times less likely to achieve the same level of education.

The report *Aboriginal People and the Labour Market: Estimates from the Labour Force Survey* (Statistics Canada, 2011) included labor statistics for Canadians over age 14. Across Canada, Native people aged 25–54 had higher unemployment rates (12.3 percent) and lower employment rates (65.8 percent) than non-Native people (6.8 and 80.9 percent, respectively). In addition, between 2008 and 2010, Native men experienced the largest employment decline. Native youth's unemployment rate was 21.1 percent; the non-Native rate was 14.6 percent. With regard to education, 34 percent of Native adults had not completed high school, and 21 percent had a high school diploma as their highest educational qualification. Further, 44 percent of Native adults between 25 and 64 had completed some form of post-secondary education compared to 60 percent of non-Native people; 8 percent of Native American people and 23 percent of non-Native American people had a university degree.

The above figures show a consistent and rather disturbing educational and employment picture for Native American peoples. Rather surprisingly, though, there has not been great deal of research directed at vocational and educational development for this population as seen in the next section.

NATIVE AMERICAN VOCATIONAL RESEARCH

Several authors have indicated that the meaning of work and career actions is embedded in both social and cultural contexts (Blustein, 2011; Blustein et al., 2004; Savickas, 1995; Young, Vallach, & Collin, 1996). However, there is a lack of research focused on Native American career development: "Because American Indian populations continue to be underrepresented in vocational psychology research, little is understood about issues that may be related to their career development" (Juntunen et al., 2001, p. 274). Merrill and colleagues (2010) echo this, and Turner et al. (2006) stressed that Native Americans report unique employment interests compared to other ethnic groups.

Juntunen et al. (2001) focused on American Indians' definitions and meanings for both career and career development. This qualitative study included 18 American Indians, aged 21 to 59, who were interviewed and asked six questions related to the meaning of career and career planning. For almost all participants, career was identified as a lifelong pursuit and included goals, planning, or activity. Some participants noted the direct link between career and promotion of traditional ways, and meaning for work was derived from sharing traditional knowledge with future generations. Most said that success could be measured by a person's ability to contribute to the well-being of another person, including family members, the next generation, and their American Indian tribe. Juntunen et al. concluded that for their sample, career seemed to be a valuable concept. It represented a lifelong endeavor that required planning, influenced personal and family goals, and had impacts on and was a part of personal identity. For those who pursued post-secondary education, all but two cited family as a support for career development and work-life. Also, educational achievement was a support for gaining employment. Juntunen and her colleagues noted that although exploration of individual interests, skills, and goals can be important, career counselors should take time to explore the role of community membership and the expression of the membership through career choice. The researchers also found that some participants experienced tension related to relocation and moving; for those living on a reserve, leaving home to study was a major consideration. Upon completion of their education, many participants had or wanted to return to their home communities to provide help. Some, however, found it difficult to return to their home communities, especially if home was located on a reserve.

Jackson and Smith (2001) conducted guided interviews with 22 Navajo high school graduates who were interested in or currently pursuing post-secondary education. The 10 males and 12 females, with a mean age of 19.4, had graduated from a high school on the Navajo Nation territory. Several family-related themes were found to impact the students' post-secondary transitions. One was family pressure to either stay home or pursue education. Another was family financial problems, which reduced the chances of pursuing post-secondary education and frequently led to individuals finding "unskilled labour to help resolve financial strain" (p. 10). Family conflicts were related to issues of divorce and alcoholism. Finally, family encouragement was tied to greater self-confidence and attributed to close family members who had graduated from college and who had found success in a particular career. Other themes included difficulties adapting to post-secondary learning environments, positive and negative experiences with faculty members, vague post-secondary and career plans, lack of knowledge about post-secondary education to career transitions, and difficulties maintaining connection to homeland and culture during their post-secondary education.

Research conducted by Marshall and colleagues involved surveys and interviews with Native students and high school graduates in several rural and coastal communities in British Columbia, Canada (Marshall, 2002; Marshall, Jackson, Drummond, & Camara, 2007; Marshall, Stewart, & Lawrence, 2011). Social and economic restructuring in these communities had led to closures and hardships in local fishing, forestry, and mining industries. Native youth both on- and off-reserve recognized the increased importance of education and training to prepare them for a different world of work than their parents and grandparents had experienced. Many wished to stay in their home communities but had to leave to find work and pursue post-secondary education. They described the often-conflicting values and priorities that they had to consider when planning their future work and career paths. These findings led to a larger study entitled "Walking in Multiple Worlds" that is discussed below.

YOUNG NATIVE AMERICAN MALES' EMPLOYMENT EXPECTATIONS

Minimal literature exists that specifically addresses the employment experiences and expectations of young Native American males. Using semi-structured interviews, Hoffmann and colleagues (2005) explored the perspectives of barriers to chosen careers for 29 Navajo Nation high school students, 14 female and 15 male. They identified a number of barriers to career development and achievement including difficulties in school, lack of finances, and negative support from family and friends. Several strategies for overcoming barriers were described: seeking academic help from teachers, seeking monetary and emotional support from family, working harder in school, and securing financial assistance in order to eliminate schooling barriers. The authors also identified complex themes that spoke to a certain level of naïveté regarding the process of achieving a career goal: ease of getting a job, few barriers listed to preferred career, lack of concern regarding barriers, and pressure to conform to perceived social pressure.

Hoffman and colleagues (2005) also spoke to specific concerns regarding the male Native American students and stated that compared to the females, the male group had more problematic future employment expectations. The male students more often believed jobs were readily available post-graduation and that little training would be required to obtain jobs. When compared to their female classmates, males listed fewer different career possibilities; the most expected type of work was trades-related, including mechanics, iron work, welding, carpentry, and engineering. Professional careers such as veterinarian, computer technician, and musician were also mentioned, but to a lesser extent. Male Native American students saw few if any barriers between their current state and their future careers; however, most could not identify how they would achieve their goal. In addition, many displayed ambivalence towards their future desired career. Hoffman et al. noted that the males seemed to have a less developed employment expectation. Their findings pointed to the need for increased support for career pathway exploration and addressing career challenges.

SUPPORTS AND OBSTACLES TO WORK AND EDUCATION

Juntunen et al. (2001) described the supportive factors and obstacles to career and educational development that their participants experienced. For high school graduates, one supportive factor was a high value placed on education by self and family, and one obstacle identified was lack of family support. For those with a post-secondary degree, supportive factors included sobriety, family influences, family support, and being a provider; obstacles were discrimination, alienation from tribal community, and restrictions of living on the reservation (such as lack of opportunities). Discrimination was experienced in both educational and work environments, which negatively impacted both career and academic experiences. In addition, lack of support could occur passively, when individuals close to the participants did not show interest in their career opportunities, or actively, when individuals who were close to the participants discouraged certain career pathways.

Merrill and colleagues (2010) identified eight barriers to successful transition into both post-secondary education and the labor market for Aboriginal youth in Canada that overlap with other researchers' findings. Each will be discussed briefly below.

The first barrier was Aboriginal people's dissatisfaction with post-secondary experiences. Lack of sensitivity regarding Aboriginal culture and peoples within the schooling context has led to a feeling of disrespect. The lack of a culturally appropriate learning environment is often cited as a barrier to positive academic experiences.

The second barrier discussed was historical impacts. The legacy of residential schools is often linked to current difficulties for Aboriginal people in post-secondary contexts. The trans-generational trauma that was intertwined with the educational system still has effects on today's education participant rates, family value placed on mainstream education, and experiences of discrimination.

The third barrier was social and personal; here the authors described a complex cycle that many Aboriginals face that has negative impacts on future employment success: Lower education levels serve as a large barrier to work placement; low socioeconomic status negatively impacts individuals' well-being; and poor self-concept can lead to feelings of powerlessness and frustration. The overall lower education of the Aboriginal population is one of the greatest barriers to successful future employment outcomes.

Family and community was the fourth barrier to education and employment success. The authors noted that "dysfunctional communities, lack of role models, language differences, peer pressure, and lack of family and community support" negatively impact success (p. 34). At the same time, they also stated that positive family events and systems, including cultural events, ceremonies, and strong family ties were helpful. Both positive and negative family issues present an ongoing impact for those living away from their home communities.

The fifth barrier was financial. Finances are a commonly cited obstacle for Aboriginal students. Despite funding assistance that is available and helpful for those who can receive it, the eligibility constraints, the amount of funding available, and the increasing needs are problematic. Qualification restraints including age, institution choice, band control of allocation, and course load further impact financial support. The report authors argue that lack of funding is one of the largest, if not the largest, obstacle to post-secondary access of Aboriginal students in Canada. Often, lack of funding leads to a decreased ability to meet other expenses such as housing, daycare, and travel to home communities. In addition, financial strain often leads to Aboriginal students picking up part-time or full-time work, which decreases the likelihood that education will be completed.

The sixth barrier is cultural; cultural differences, discrimination, and racism are commonly cited problems that Aboriginal individuals encounter in their transitions to and experience in their school and work environments. Lower rates of educational success for Aboriginal students are linked to inappropriate cultural content, teaching methods, and assessment. Often, mainstream education does not take into account culturally appropriate ways of learning, including the oral translation of knowledge, traditional knowledge, and the holistic worldviews of Aboriginal peoples. Transition to employment is also complicated by cultural differences. In many Native communities, cooperation, interdependence, and communal responsibility conflict with typically individually oriented career expectations such as competitive employment and leaving home to seek new opportunities. In addition, "stereotypes, presumptions, and different values and attitudes, including some that may be embedded in rules, restrictions, and structures, may lead to misunderstandings between Aboriginal people and their employers or other workers in forms of rules, restrictions, and structures that do not appeal to Aboriginal people" (p.38). It is useful for work sites to have awareness of this barrier; discussions of cultural differences can facilitate more compatible opportunities. Role models and mentors are highly useful to support individuals entering and engaging in both schooling and employment.

The seventh barrier is geographic location. Rural and/or on-reserve individuals can face particular challenges in their transition. Many have a strong desire to work in their home communities; research has pointed to living preferences, culture, identity, and tradition having strong influences on this desire. However, fewer employment and educational opportunities exist outside of larger centers; this situation adds to the existing geographic tension for those people from smaller communities.

Education-labor force linkages is the eighth barrier. There is often a mismatch between educational attainment and specific job requirements; the obtained degree or diploma is inadequate to gain preferred work placement. The authors noted that that 42 percent of Aboriginal individuals have jobs that match their educational training compared to 48 percent of non-Aboriginal individuals; 35 percent of Aboriginal individuals have a full-time job for which they were overqualified compared to 32 percent of non-Aboriginal individuals; and 24 percent hold jobs for which they are under-qualified compared to 20 percent for non-Aboriginals. Merrill et al. (2010) stated that although post-secondary education may not prepare all students adequately for the reality of future employment, Aboriginal individuals, especially those living on reserve, are especially impacted.

The Canadian Education Statistics Council (2010) released a report that highlighted trends in Aboriginal post-secondary education in Canada. It was noted that while Native people have experienced increased participation rates in college and trade schools, a notable gap in university attendance remains. Two major challenges were identified: lack of funding or the financial means to pursue education and limited academic preparation coupled with low high school graduation rates. Rural and remote communities experience even further financial hardships due to travel costs and additional living costs associated with living away from families. Additional challenges included cultural safety issues; limited numbers of Native role models and teachers with post-secondary credentials; historical assimilation practices (including residential schools); differences in communication models, teaching, language, and learning styles between culturally traditional approaches and mainstream post-secondary approaches to learning and teaching; and personal issues.

"WALKING IN MULTIPLE WORLDS" RESEARCH STUDY

"Walking in Multiple Worlds: Aboriginal Young Adults' Work-Life Narratives" (WIMW) was a three-year study conducted in two Canadian urban centers: Victoria, British Columbia, and Toronto, Ontario. The focus of this project was emerging Native adults' experiences of life and work transitions. More specifically, we were interested in learning about the impacts of culture and community and the supports and barriers that were experienced in finding and maintaining employment (Marshall, Stewart, Coverdale, Spowart, & LeBlanc, 2012). Specifically, the research question being asked is this: "Which supports, challenges, and barriers do Indigenous young adults experience with regard to finding and keeping work?" For the project, we utilized a culturally informed narrative orientation to data collection since Native American people typically describe themselves as utilizing an oral-based storytelling tradition (Medicine-Eagle, 1989; Stewart, 2008). Both individual and group interviews were conducted with over 100 young Aboriginal men and women aged 18 to 33. The findings from the Toronto site and from the Victoria site group interviews and individual interviews with young women are reported elsewhere (Coverdale, 2012; Marshall, Stewart, & Coverdale, 2013; Marshall, Stewart, Popadiuk, & Lawrence, 2013; Overmars, 2011). In this chapter, we present the findings from in-depth individual interviews with eight young Aboriginal men.

The individual interviews with the young Native men were conducted by the first author (Spowart, 2013). They took place in a mutually agreed-upon location (usually away from campus) and lasted between one and one and one-half hours. Participants were invited to tell their stories of finding and keeping work, with specific prompts to describe examples of supports and barriers they had experienced. The audio-taped interviews were transcribed using a process developed within the research team (Marshall et al.,

2012). A condensed version of each participant's story was crafted using a process called *ghostwriting* (Rhodes, 2000); this involves a co-construction by the researcher of the participant's story in the first person. The *ghost story* is sent back to the participant for additions and changes as a form of member-checking. Then, for the thematic transcript analysis across all the participants, Braun and Clarke's (2006) approach was utilized. Two of the major meta-themes identified in the data, employment and education, together with related specific themes and subthemes, are summarized below.

Employment

The young Native men were eager to share stories related to their experience of finding and maintaining employment. Across the group, there was a wide range of work experiences; some participants had had only one previous job while others had had several and across a variety of fields such as construction, food service, and band office work. There were four major themes: searching for work, the experience of working, their future work-related plans, and the challenges they experienced related to finding and maintaining employment.

Searching for Work

Everyone spoke about their experiences of looking for and securing work. For the majority, searching for work was a time-consuming and often difficult task. Most said that it took a tremendous amount of time and effort to actually get a job; for some, the search for work presented more challenges than working at the job itself. As one young man put it, "It's hard to find work, and there are a lot of obstacles to go through with finding a job . . . once I'm working, that's the easier part." Finding work required persistence, specific skills, and know-how. This is consistent with findings from Juntunen et al. (2001) and Hoffman et al. (2005) and echoes the often-cited observation that looking for work is a full-time job.

The young men spoke extensively about how their limited training, work experience, or lack of a high school education was a major barrier to finding new employment. Some were actively pursuing specific training and certifications in food preparation, workplace safety, and first aid to make themselves more marketable to future employers and to enable them to apply for certain jobs. These participants credited community agencies and their reservation band office with providing programs that offered specific trainings and job search skills and stated that this support allowed them to make progress in their search for employment. One man recounted, "The band was really helpful because they helped me get my driver's license last year, and they help with resumes, your cover letters, or if you want work experiences or anything."

The Experience of Working

There was a wide range of work experiences, and the young men described the benefits they received from their day-to-day work. Each detailed his job history. Six had worked in the food service industry, three had worked for their band, three had manual labor jobs, two had janitorial-specific jobs, and two had sold Native artwork. Other jobs included being a youth program coordinator, a worker at a foster home, and a research assistant.

When discussing some of the benefits of working, participants talked about the on-site training that they received at their jobs. They took pride in the development of their various proficiencies. One talked about his construction job and what his uncle had taught him: "He taught me a lot of things . . . when I buy a house I don't need to hire someone to fix the plumbing or fix the drywall, I know how to do it." They realized that the transferable skills and formal certificates gained through employment would increase their marketability to future employers and that certain skills such as carpentry could be utilized across their lives.

Financial gain was consistently cited as a major reason for being employed, which Blustein (2006) characterizes as *working for survival*. All eight participants said that at one time or another, the main reason for working was to earn and keep earning money. There were a range of reasons provided as to why money was needed: covering living expenses; supporting their family; and paying for education, travel, and luxury items. One young man noted, "As long as I could remember, I've always worked, I've always had some kind of income . . . I was really poor so it was nice to have any kind of income." Another said, "I'll just try to find a job that is the smallest job I can do to make money."

Money was not the only reason why people worked; however, not surprisingly, it was a key motivating factor in why the men participated in the workforce. Ultimately, financial gain and working are linked. Securing money through work helped the participants meet current and future financial needs. For this participant group, wages were not a determining factor in job selection, and they would take any paying job that they could get.

Future Work-Related Plans

Several of the young men spoke directly to future work goals; some were actively making plans about how they would help their own people. There were varying degrees of certainty related to their next steps and future employment. Some had a specific route, plan, and job in mind while others had much less concrete plans.

Pursuing Native American–related work was highly desired among this sample. Similar to Juntunen et al.'s (2001) findings, many desired to return to and support their home communities after they completed their education. Half of the young men said that they were interested in and hoped for

Aboriginal-related work in their future. Of these, three had a particular job in mind along with a specific plan of how they could achieve their goal. One participant who was enrolled in a graduate degree program wanted to complete a clinical practicum focused on counseling "the survivors of" and the "children of residential school survivors." Two others also shared their hopes for future work: "I am currently in the process of getting grant money and starting my own business so I can be my own self-employed artist and make my own stuff, and I'm hoping I can do my community internship working at an organization which focuses on urban populations of indigenous people." This commonality regarding working with Native communities was highlighted when one participant reflected on previous work experiences and future directions: "I've always said from the get go, as long as I'm working with other Natives, I don't care what I'm doing." These findings echo Juntunen et al. (2001), who stated that many of the participants in their study had a desire to provide help to their home communities through their future employment. These authors urged career counselors not only to explore individual interests, skills, and goals with young Native people but also to take time to explore the role of community membership and the expression of the membership through career choice.

Participants also spoke about a sense of uncertainty that they experienced when considering future jobs. Even for some of those who did have specific work plans, there was an element of caution that was present as explained by one participant who said: "[T]here is the dream, and then there is a reality, and I am trying to prepare for both." Some individuals had particular plans: "There are three separate things I want to be doing. I don't know which one yet, and I'll probably try to find a job at a grocery store . . . any place that I can find that involves cooking or, like, janitorial work." Another felt much less clear about what his future employment would be: "I'm thinking, where do I fall in all this? How can I best serve my community and my people? Where do I fit in all of this?" Participants also shared that in the past and currently, they had little to no idea about what job they would head toward. Being unsure of future employment was highly stressful, especially for those who experienced financial pressure. Uncertainty is an ongoing theme in the lives of most emerging adults (Arnett, 2004), and work uncertainty seemed salient for these Native participants.

Work Challenges

The young men also shared some of the challenges and obstacles that they have had and continue to endure in their work experiences. The most frequently cited obstacles were discrimination, limited options, and geographic location.

Five of the participants said that they felt that they had experienced discrimination while they were working or searching for work. Some participants had been subject to this in very specific industries or jobs while others had a broader and more pervasive experience of it. One young man stated that he felt that most people do not understand the widespread nature of discrimination and racism that Native people face in the workplace and said, "One thing that's clear in working life for Aboriginal people is that there's always that something that everyone else won't realize cause they just have no conception of it." This young man saw ignorance and discrimination as central obstacles that he and others faced in their work experiences.

Another participant described how he thought ignorance fostered the discrimination he experienced at the hands of his coworkers and employers:

> Keeping work's not really the problem; it's just been dealing with the people at work and what they were saying . . . It's dealing with ignorance . . . It seems to be more from specific people rather than jobs as a whole. I found there's often at every job there's a person who gives me a hard time like, 'Oh, you look white, so why should you get these things?' But it is kind of a pressure in the job to deal with these people cause I really don't want to work with people if they're going to be trying to bring awkward conversation to things like that.

This participant took pride in using his educational background and life experience to educate people but found it frustrating that he had to take on that role in the first place.

A third participant shared that a combination of discrimination and minimal local opportunities lay behind the difficulty he had with finding work: "It's hard enough getting work in Victoria, let alone being Native." He went on to talk more specifically about a major industry that he had been a part of during his earlier employment history:

> In the cooking industry, I can tell you right now, racism is one of the biggest barriers you have to deal with. Nobody wants to hire a Native, and nobody would say that. The cooks were racist . . . they were just overall abusive. I experienced a lot of racism in that job . . . Those attitudes, those layers are there before you even say a word. But those I see as barriers, kind of like that false identity created by the mainstream population. It's kind of like onions, they don't really know what's under there.

Participants clearly stated that discrimination exists, has negatively impacted their work experiences, and is a significant experience that they and people that they knew endure. This situation has also been highlighted by previous researchers, who have found that cultural differences, discrimination, racism, and the impacts of colonialism are experienced by Native people within the work environment and the educational system and are major barrier to success (Coverdale, 2012; Hoffman et al., 2005; Juntunen et al., 2001; Kirmayer, Brass, & Tait, 2000; Merrill et al., 2010; Stewart, 2008). This topic clearly needs to be addressed.

Participants also talked about their experiences of limited job options. Gaining employment was very important; however, finding a job and being hired was a major challenge, which reflects the government census data cited above. Across the young men interviewed, there were three explanations for why getting a job either currently or in the past was difficult: lack of previous work experience, lack of education, and lack of job availability. One participant shared his frustration with an ongoing cycle that he has endured of wanting a job but not having the necessary experience to be competitive enough to get hired: "I've been applying for all sorts of jobs, and not a lot of interviews coming my way . . . it's kind of hard to get that experience if no one will hire me . . . it's kind of discouraging." All participants were motivated to work; however, many were faced with limited options and availability of attainable or suitable jobs. Despite these challenges, participants were able to identify resources that would help, including seeking support from family and furthering their education.

Participants talked about their geographical locations as a potential barrier, which echoed Merrill et al.'s (2010) observation that geographical location impacts education and employment experience. Several of the young men said that there were fewer opportunities in their smaller home communities when compared to larger cities and that certain jobs required a great amount of travel to the work site. One participant described riding the bus for four hours each day to get to and from work: "I got a job at a fish plant, two hours from town. So I lived in one town and in the mornings had to wake up at roughly 3:00 in the morning and took a bus." As access to public transportation is limited in small communities compared with metropolitan areas, getting to work in smaller communities presented additional challenges. Geographic location has particular implications for many Native Americans seeking employment, especially for those living on reserve. Connection to land, family, culture, and housing play important roles when considering where to live. Many of the men recognized this interplay and how it influenced both their job pursuits and their opportunities.

Education

Participants described their experiences of past, present, and future educational experiences and plans. Formal educational levels ranged from grade 10 completion to enrollment in graduate school. Two data themes were identified: academic aspirations and challenges.

Academic Aspirations

Every participant spoke about the importance of education and said that it was a necessary and valued component of their pursuit of future employment options and opportunities. Similarly, Juntunen et al. (2001) stated that education at the high school and the post-secondary education levels was seen as a major support for future employment. Participants who had not yet completed high school stated that it was incredibly hard to get anything more than entry-level jobs and that completing high school was a priority. For those attending post-secondary education, their schooling was seen as a way to open up opportunities that would otherwise be unavailable. Those pursuing education also spoke about financial support and shifting priorities as important elements of their academic pursuits. Most had dreams about furthering their education beyond the current level that they were trying to complete, ranging from completing a post-secondary diploma to completing a doctoral degree. This focus on the importance of education is encouraging, given the strong correlation between higher education completion and increased access to employment opportunities.

Several participants spoke about the academic funding that they received to pursue their education and recognized that this was a major component of their educational and future employment success. Many Native people are eligible for educational and training funding. This, however, varies based on ancestry (status vs. non-status, First Nations vs. Métis) and funding streams (Nations vs. Government) and can range from a few hundred dollars to several thousand (Coverdale, 2012). One participant reflected on how the funding enabled him to dedicate his energy to pursuing his degree and said, "I'd say that scholarships and bursaries are a huge support because it means I don't have to work as much, so it takes off the added pressure. Another said, "I went to school for a year without working, but I had band funding . . . they give you a small amount of money, just enough to get by on." A third said, "My mom is currently paying for my schooling." The funding provided a great sense of relief for many of the participants and allowed several to entertain the idea of pursuing post-secondary and graduate level schooling.

In addition to the relief from financial pressure, funding also ensured less debt upon graduating for these individuals; this would also help reduce future financial hardship. Across participants, it was noted that pursuing further education would have been much less feasible without the financial support that they currently received, similar to findings by Merrill et al. (2010) and Hoffman et al. (2005), who stated that lack of finances was a major barrier to post-secondary education.

Several participants also spoke about the pull between continuing with a particular job and pursuing further education. Stepping away from a job is not always a realistic option, however, and participants indicated that the prospect of financial instability was a challenge that was considered when making the decision to either stay with their job or leave to pursue further education. For those with financial support, leaving work or reducing hours to continue with education was not only a priority but also a realistic option. Only one participant who was currently taking a post-secondary degree had part-time employment. He spoke about the effort it required to juggle several roles and recognized that while being employed was very meaningful to him, it lengthened the time it would take to get through his degree.

Challenges

Academic challenges among Native American youth are well documented within the literature (Jackson & Smith, 2001; Juntunen et al., 2001; Merrill et al., 2010); the young men in WIMW spoke about a variety of difficulties that they experienced throughout their education pursuits. Graduating from high school was the most commonly cited challenge, and at the time of the interviews, three participants were still making efforts to do so. They cited several specific historical and present reasons for their challenges with completing high school. This included family turmoil, drug and alcohol use, mental health concerns, and academic struggles. One of the participants described his continued difficulties with school: "I had troubles during school. I've been trying to catch up. Got a few years behind . . . I wasn't doing the greatest in school." He also recounted his current efforts to get his grade 12 education. Another said,

> I guess around 17 I was doing really horrible in school cause I got a lot of stuff at home. And so I got into some program. I remember it was for, basically it was for kids who they thought weren't going to amount to anything . . . and then I dropped out of school because I wasn't going to pass.

The challenges with graduating from high school are not unique to this participant group; educational completion rates for Native Americans are lower than for non-Natives. What is encouraging is that these participants had high hopes about their educational future and stated that education was a priority.

Another challenge that was discussed was the difficulty with choosing future directions. Jackson and Smith (2001) noted that their research participants had "limited understanding of post-secondary education and its relationship to specific careers." The WIMW participants spoke about multiple educational options, the daunting task of selecting an educational direction, and the uncertainty that came along with the variety of choices. There would also be financial implications related to prolonged schooling or changing programs, given the increased costs with lengthening educational enrollment. Of the two participants who had a more specific plan about how their academic career would progress, there was still recognition of the multiple academic directions they could pursue after the completion of their current level of schooling, which was accompanied by a sense of ambivalence about committing to a final decision.

Overall, the work and educational experiences of these young Native men were similar to others presented above. Alongside every story of the challenges related to work and education were stories of hope, perseverance, and success. Following this research and the larger project's findings, we have several recommendations pertaining to career development practices and conducting research with Native American populations.

IMPLICATIONS FOR RESEARCH

Conducting research with Native Americans requires a high level of awareness and commitment to ethical practice. Cochran et al. (2008) stated that "an extensive body of health-related research has been conducted on Native American populations around the world, but it appears to have had little impact on their overall well-being," (p. 22) and he argued that the *how* of doing research with these communities is equally as important as the outcomes. Rather than conducting research *on* these populations, Cochran urges researchers to conduct research *with* these groups. Marshall and Guenette (2011) underscore the importance of collaboration between researchers and Aboriginal communities. Before entering a community, it is absolutely imperative to spend time becoming familiar with protocol, local agencies, and key contact people and to maintain constant and respectful communication throughout.

In addition, there is a certain level of disclosure that is appropriate when working with Native American communities. With regard to introductions, for example, it is important that researchers explain who they are and why they are there as well as what they are doing. For example, sharing where your parents and grandparents are from is culturally appropriate and expected. It is also important to acknowledge the local land and traditional territory names. These respectful practices help to build trust and a spirit of collaborative relationship. We recommend connecting with a member from the specific community of interest to obtain guidance and make sure that protocols are followed.

IMPLICATIONS FOR CAREER DEVELOPMENT PRACTICE

Relational Focus

Throughout our own and others' research, it has become clear that relational supports are of the utmost importance throughout employment and educational pursuits. Helping Native communities build capacity to better support their members would be a worthwhile endeavor and a valuable investment of resources. For those already providing support, such as elders, family members, and tribal or band employees, honoring their contributions and *supporting the supporters* will help maintain existing resources. For those that are not doing so already, encouraging young people to seek support from their relational network would be beneficial.

For young Native Americans who feel disconnected or are living away from their home communities, providing additional and accessible relational supports is recommended. Local friendship centers and Native social service agencies were often cited as places to access multiple forms of support. Expanding the awareness of and advocating for increased funding for these key resources will allow for more people to connect and be supported.

Employment Support

Many of the men noted that culturally related work experiences were highly valued because they provided culturally meaningful experiences. Increasing access to these types of job opportunities would be beneficial. It is important that teachers, job counselors, placement workers, and others who are supporting these young people are aware of a wide range of opportunities and maintain relationships with communities in order to help facilitate these opportunities.

It was also made clear that lack of resume writing and specific employment search skills created challenges to gaining employment. Further, many of the men had a limited awareness of possible job opportunities that they could pursue as well as little know-how of how to advance beyond entry-level job positions. For these individuals, this fact resulted in a limited perception of employment opportunities. Some had been able to connect with Native American community agencies, which provided not only the technical skills related to searching for and obtaining a job but also specific information on various job opportunities along with the steps that would be needed to obtain a certain position. This feedback provided participants with a realistic idea and plan of what would be needed to obtain jobs in trades and non-trade work fields. Increasing awareness of and access to community employment support programs and structured work search resources could help those struggling with the initial needed elements in looking for work as well as those who are looking to expand their job opportunities. Intervention through community programming, both on and off reserve, and in high school curricula would also be fundamental components of supporting youth in their job search development.

Educational Completion

Educational completion was consistently cited as a major factor for gaining employment. Completion of both high school and post-secondary degrees is significantly lower in the Native American population when compared to non-Native national averages. Building on and building in additional educational resources for Native American youth needs to be a priority. Young people have said that without in-school supports such as resource rooms, educational assistants, and tutoring, they would find it much harder to stay in school and obtain the grades needed for post-secondary entrance. As found by Juntunen et al. (2001), students from communities that place high value on educational goals experience relational support throughout their academic pursuits. Communities that are supportive of education will result in increased numbers of people attaining it; this support has positive impacts for both current and future generations through a cascading effect. Encouraging schools to partner with communities in the development of culturally based curricula could, in turn, increase community support of education as well as encourage academic and vocational aspirations.

At the post-secondary level, increasing the ease of access to funding and increasing funding dollars would allow more students to consider and pursue post-secondary education. Having Native American–specific services and contact people at recruitment and advising centers could prove useful. Increasing the availability of Native American academic programs and courses has also been shown to have a positive impact on student enrollment and retention.

CONCLUDING THOUGHTS

This chapter has highlighted the work-related issues and experiences of young Native men. Relational and social constructionist theories were deemed particularly relevant to career development practice and research with this population. It was important for us to present a balanced picture—statistical reports and the scholarly literature seem to focus on the problems and deficits among Native Americans; however, we also encountered stories of resilience, pride, great strength, and commitment to culture and community. It is imperative that these successes are acknowledged and shared. We would like to close with a quote from one of our participants: "The barriers and obstacles are now easier to remove because I have options, I have a stronger identity, I have resources, I have people behind me. It's just a matter of me making that move and just finding that direction."

REFERENCES

Arnett, J. J. (2004). *Emerging adulthood: The winding road from the late teens through the twenties.* New York, NY: Oxford University Press.

Blustein, D. L. (2006). *The psychology of working: A new perspective for career development, counseling, and public policy.* Mahwah, NJ: Lawrence Erlbaum Publishers.

Blustein, D. L. (2011). A relational theory of working. *Journal of Vocational Behavior, 79*(1), 1–17.

Blustein, D. L., Kenna, A. C., Gill, N., & Devoy, J. E. (2008). The psychology of working: A new framework for counselling practice and public policy. *Career Development Quarterly, 56,* 294–308.

Blustein, D. L., Kenna, A. C., Murphy, K. A., DeVoy, J. E., & DeWine, D. B. (2005). Qualitative research in career development: Exploring the center and margins of discourse about careers and working. *Journal of Career Assessment, 13*, 351–370.

Blustein, D. L., Schultheiss, D. E. P., & Flum, H. (2004). Toward a relational perspective of the psychology of careers and working: A social constructionist analysis. *Journal of Vocational Behavior, 64*, 423–440.

Braun, B., & Clarke, V. (2006). Using thematic analysis in psychology. *Qualitative Research in Psychology, 3*, 77–101.

Cochran, P. A. L., Marshall, C. A., Garcia-Downing, C., Kendall, E., Cook, D., McCubbin, L., & Gover, R. M. S. (2008). Indigenous ways of knowing: Implications for participatory research and community. *American Journal of Public Health, 98*(1), 22–27.

Coverdale, J. (2012). *Walking in multiple worlds: Aboriginal young people's life work narratives*. (Master's thesis). University of Victoria, Victoria, Canada.

Gergen, K. (1999). *An invitation to social construction*. Thousand Oaks, CA: Sage Publications.

Hoffmann, L. L., Jackson, A. P., & Smith, S. A. (2005). Career barriers among Native American students living on reservations. *Journal of Career Development, 32*(1), 31–45.

Jackson, A., & Smith, S. (2001). Postsecondary transitions among Navajo Indians. *Journal of American Indian Education, 40*(2), 1–32.

Jordan, J. (2008). Recent developments in relational-cultural theory. *Women & Therapy, 31*(2/3/4), 1–4.

Juntunen, C. L., Barraclough, D. J., Broneck, C. L., Seibel, G. A., Winrow, S. A., & Morin, P. M. (2001). American Indian perspectives on the career journey. *Journal of Counseling Psychology, 48*(3), 274–285. doi:10.1037/0022-0167.48.3.274

Kirmayer, L., Brass, G., & Tait, C. (2000). The mental health of aboriginal peoples: Transformations of identity and community. *Canadian Journal of Psychiatry, 45*(7), 607.

Marshall, A., Jackson, L., Drummond, D., & Camara, S. (2007). The human voice of social-ecological restructuring II: Youth, restructuring, education and health. In R. E. Ommer & the Coasts Under Stress Research Project Team (Eds.), *Coasts under stress: Restructuring and social ecological health* (pp. 241–295). Montreal, Quebec, Canada: McGill-Queen's University Press.

Marshall, E. A. (2002). Life-career counselling issues for youth in coastal and rural communities. The impact of economic, social and environmental restructuring. *International Journal for the Advancement of Counselling, 24*(1), 69–87

Marshall, E. A., & Guenette, F. (2011). Cross-cultural journeys: Transferring and exchanging knowledge among researchers and community partners. In E. M. Banister, B. J. Leadbeater & E. A. Marshall (Eds.), *Knowledge translation in context* (pp. 35–55). Toronto, Ontario, Canada: University of Toronto Press.

Marshall, E. A., Stewart, S. L., & Coverdale, J. (2013, January). *Walking in multiple worlds: Aboriginal youths' worklife experiences*. Presentation at Cannexus 2013, Ottawa, Ontario, Canada.

Marshall, E. A., Stewart, S. L., Coverdale, J., Spowart, J. P., & LeBlanc, J. (2012, May). *Worklife and mental health for Aboriginal youth*. Presentation at the annual conference of the Canadian Counselling and Psychotherapy Association, Calgary, Alberta, Canada.

Marshall, E. A., Stewart, S. L., & Lawrence, B. C. (2011, November). *Transitions and possible selves: Research and counselling with rural youth and families.* Paper presented at the New Zealand Association for Research in Education Conference, Tauranga, New Zealand.

Marshall, E. A., Stewart, S. L., Popadiuk, N., & Lawrence, B. (2013). Walking in multiple worlds. Successful school-to-work transitions for Indigenous and cultural minority youth. In G. Tchibozo (Ed.), *Cultural and social diversity and the transition from education to work* (pp.185–202). Rotterdam, Netherlands: Springer.

Medicine-Eagle, B. (1989). The circle of healing. In R. Carlson & J. Brugh (Eds.), *Healers on healing* (pp. 58–62). New York, NY: Penguin.

Merrill, S., Bruce, D., & Marlin, A. (2010). *Considerations for successful transitions between postsecondary education and the labour market for aboriginal youth in Canada final report.* Sackville, New Brunswick, Canada: Rural and Small Town Programme, Mount Allison University.

Overmars, D. (2011). *Finding a path among the concrete: Work-life narratives of urban Aboriginal young adults* (Master's Thesis). University of Toronto, Toronto, Canada.

Rhodes, C. (2000). Ghostwriting research: Positioning the researcher in the interview text. *Qualitative Inquiry, 6*(4), 511–525.

Savickas, M. L. (1995). Constructivist counseling for career indecision. *The Career Development Quarterly, 43*(4), 363–373.

Schultheiss, D. E. P. (2007). The emergence of a relational cultural paradigm for vocational psychology. *International Journal for Educational and Vocational Guidance, 7*(3), 191–201.

Schultheiss, D., Watts, J., Sterland, L., & O'Neill, M. (2011) Career, migration and the life CV: A relational cultural analysis. *Journal of Vocational Behavior, 78,* 334–341.

Spowart, J. K. P (2013). *Young Indigenous men's work narratives.* (Master's Thesis). University of Victoria, Victoria, Canada.

Statistics Canada. (2011). *Aboriginal People and the labour market: Estimates from the Labour Force Survey, 2008–2010.* Retrieved from http://www5.statcan.gc.ca/bsolc/olc-cel/olc-cel?catno=71-588-X2011003&lang=eng

Stewart, S. (2008). Promoting Indigenous mental health: Cultural perspectives on healing from Native counsellors in Canada. *International Journal of Health Promotion and Education, 46*(2), 49–56.

Turner, S. L., Trotter, M. J., Lapan, R. T., Czajka, K. A., Yang, P., & Brissett, A. E. A. (2006). Vocational skills and outcomes among Native American adolescents: A test of the integrative contextual model of career development. *The Career Development Quarterly, 54,* 216–226.

U.S. Census Bureau. (2013). *American FactFinder.* Retrieved from http://factfinder2.census.gov/faces/nav/jsf/pages/index

Whiston, S. C., & Rahdjya, D. (2005). Qualitative career assessment: An overview and analysis. *Journal of Career Assessment, 13*(4), 371–380.

Young, R. A., Vallach, L., & Collin, A. (1996). A contextual explanation of career. In D. Brown & L. Brooks (Eds.), *Career choice and development* (pp. 477–512). San Francisco, CA: Jossey-Bass.

9 Building Tomorrow's Tribal Public Health Workforce

Jennifer Pharr and Michelle Chino

Public health has always been part of improving the human condition. Even the earliest recorded civilizations understood the importance of sanitation and regulating behaviors that could compromise the health and well-being of the community. Definitions of public health, however, are as diverse as the field itself, and even public health professionals struggle to precisely define what has been referred to as an invisible profession. One of the earliest definitions of public health may also still be the most helpful in understanding this multi-dimensional, multi-faceted field:

> Public health is the science and art of preventing disease, prolonging life and promoting health and efficiency through organized community efforts for the sanitation of the environment, the control of community infections, the education of the individual in the principles of personal hygiene, the organization of medical and nursing services for the early diagnosis and preventive treatment of disease, and the development of the social machinery which will ensure to every individual in the community a standard of living adequate for the maintenance of health.
> (Winslow, 1920, p. 30)

By the end of the 20th century, the field could boast of the Ten Great Public Health Achievements including the control of infectious diseases, immunizations, motor-vehicle safety, safer food supplies, fluoridated water, and declines in heart disease. These achievements, however, led to complacency and a shift in focus to biomedical advances. For several decades the public health workforce was largely overlooked as an essential part of the continuum of health promotion, prevention, and clinical care. As we entered the 21st century, several major events quickly brought public health back into the public's eye and the need for a skilled workforce back to the forefront. A resurgence of infectious diseases (AIDS, SARS, H1N1, and others) along with natural disasters such as Hurricane Katrina and the threat of bioterrorism after 9/11 propelled public health back into action. Today, public health is defined by three core functions and ten essential services that together can ensure conditions in which people can be healthy (Institute of Medicine, 1988) (Table 1).

Table 9.1 Core Functions and Ten Essential Services of Public Health

Core Functions	Ten Essential Services of Public Health
Assessment	1. Monitor health status to identify and solve community health problems
	2. Diagnose and investigate health problems and health hazards in the community
Policy Development	3. Inform, educate, and empower people about health issues
	4. Mobilize community partnerships and action to identify and solve health problems
	5. Develop policies and plans that support individual and community health efforts
Assurance	6. Enforce laws and regulations that protect health and ensure safety
	7. Link people to needed personal health services and assure the provision of health care when otherwise unavailable
	8. Ensure competent public and personal health care workforces
	9. Evaluate effectiveness, accessibility, and quality of personal and population-based health services
	10. Research for new insights and innovative solutions to health problems

Today's public health workforce protects and improves the health of a community through education, promotion of healthy lifestyles, and research for disease and injury prevention much the same as in Winslow's day. Even with clearly defined professional objectives, new roles and responsibilities and new demands for technology, communications, and partnerships (Kurland, 2000), career paths for public health workers are not well defined (Trust for America's Health, 2008). Many public health workers lack formal training and public health degrees. While the number of academic institutions offering degrees in public health has increased, many graduates do not work in public health departments.

Public health is necessarily both proactive and responsive and as such requires a diverse workforce with a continuum of skills. When there is a natural disaster, disease outbreak, or other threat to the well-being of a community, public health workers must be prepared to fill myriad responsibilities, from communications to laboratory research, from coordination with first responders and care providers to enforcing laws and following protocols for response. A major challenge for public health is maintaining a balance between the progress made in the last century and preparing for the challenges of this century. This balance is a challenge for tribes and further complicated by the political nature of public health. As sovereign nations, American Indian tribes have a unique political status and relationship with the United States government. To understand any issue in tribal communities, one must understand the underlying political, economic, and socio-cultural issues that stem from the government-to-government relationship that exists between tribes, the federal government, and state and county governments.

THE TRIBAL PUBLIC HEALTH CONTEXT

Health care services and support for the tribal health workforce have undergone many changes in the past few decades. Sovereignty allows tribes a certain degree of autonomy when it comes to community health and wellness services, often defined legislatively and subject to the availability of funding. From the Snyder Act of 1921 (PL 67–85) to the permanent reauthorization of the Indian Health Care Improvement Act (IHCIA), enacted in 2010 as part of the Patient Protection and Affordable Care Act (P.L. 111–148), Congress has established legislative authority for the appropriation of funds for general support, including education, and for the conservation of health of Indian people.

The Snyder Act included public health–related expenditures to fund improvement of water supplies, control of alcohol and drugs, and employment across key positions including inspectors, supervisors, superintendents, clerks, field matrons, farmers, physicians, Indian police, and Indian judges. The IHCIA established objectives for addressing health disparities and provisions for recruiting and retaining qualified health professionals. Over time, other laws, court cases, and executive orders have continued to reaffirm the unique relationship between tribal governments and the federal government along with the government's responsibility for the health of Indian people. In 1975, the Indian Self-Determination and Education Assistance Act (PL 93–638) changed the landscape of Indian health by enabling tribes to administer tribal programs and assume responsibility for services previously administered by the federal government.

Disparities in health, education, and income experienced by the four million American Indian/Alaska Native people living in Indian Country underscore the need for tribe-specific public health services and infrastructure (CDC, 2013; U.S. Census, 2000). For many health indicators, Native populations fare worse than the general population in the U.S. Access to education, income, and basic necessities such as adequate housing influence the health of people living in a community. A summary of current status indicators for Native people in terms of health, education, and income are presented below (Russell, 2004; U.S. Department of Education, 2005).

The tribal public health workforce is now challenged to provide basic services to communities whose health status is decades behind the mainstream and to meet the demands of a new century. A skilled tribal public

Table 9.2 Current health status of American Indians

Health	U.S. government spends about twice as much on health care for a federal prisoner as for American Indian.
	The tuberculosis rate is 750 times greater in Native populations than among all other Americans.
	The diabetes rate is 6.8 times greater in Native populations than among all other Americans.
	The prevalence of pneumonia and influenza is 61 percent greater in Native populations than among all other Americans.
	Asthma prevalence is greater among Native adults and children than among other groups (healthier tribal housing).
	Native children have higher rates of oral disease than non-Native children.
	Natives die six years earlier, on average, than other Americans.
Education	Only 52 percent of Native teens finish high school.
	Only 17 percent attend college, and only 4 percent graduate.
	Only 2 percent attend graduate school.
	Native high school students are more likely than students in general to report having been threatened or injured with a weapon on school property.
	Native high school students are more likely than students in general to be in a physical fight on school property.
Income	Poverty among Indians has actually risen during the past decade.
	More than half of all reservation Natives live below the poverty line (four times the national average).
	45 percent of Native persons live at or below the poverty line.
	75 percent of the Native workforce earns less than $7,000 each year.
	The average unemployment rate on reservations is 45 percent.
	On some reservations, the unemployment rate is upward of 90 percent.

workforce is essential as tribes increasingly take responsibility for an array of prevention and intervention services. Training and educational opportunities have not kept pace, with few clearly defined opportunities for the tribal public health workforce. While some public health workforce training is available to tribes, it may not reflect what tribes need most.

Many tribes lack essential technology, not to mention paved roads and clean running water. The health threats from polluted water are likely to be of greater urgency than the threat of a chemical weapons attack. Additionally, given the small population size and isolation of many communities, they are unable to compete for anything but the smallest grants. Even when funding can expand existing services or develop new resources, filling workforce needs can be a major challenge. Workforce shortages translate into a shortage of essential services (Morrissey, 2011). Tribes face additional challenges due to factors such as remote locations, a lack of a clearly defined infrastructure for public health services, and the challenges of cross-cultural communication and culturally relevant resources.

The recognition that the tribal public health workforce may not be equipped to respond to a public health crisis has not gone unnoticed. Scholarship opportunities for educating the next generation of health care professionals and training opportunities for the current health workforce have been instituted. New strategies, however, are needed that address the underlying impediments that make it difficult for workers to access even those resources designed specifically for the tribal workforce.

There is now added pressure and incentive to strengthen the tribal public health workforce. Public health accreditation is the newest initiative for standardizing public health across the nation with a set of accreditation standards that would apply to all state, tribal, local, and territorial health departments. The Public Health Accreditation Board (PHAB) standards indicate the required level of achievement for service provision with the understanding that the actual mechanisms of service delivery will differ by organizational structure. The benefits of a national accreditation process would include consistency, accountability, and continuous quality improvement. Accreditation could also help the public better understand the functions of public health and increase a department's credibility. The implications for workforce training and education are huge (Gebbie & Turnock, 2006).

Like many state and local health departments, tribes are interested in the accreditation process but often lack the basic elements to start the process. In addition to forming an accreditation team, there is the expectation that applicants will have electronic filing and data systems. The PHAB notes that accreditation requires an ongoing commitment to quality improvement and adherence to national standards. For a tribal public health workforce struggling to provide for basic needs, even the fundamental requirements for accreditation may be out of reach for all but the largest tribal health departments.

TRIBAL PUBLIC HEALTH WORKFORCE EDUCATION ISSUES AND TRENDS

The public health workforce is vast and inclusive and requires a wide array of skilled and knowledgeable people to promote health and prevent disease. Health educators, inspectors, epidemiologists, first responders, administrators, scientists, and environmental health specialists are all part of maintaining a healthy population. These varying roles require different levels of educational attainment ranging from high school to doctoral degrees in fields that span the social, health, and physical sciences as well as communications, law, and public administration. Furthermore, the public health workforce regularly and necessarily collaborates with clinicians, government officials, and nonprofit organizations.

The full complement of skills needed to support the three core functions and ten essential services was defined through a collaborative effort between the Centers for Disease Control and Prevention (CDC), the Health Resources and Services Administration (HRSA), and the Public Health Foundation (PHF). Eight skill domains and three career development tiers that reflect the broad practice of public health in any setting provide a foundation for public health practice and offer a starting point for public health entities to better understand and meet workforce development needs. The eight domains include the following: 1) analytical and assessment skills; 2) policy development/program planning skills; 3) communication skills; 4) cultural competency skills; 5) community dimensions of practices skills; 6) public health science skills; 7) financial planning and management skills; and 8) leadership and systems thinking skills. Each tier uses more precise verbs to describe the desired level of competence. Tier 1 includes skills relevant for entry-level public health professionals, Tier 2 skills for those in program management or supervisory roles, and Tier 3 skills for senior management or executives (Public Health Foundation, 2010).

The core competencies framework provides a set of standards by which health departments can better assess workforce knowledge and skills, identify training needs, develop training plans, craft job descriptions, and conduct performance evaluations. According to the Public Health Foundation, these core competencies can support workforce development to improve performance, prepare for accreditation, and support community health needs. This framework, however, is based on assumptions about the local public health infrastructure that may not fit the realities of public health in tribal communities.

In mainstream communities, public health is generally well defined with a network of resources led by a central health department (PHAB, 2011). In tribal communities, those functions that exist are often scattered and fragmented as the tribal public health workforce is not always identifiable as a distinct unit and may not have a defined public health person or office. Tribal health departments vary as much as tribes themselves. Larger ones may include an array of public health services, which may or may not be defined as such. Smaller tribes may rely heavily on county and state services to fill in the gaps. In addition to caring for the local population, tribes must also be prepared to care for the needs of tribal members who may not always reside on the reservation.

It is estimated that two-thirds of American Indians live off reservation but that many return to their tribal communities on a regular basis. These transitory patterns have important implications for public health, such as disease transmission, continuity of care for chronic conditions, and the use of traditional medicine and healing ceremonies. In particular, Indian people with conditions such as HIV/AIDS, who may have always lived in an urban setting, are now returning to their home reservations for health services not available or affordable in the cities (NNAAPC, 2002). Tribal public health services are scrambling to be prepared to address the need for health education, prevention and screening services, and surveillance.

Preliminary efforts to identify and document the state of public health services, gaps, and workforce needs included a report by the National Indian Health Board (NIHB, 2010). According to the NIHB study, almost half of tribal health organizations serve populations of fewer than 5,000 people with budgets of under $500,000 per year. These funds come from multiple sources, including the Indian Health Service, federal grants from a variety of agencies, and state program support for programs such as Women, Infants, and Children (WIC). The report also states that public health functions are part of a tribal health department that may be part of Indian Health Service functions or, increasingly, an independent, tribally operated program.

Often tribal public health is a combination of workers and activities from health care, social services, environmental health, and a variety of other entities that serve a tribal community. With smaller tribes, gaps may be filled through collaboration with tribal health consortia or with county or state public health entities. Reservation boundaries often cross multiple state and county borders, and this jurisdictional overlap requires relationships with multiple state and county services, including agencies that provide enforcement, investigation, services, and support for public health–related issues. Federal policy and jurisdictional issues impact services needed and offered. A lack of cross training and systems-level training further fragments an already fragmented system.

In the tribal public health workforce, people wear many hats, and one person may serve multiple roles that fall into the different tiers described earlier. In one role, the skill requirements might fall into Tier 1 or entry-level while in another role, the skill requirements might fall into Tier 3 or senior management/executive. The workforce needs the agility to adapt to the varied skill levels required within the context of their tribal community. Training and education, however, usually follows the tier structure, leaving critical gaps in needed knowledge, skills, and abilities. While these issues are impediments to any well-trained workforce, there are additional underlying issues for the tribal workforce to consider: culture, tradition, and the factors that impact community capacity.

The Cultural Divide

Tribal culture and tradition is a defining characteristic of American Indian and Alaska Native communities and is the foundation for understanding the complexities of service delivery, resource management, and almost every facet of community life. There have been concerted efforts over the past few decades to ensure a culturally competent workforce; in fact, it is one of the eight skill domains. From a tribal perspective, however, cultural competence is a two-way street.

This divide was illuminated in a recent pilot study of tribal and non-tribal public health workers (Chino, 2013). To better understand public health training needs, a convenience sample of more than 100 public health workers piloted an assessment tool based on the PHF workforce skill domains. The sample included 57 tribal public health workers and 54 non-tribal public health workers. Individual and team skill levels on the eight skill domains of public health workforce competency were assessed along with individual and team-level training needs. Initially, the purpose of the project was to ask the standard questions: Are training needs different? Are priorities different? While these questions were answered, a bigger question emerged: Is there a difference in how the competencies are conceptualized and interpreted?

The project used one of the tools designed to assist communities in workforce development planning, the PHF 3-Step Competency Prioritization Sequence (PHF, 2012), to identify strengths and areas of need. As expected, there were some statistically significant differences between the tribal and non-tribal participants. However, there were also three competency areas where both groups scored the same (see Figure 9.1).

The assumption was that where both scored equally, each would request equivalent types of training. Both tribal and non-tribal groups scored equally in three of the eight domains: communication, policy development, and cultural competence. Each group's related training requests, however, showed important differences not only in how the domains were conceptualized but also in the focus and direction of areas of need.

The communication skills domain includes skills such as health literacy, transmission of public health information both to community and

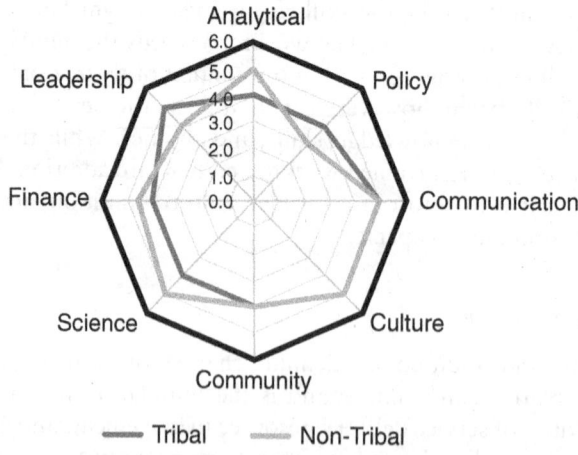

Figure 9.1 PHF 3-Step Competency Prioritization Sequence revealing strengths and areas of need (PHF, 2012)

professional venues, group communication skills such as conflict resolution and risk communication, and, ultimately, communication of the role of public health within the overall system. The non-tribal group requested training focused on building these skills within their staff and work groups. Managers (higher tier workers) requested training to increase the ability of their staff to communicate the concepts of public health more effectively to communities and use multiple mediums.

The tribal-group-requested training focused in a different direction. Tribal workers requested training that would inform and educate their managers and administrators about public health and about how the workforce needs to operate in a tribal environment. With public health functions scattered across agencies and job descriptions, tribal workers wanted managers and administrators, rarely trained in public health, to better understand roles and responsibilities in the workforce. Those at the higher tiers wanted to better understand how to support and integrate public health services within the existing infrastructure.

The Policy Development/Program Planning Skills domain includes understanding and ensuring activities align with public health laws, informing policy through data analysis, and understanding the outcomes of policy options. The non-tribal group requested training focused particularly on the development of interagency policies. Their greatest needs were focused on data sharing, cooperative agreements, and gaining consensus on roles and responsibilities.

The tribal group requested training on state and federal laws and policies as they relate to tribal government and health policy. The tribal group also wanted state and federal partners to better understand tribal sovereignty and self-determination and ways to develop policies to fill critical gaps in the continuum of public health services.

The cultural competency domain includes the recognition of the role of culture and interaction with persons from diverse backgrounds. This domain also emphasizes the importance of a diverse workforce. As might be expected, the non-tribal group requested skills to better understand and communicate with tribal populations. The tribal group wanted training to help them better understand and communicate with county, state, and federal entities and to help these entities understand that protocols for program and policy development are different for tribes than for mainstream organizations. They needed not only different mechanisms for delivering workforce training and education to tribal practitioners but also assurance that these resources are in alignment with the tribe's definition and directionality.

Community Capacity

The cultural divide can isolate tribes from accessing and integrating with non-tribal entities and make them struggle to compete with mainstream health departments for limited resources. There are other forms of isolation that also impede the ability of tribes to obtain needed training and educational resources. Geographic isolation has a ripple effect that impacts access to resources, information, and technology—all of which affect the development of a strong infrastructure for public health.

Many reservations encompass large geographic areas and are far from urban hubs. Small, remote tribal populations are hard pressed to provide the full continuum of public health services. Distance exacerbates the challenges of the tribal public health workforce to engage in continuing education or training activities. High school graduates who want to pursue degrees in public health are forced to either leave the reservation or travel long distances to tribal colleges. Although online degrees in public health and online public health workforce training options have increased over the past five years, a lack of technology infrastructure reduces the viability of this option as an alternative for Native students who do not want to leave the reservation or who for myriad reasons are unable to attend school away from home.

As a result of fragmentation and formed reliance on the Indian Health Service or state-level services, public health is not on the minds of Native people, either as a career or as a priority. The need for a tribal public health workforce is a relatively new phenomenon. It will take time for mentors to develop, jobs to be added, and employment options to be more readily available. Many positions require credentials and certifications that are difficult for people to acquire in remote communities.

When a skilled workforce is not locally available, tribes recruit from outside the area, primarily non-Indians. Salaries that tend to be lower than in urban areas hinder recruitment efforts, and retention is an issue for programs that rely on grant funding and on non-Indians, who may have difficulty adjusting to life in a rural tribal community.

Lack of infrastructure is also an artifact of funding for prevention and health promotion programs. Most rely heavily on competitive government grants, contracts, and pass-through funding. When funding streams are inconsistent, services come and go and do not become established within the community. Many tribes rely on these funding mechanisms for services that other communities take for granted, such as mammogram screening, child car seats, and violence prevention.

Underlying many of the challenges presented by geography and often limited infrastructures for public health is the technology divide. The lack of basic computer technology challenges the daily assumptions of those who take resources like the Internet for granted. Many training opportunities are offered through computer-based technologies, including webinars, CD-ROM, and online tutorials. The infrastructure to support online or e-learning technology, however, is often missing on reservations, leaving the tribal public health workforce without these important workforce development tools. While access to technology is improving in Indian County, it still lags far behind the rest of the country. Fewer than 10 percent of Native

American communities have broadband access, compared to a national average of almost 70 percent. Broadband access is either not available or too expensive for many living on reservations, especially those in very rural settings. In addition to lacking Internet access, fewer than three-quarters of those in Indian country have a telephone, while the national average is 98 percent (Morris & Meinrath, 2009).

The primary challenge for any health program is funding. Health services for American Indians are notoriously underfunded. A report issued by the Indian Health Service in 2003 showed that Indian tribes are chronically underfunded, resulting in unmet healthcare needs of Native people. In contrast to other federally funded health care recipients such as veterans and Medicaid recipients, severe funding disparities exist for American Indians (Figure 9.2). Even federal prisoners receive more than twice the amount spent on American Indian/Alaska Native health care. The poor health status of American Indians further amplifies the disparities. Funding for basic sanitation, water, and sewage disposal—an essential facet of public health—is a fraction of the amount that would be needed to bring tribal communities on par with other U.S. communities. It is estimated that about 8 percent of Native homes lack safe water (USCCR, 2003). Additionally, the vacancy rate for Indian Health Service professional positions remains high, with critical shortages in some areas. Despite the high level of need, the IHS has experienced regular decreases in health professional training funds over the past decade.

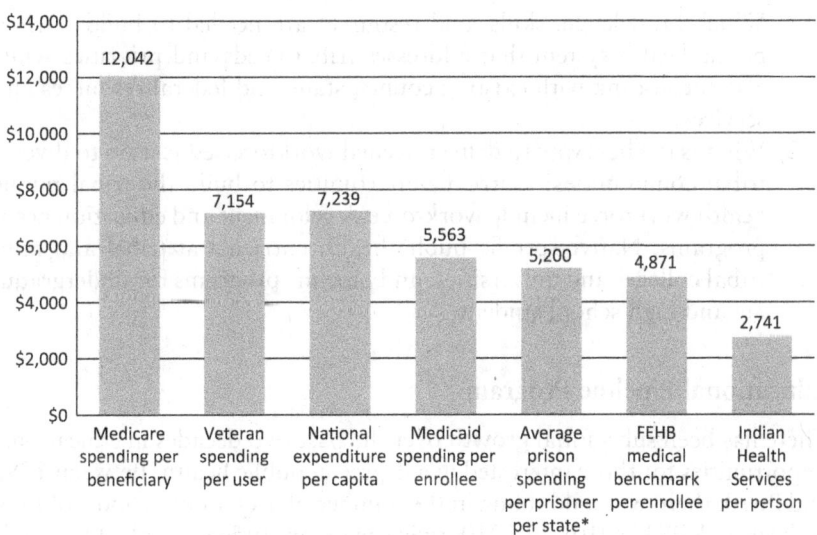

Figure 9.2 2012 Indian Health Services Spending per Capita Compared to Other Federal Healthcare Expenditures.

*Average per-prisoner spending per state included 44 states that reported data. (Henry Kaiser Family Foundation, 2012; NCAI, 2013; Pew Charitable Trust, 2013)

When primary care is underfunded, then public health functions at even lower levels of funding. It is estimated that for every dollar spent on clinical medicine, 10 cents is spent on public health (Association of Schools and Programs of Public Health, 2010). Further, because public health is funded by the government, when the economy lags, so does funding for public health. According to Morrissey (2011), the recent economic downturn has accelerated declines in the public health workforce with more than one in five jobs lost. Despite one-time funding efforts such as the American Recovery and Reinvestment Act of 2009 (ARRA), the shortages of workers means public health functions at all levels have to do more with less. This is particularly true for tribal communities where resources are limited to begin with and recruitment and retention for public health jobs are a major challenge.

Tribes are cognizant of the limitations of government funding and have taken advantage of revenues from tribal businesses, including gaming, to fund health and education for their communities. The funding from these sources, along with innovative approaches, is beginning to bridge the gaps.

PROMISING PRACTICES AND WAYS FORWARD

Tribes need to define workforce competencies on their own terms but also have them be comparable to the mainstream entities with whom they interact. Important questions for tribal communities to answer are these:

1) Which knowledge, skills, and resources are needed to build a tribal public health system that addresses tribal needs and priorities while also integrating with existing county, state, and federal resources and services?
2) What is the best way to deliver needed workforce education to diverse tribal communities? Current opportunities to build the tribal public health workforce include workforce development and education grant programs, Native-specific public health curricula at tribal and non-tribal colleges and universities, and pipeline programs for undergraduate and high school students.

Educational Pipeline Programs

There has been substantial growth over the past two decades in educational opportunities for those interested in a degree in public health. Between 1990 and 2010, there was a doubling in the number of accredited schools of public health (ASPH, 2010). In 2010, twice as many students applied to public health programs as compared with 2000. Although public health needs an ethnically, linguistically, and geographically diverse workforce, disparities are evident when considering the representation of students in public health academic programs. Less than 1 percent of Master's of Public Health (MPH, the terminal degree) applicants are American Indian/Alaska Native. This raises concerns about having a future public health workforce knowledgeable about the unique needs of tribal communities.

The vast majority of resources, programming, and education available for the health workforce has been focused on medical care and on increasing the number of clinicians working in tribal communities. Increasingly, there is an awareness of the need for disease prevention programs such as diabetes and cardiovascular disease prevention or smoking cessation. While many of these programs fall into the realm of public health, the primary focus has traditionally been on the severe disparities in clinical care services and educating the clinical healthcare workforce. Several universities and tribal colleges are now developing programs to educate the next generation of tribal public health professionals with some very positive results.

The CDC, tribal colleges, and other universities have begun to develop pipeline programs to deliver the needed workforce education to tribal communities and increase the interest of Native students in health professions, but with mixed results (Zaback, Becker, Dignan, & Lambert, 2010). A number of tribal colleges now offer Associate and Bachelor's degrees in public health–related fields. In addition to Associate and Bachelor's degrees in public and environmental health offered through tribal colleges, a few non-tribal colleges and universities offer degrees and programs specific to Native public health. These include Johns Hopkins University, North Dakota State University, and Oregon Health & Science University.

Johns Hopkins Center for American Indian Health Training & Scholarship Program

This program supports Native health professionals in their academic pursuit to address health needs in Indian Country. Offerings include a Summer Research Institute, a Winter Research Institute, a Public Health Training Certificate in American Indian health, a Public Health Training Certificate scholarship, an Annie Wauneka Visiting Faculty Fellowship, a postbaccalaureate fellowship for AI/AN applying to a public health graduate program, a diversity summer internship program for undergraduates that provides research experience in the public health or biomedical field, and a Training of Field Staff Center that promotes educational and professional development opportunities for all center field staff (Johns Hopkins School of Public Health, 2013).

North Dakota State University

North Dakota State University offers a Master's of Public Health with a specialization in American Indian public health. This program prepares graduates to work to improve the health of Native people and reduce health disparities (NDSU, 2013).

Oregon Health & Science University

Oregon Health & Science University offers a Summer Research Training Institute for American Indian/Alaska Native health professionals. This program is designed to meet the needs of professionals currently working in Native health. The training emphasizes research skills and program design and implementation for community health workers, physicians, nurses, researchers, and program managers (OHSU, 2013).

Attracting Undergraduate Native Students

Other examples of pipeline programs aimed at getting undergraduate Native students interested in public health careers include the Diné College Summer Research Enhanced Program in Public Health and Health Research and a program called Launching Native Health Leaders.

Diné College Summer Research Enhanced Program in Public Health

Diné College has a ten-week summer program for freshman and sophomore Native undergraduate students interested in public health research. The goals of this training program are 1) to provide health-related research training and research experiences to Native American students and 2) to provide students with a firm grasp of the health and living concepts embedded in traditional Native American life and how these relate to those taught in western academia (Diné College, 2013). Through this program, Native students develop a multicultural approach to public health in a culturally supportive atmosphere.

Launching Native Health Leader (LNHL)

Over 60 undergraduate students pursuing community service careers were recruited through college and university student service programs to attend health and research conferences. Conference discussions led by tribal community leaders focused on tribal health issues such as tribal wellness, health knowledge, and cancer control. Additionally, students worked with professional and tribal mentors. This program reduced academic isolation of Native students, provided mentoring and empowerment, and developed a pathway to serve Indigenous peoples (Segrest, James, Madrid, & Fernandes, 2010).

Attracting Native Students in High School

A key issue in ensuring a tribal public health workforce is getting students interested in public health professions prior to starting their undergraduate degree. However, many Native students do not see themselves as researchers, scientists, or health professionals or cannot imagine going into careers that require a science background. Three programs that expose Native high school students to careers in public health and health professions are STEP-UP, Hawaii Teen Health Camp, and Diabetes Education for Tribal Schools (DETS).

STEP-UP

STEP-UP is a hands-on summer research experience for high school students from racial/ethnic groups underrepresented in biomedical fields but interested in exploring research careers in the biomedical, behavioral, clinical, and social sciences. Universities offering the STEP-UP program include the University of Hawaii at Manoa, Charles Drew University of Medicine and Science, the University of California-San Francisco, and the University of Nevada Las Vegas (STEP-UP, 2013).

Hawaii Teen Health Camp

Nearly 500 middle and high school students participated in the program run by the John A. Burns School of Medicine (JABSOM). At camp, students learn about different health care professions, local organizations involved in providing health services in their community, and academic preparation for college and post-graduate health professional programs. The goal of this program is to motive high school students to consider a career in the health professions (Dunn, Duques, Shiff, Lau, Malate, & Withy, 2013).

Diabetes Education for Tribal Schools (DETS) K-12

Development of the DETS Health Is Life in Balance K-12 curriculum was a unique collaborative effort between the National Institute of Diabetes and Digestive and Kidney Diseases (NIDDK), the Indian Health Service's Division of Diabetes Treatment and Prevention (IHS/DDTP), the CDC's Native Diabetes Wellness Program (CDC/NDWP), eight tribal colleges and universities (TCUs), and the NIH Office of Science Education (NIH/OSE). The purpose of the DETS curriculum is to 1) increase the understanding of health, diabetes, and maintaining life in balance among American Indian/Alaska Native students (teach about diabetes), 2) increase American Indian/Alaska Native students' understanding and application of scientific and community knowledge (value and use scientific and traditional knowledge), and 3) increase interest in science and health professions among American Indian/Alaska Native youth (encourage science and health careers) (NIDDK, 2013).

Leadership Development

An example of tribal public health leadership development is the Tribal Public Health Summit, which is hosted by the National Indian Health Board.

The summit allows for tribal public health leaders, researchers, professionals, and other stakeholders to discuss successes, challenges, opportunities, and the future of the health of Native people. Participants are given the opportunity to network and develop mentoring relationships with tribal leaders, tribal health directors, medical practitioners, mental health professionals, advocates, epidemiologists, and researchers (National Indian Health Board, 2015). Five areas of focus for the summit workshops include health promotion/disease prevention, workforce development, accreditation and quality improvement, tribal public health law and policy, and behavioral health. Topics discussed during the 2015 summit included tobacco, diabetes and obesity prevention, prescription opiate drug abuse, tribal community health assessment and improvement planning, the basics of public health program evaluation, hepatitis C outbreaks, and the integration of health protection and health promotion. Summits such as this one provide an excellent opportunity for public health professionals and leaders to network and be mentored or mentor others.

One of the goals of Healthy People 2020 is to ensure that tribes have the necessary infrastructure to effectively provide the public health services needed. An improved infrastructure allows tribes to build a capable and qualified public health workforce (Healthy People, 2020, 2013). One way to ensure that the necessary infrastructure is in place is through community capacity building. Community capacity building provides a foundation for building knowledge, skills, and abilities in tribal communities. The tribal workforce benefits greatly when education is combined with skills for building capacity. An example of community capacity building for the tribal public health workforce was the CDC Tribal Support Unit's grant for tribal public health capacity building and quality improvement, awarded in 2013. This grant awarded up to $97,000 per year for five years to six federally recognized tribes. The CDC recognized this:

> Tribal public health infrastructure is strengthened when each tribe, as an independent sovereign government, adopts local strategies to meet its public health challenges. Interventions are tailored to the cultural beliefs and practices of the population, ultimately leading to decreased morbidity and early mortality and improved quality of life.
>
> (CDC, 2013, p. 3)

Through grants such as this, there is an understanding that the tribal public health system must receive culturally appropriate capacity building. In addition, culturally competent integration of information and resources is needed at the various levels of public health as tribal public health professionals often collaborate with these entities. Cultural competencies and knowledge about tribal populations are necessary in local health departments and organization that support county- and city-level public health officials such as the National Association County and City Health Officials

(NACCHO), state health divisions, federal health divisions such as the CDC or the National Institutes of Health, and global health agencies which serve indigenous populations such as the World Health Organization (WHO) and the Pan American Health Organization (PAHO).

Building public health workforce capacity is necessarily a process that engages the community on its own terms, takes advantage of individual skills and collective assets, focuses on issues unique to AI/AN people, and creates effective linkages to other community and mainstream initiatives (McNeely, 1999). An indigenous model must reflect indigenous reality. It must integrate the past, the present, and the people's vision for the future. It must acknowledge resources and challenges and allow communities to build a commitment to identifying and resolving health concerns and issues (Chino & DeBruyn, 2006). Key elements of that process include the need to engage and involve community in the concept and the process of public health.

The tribal workforce needs to engage all facets of public health services in a community to understand the scope of opportunities and responsibilities to prepare and support current and future generations for the public health workforce. The workforce will need to be able to assess the readiness of the current system to adapt to tribal definitions of a healthy community, identify and build essential skills, redefine "credentials," and revisit workforce priorities. Public health readiness will mean identifying what is needed, what works, and what makes sense for Indigenous populations. Information sharing, sharing experiences, and communication pathways will be essential. Tribes do not have the time to re-create the public health infrastructure, nor do they have to. Tribal communities share histories, challenges, and perspectives and can learn from one another and adapt good ideas to the needs of the local community. This implies that there is a process for ensuring that the Indigenous public health workforce can integrate existing knowledge with new knowledge and pass down that knowledge from one generation to the next, raising a new generation of thinkers, scholars, researchers, and practitioners who can envision and promote public health.

WAYS FORWARD—IMPLICATIONS OF THE AFFORDABLE CARE ACT

The Patient Protection and Affordable Care Act of 2010 (ACA) promises new opportunities for building the tribal public health workforce capacity and for expanding successful training and educational initiatives. In addition to insurance reform, the ACA includes health system reforms that include a focus on the public health workforce, including workforce training, strengthening the capacity of the public health infrastructure, and new community-based programming. The Act raises the profile of public health (Blumberg, Buettgens, Feder, & Holahan, 2012), and its prevention and public health fund is the first mandatory funding for public health that includes workforce and infrastructure as one of its major funding goals.

One of the workforce-related entities that has reached out effectively to tribes is the National Public Health Improvement Initiative (NPHII), providing support for health departments to build capacity and improve systems that will improve the delivery and impact of public health services. There is a strong focus on accreditation, quality improvement, and systems change with technical assistance available by national organizations. To date, eight tribal entities have been funded to help support accelerating public health accreditation readiness activities, implementing performance and improvement management practices and systems, and implementing and sharing practice-based evidence (CDC, 2013).

The ACA allows the Health Resources and Services Administration (HRSA) and the U.S. Health and Human Services Department (HHS) to fund the National Public Health Training Centers (PHTC) Network. The purpose of these university-based centers is to deliver public health workforce training to "strengthen the technical, scientific, managerial and leadership competence of current and future public health professionals" (HRSA, 2013, para. 2). Many of the training sessions offered through the PHTCs are available online, through e-learning, or as a CD-ROM. The intent is to make these training sessions accessible to many in the public health workforce, so several of these centers offer free or low-cost public health training for the tribal public health workforce. To make these training sessions a viable alternative for tribal public health professionals, increased technology resources such as computers and Internet must be available in their community.

PHTCs located in states with large tribal populations have helped to bridge the technology gap and bring training directly to tribal communities. An example is the training offered by the California-Nevada Public Health Training Center (CA-NV PHTC). This center, whose faculty includes American Indian public health professionals and faculty with long-standing working relationships with area tribes, has offered a variety of training programs designed specifically for the tribal workforce. Frequently requested training topics include public health fundamentals, grant writing, evaluation, grant management, and leadership. Most have been provided on-site in tribal communities or as workshops at tribal public health conferences to facilitate access by tribal public health workers.

While promising, these initiatives will need to be fully funded if they are to be successful. Because of the dual focus of the ACA, the public health workforce may have to continue to compete with the clinical care workforce for limited funding (Morrissey, 2011).

* * * * *

Building tribal public health workforce capacity goes far beyond the classroom. Training and education needs to be ongoing and comprehensive and build skills at all levels. Communities also need to understand and participate in the process of defining public health services. Any strategy for training and education must engage tribal communities on their own terms, make good use of local skills and assets, and integrate public health into other community initiatives and into mainstream efforts to support community health and well-being. While the capacity of the current workforce needs to be enhanced and strengthened, support is also needed for students to progress through undergraduate and graduate programs and then bring their knowledge and skills to further enhance the tribal public health workforce. Tribal workforce education is a two-way street. Non-tribal public health departments and agencies need to have an understanding of tribal populations, and the tribal workforce needs to know about mainstream strategies, resources, and requirements of local, state, and national public health organizations.

As tribes continue to build their public health capacities and prepare for accreditation through PHAB, it will be important to support tribal interpretations of workforce competencies, define roles and responsibilities in terms of tribal needs and realities, and ensure continuity with non-tribal assessment metrics for accreditation and full participation. Lastly, funding for public health generally and tribal public health specifically is necessary to build and maintain a public health workforce that can be both proactive and responsive to the health needs of Native populations.

REFERENCES

Association of Schools and Programs of Public Health. (2010). *Annual data report.* Retrieved from http://www.asph.org/UserFiles/DataReport2010.pdf

Blumberg, L., Buettgens, M., Feder, J., & Holahan, J. (2012). *Implications of the Affordable Care Act for American business.* Retrieved from Urban Institute website at http://www.urban.org/UploadedPDF/412675-Implications-of-the-Affordable-Care-Act-for-American-Business.pdf

Centers for Disease Control and Prevention (CDC). (2013). State, tribal, local, and territorial public health professionals gateway. *National Public Health Improvement Initiative.* Retrieved from http://www.cdc.gov/stltpublichealth/nphii/

Centers for Disease Control and Prevention (CDC). CDC RFA OT13-1303 (2013a). *Tribal public health capacity building and quality improvement.* Retrieved from http://www.grants.gov/web/grants/view-opportunity.html?oppId=234133

Centers for Disease Control and Prevention (CDC). (2013b). Minority health. *American Indian & Alaska Native Populations.* Retrieved from http://www.cdc.gov/minorityhealth/populations/REMP/aian.html

Chino, M. (2013, November 5). *Building the tribal public health infrastructure through workforce development.* Paper presented at the 141st Annual Meeting of the American Public Health Association. Boston, MA.

Chino M., & DeBruyn, L. (2006). Building true capacity: Indigenous models for indigenous communities. *American Journal of Public Health, 96*(4), 596–599.

Diné College. (2013). *Summer research enhanced program in public health.* Retrieved from http://www.dinecollege.edu/institutes/SREP/srep.php

Dunn, B., Duques, E., Shiff, T., Lau, N., Malate, A., & Withy, K. (2013). Teen health camp Hawai'i: Inspiring Hawai'i's youth to be healthcare leaders of tomorrow. *Hawaii Journal of Medicine and Public Health, 72*(4), 140–142.

Gebbie, K., & Turnock, B. J. (2006). The public health workforce, 2006: New challenges. *Health Affairs, 25*, 923–933. doi:10.1377/hlthaff.25.4.923

Health Resources and Services Administration (HRSA). (2013). *Public health training centers network*. Retrieved from http://bhpr.hrsa.gov/grants/publichealth/trainingcenters/index.html

Healthy People 2020. (2013). *Public health infrastructure*. Retrieved from http://www.healthypeople.gov/2020/topicsobjectives2020/overview.aspx?topicid=35

Henry Kaiser Family Foundation. (2012a). *Medicaid and CHIPS*. Retrieved from http://kff.org/state-category/medicaid-chip/

Henry Kaiser Family Foundation. (2012b). *Medicare spending per enrollee by state*. Retrieved from http://kff.org/medicare/state-indicator/per-enrollee-spending-by-residence/

Institute of Medicine. (1988). *The future of public health*. Washington, DC: The National Academies Press.

Johns Hopkins School of Public Health. (2013). *Center for American Indian Health training and scholarship program*. Retrieved from http://www.jhsph.edu/research/centers-and-institutes/center-for-american-indian-health/Programs/Training%20Folder/training.html

Kurland, J. (2000). Public health in the new millennium III: Global health and the economy. *Public Health Report, 115*, 398–401.

McNeely, J. (1999). Community building. *Journal of Community Psychology, 27*, 741–750.

Morris, T. L., & Meinrath, S. D. (2009). *New media, technology and internet use in Indian country: Quantitative and qualitative analyses*. Native Public Media and New America Foundation. Retrieved from www.newamerica.net

Morrissey, T. (2011). *The Affordable Care Act's public health workforce provisions: Opportunities and challenges*. Retrieved from the American Public Health Association website at http://www.apha.org/NR/rdonlyres/461D56BE-4A46-4C9F-9BA4-9535FE370DB7/0/APHAWorkforce2011_updated.pdf

National Congress of American Indians. (2013). *FY2014 Indian country budget request*. Retrieved from http://www.ncai.org/resources/ncai-publications/indian-country-budget-request/fy2014/07_NCAI_2014_Budget_Request_Health.pdf

National Indian Health Board. (2010). *2010 Tribal public health profile. Exploring public health capacity in Indian country*. Retrieved from http://www.nihb.org/docs/07012010/NIHB_HealthProfile%202010.pdf

National Indian Health Board. (2015). *2015 Tribal public health summit*. Retrieved from http://www.nihb.org/communications/phs_2015.ph

National Native American AIDS Prevention Center (NNAAPC). (2002). *Working with Native Americans living with HIV*. Retrieved from http://www.ihs.gov/hivaids/docs/Cliniciansguide.pdf

North Dakota State University. (2013). *Masters of public health*. Retrieved from http://www.ndsu.edu/publichealth/

Oregon Health & Science University (2013). *Summer research training institute for American Indian/Alaska Native health professionals*. Retrieved from http://www.ohsu.edu/xd/education/schools/school-of-medicine/departments/clinical-departments/public-health/education-programs/summer-research-training.cfm

Pew Charitable Trust. (2013). *Managing prisoner healthcare spending*. Retrieved from http://www.pewstates.org/uploadedFiles/PCS_Assets/2013/SHCS_Pew-Managing_Prison_Health_Care_Spending_Report.pdf

Public Health Accreditation Board (PHAB). (2011, May). *2011 standards: An overview*. Retrieved from http://www.phaboard.org/wp-content/uploads/PHAB-Standards-Overview-Version-1.0.pdf

Public Health Foundation. (2010). *Core competencies for public health professionals*. Retrieved from http://www.phf.org/resourcestools/Pages/Core_Public_Health_Competencies.aspx

Public Health Foundation. (2012). *3-Step competency prioritization sequence*. Retrieved from http://www.phf.org/resourcestools/Pages/3Step_Competency_ Prioritization_Sequence.aspx

Russell, G. (2004) *American Indian facts of life: A profile of today's population, tribes and reservations*. Phoenix, AZ: Native Data Network.

Segrest, V., James, R., Madrid, T., & Fernandes, R. (2010). Launching native health leaders: Students as community campus ambassadors. *Progress in Community Health Partnership*, 4(1), 81–86.

STEP-UP. (2013). *High school program*. Retrieved from https://stepup.niddk.nih.gov/hs.aspx

Trust for America's Health. (2008). *Blueprint for a healthier America: Modernizing the federal public health system to focus on prevention and preparedness*. Retrieved from http://healthyamericans.org/assets/files/Blueprint.pdf

U.S. Census. (2002). *United States census 2000*. Retrieved from http://www.census.gov/census2000/states/us.html

U.S. Commission on Civil Rights. (2003). *A quiet crisis. Federal funding and unmet needs in Indian country*. Retrieved from http://www.usccr.gov/pubs/na0703/na0204.pdf

U.S. Department of Education. (2005). *Status and trends in the education of American Indians and Alaska Natives*. Retrieved from http://nces.ed.gov/pubs2005/2005108.pdf

Winslow, C. E. (1920). The untitled fields of public health. *Science*, 51(1306), 23–33.

Zaback, T., Becker, T., Dignan, M., & Lambert, W. (2010). A program evaluation of a summer research training institute for American Indian and Alaska Native health professionals. *American Indian Culture and Research Journal*, 34(3), 93–106.

Conclusion

Carsten Schmidtke

Workforce education, economic development, and sovereignty have been shown to be closely linked with one another. None can exist without the others. Economic development without sovereignty will likely benefit only the mainstream economic system and be a potential threat to cultural and community survival; sovereignty without economic development may lead to Native people's being mired in paraeconomic survival. The tiebreaker, as it were, is workforce education. Only an educated and skilled workforce can attract businesses to tribal communities or make it possible for Native people to create strong reservation and community economies that can achieve maximum independence from federal, state, and tribal governments and from the influences of off-reservation, non-Native businesses.

At the same time, workforce education is no panacea. As the chapters in this book outline, the challenges are quite formidable. One of the major challenges is the realization that despite its focus on workplace skill development, workforce education is not value-neutral. The trauma of the boarding school experience in particular and of white-Indian relations in general is always present, even when skills training is being discussed. Workforce education professionals must always be keenly aware of skepticism resulting from the sometimes open, sometimes hidden agenda of past attempts to train Native people for jobs. Overcoming fears that the next program will once again be a thinly veiled attempt at assimilation and cultural destruction is crucial, as is having clear evidence that training will not just turn Native people into semi-skilled labor that can easily be exploited but make them truly competitive in the job market.

Furthermore, considering the fact that at present and likely for the foreseeable future, Native trainees will be taught by non-Native, mostly white, instructors will make it necessary for such instructors to be aware of the betrayals, broken promises, and attempts at cultural and physical genocide that characterize the history of Indian-white relations. Not acknowledging the pertinence of past events will only foster suspicions that current programs are just so much more of the same and lead to reluctance to participate in job training if not outright rejection of such programs. Cultural integrity and survival in un- or underemployment may strike many as preferable to employment at the cost of giving up one's culture and identity. The lesson then is that no matter how qualified a program designer or developer, it is crucial that tribal community members be closely involved in program development and implementation. As stated above, in a relationship that has experienced so many breaches of faith, even job skills are not neutral. Instead, they must be placed within a culturally appropriate framework and be related not only to individual advancement but also to community, reservation, and tribal development. Considering the overall collectivist orientation of most American Indian cultures, building a workforce training program on mainstream values and goals is unlikely to find support and success.

This awareness has to be present at the very beginning of the career journey, that is, in the career development path. Showing Native students that career planning and choice can indeed have positive influences on their communities and families is crucial; why expend time and effort on something that is likely to benefit mostly outsiders? Here, too, communities and families have to be part of the process, not just as passive observers but as active participants with a real voice in the career choices of their young people and the design of programs that can teach the needed job skills. One approach to workforce training has been to bring tribal colleges into the process of economic development. Considering that tribal colleges are Native-controlled institutions, their administrators can take advantage of their unique situation and take on a leading role in economic development. Rather than focusing most of their energy on being transfer institutions, these colleges have explored and should continue to explore how they can help their communities become economically stronger and more independent.

In addition, the unique situations of many communities, be they urban or on remote reservations, must be considered. If program developers and administrators are serious about cultural sensitivity in program design, then issues such as transportation, child care, financial support, and others must be considered. For example, as shown in the chapters here, many Native people are reluctant to engage in workforce training if such training or the subsequent job will take them away from their home communities, however remote each community may be. Matters such as local training centers and local economic development are crucial to a successful training program. The same applies to family and community support. In addition to providing tuition assistance for a student or trainee, the fact that a Native person may have responsibilities toward other family members must be considered in offers of financial support. Once again, a holistic approach is warranted that looks not only at the educational needs of the trainee but also at family and community benefits and needs and takes the trainees' cultural context into account.

This volume is the first of its kind that examines contemporary workforce education for American Indians. As a result, instead of getting into specifics on how to design, implement, and administer workforce programs, the authors have had to grapple with fundamental issues, particularly how to overcome legacies of the past and how to make sure that even though the issue is workplace skills, cultural issues are accorded their appropriate emphasis. We hope that this volume will serve as a springboard from which specific workforce education and training initiatives may be discussed as an integral part of building and maintaining tribal sovereignty rather than looking at them through the lens of old stereotypes and as a vestige of nefarious past initiatives.

Contributors

G. S. Briscoe (Comanche) is executive director of Suahbetainu Kahni, a non-profit organization. His academic preparation was completed at Oklahoma State University in Business Administration. Mr. Briscoe has over 20 years' experience providing technical assistance to tribes and individuals throughout Indian Country. He has held various administrative positions in national corporations and in post-secondary institutions.

Michelle Chino is an American Indian researcher and Professor Emeritus of Public Health at the University of Nevada Las Vegas. Dr. Chino has dedicated her career to promoting health and social justice for American Indians and other underserved populations. Her work focuses on building community capacity to address the social determinants of health, particularly issues that cross health and justice paradigms such as environmental justice and violence prevention. Her research explores new ways of thinking about achieving health equity such as employing a complex adaptive systems approach to better understand disparity and health problem solving. Dr. Chino's research has earned her national and international recognition with multiple prestigious research grants from the National Institutes of Health and other federal granting agencies. At UNLV, Dr. Chino's dedication to teaching, mentorship, and service has earned her a tenured professorship and multiple awards from the School of Community Health Sciences.

Amy Fann is Assistant Professor in Counseling and Higher Education at the University of North Texas, Denton, Texas. She completed her degree at The University of California, Los Angeles. Her research focuses on post-secondary access for underrepresented students with an emphasis on American Indian communities. This work includes looking at the complex nexus of barriers to college and the role of higher education in advancing economic development and self-determination.

John A. Goodwin is a Ph.D. Candidate in History at Arizona State University. He is trained in American history with specializations in Native

American history and comparative colonialism. His research interests center on American Indian education and activism, especially in the 20th century. He was recently awarded the Valeen T. Avery Award from the Arizona Historical Society for his presentation of the paper "Walking in Beauty: Navajo Community College as a Protected Space for Modern American Indian Identity" at the 2014 Arizona History Convention. He is currently researching the intellectual origins, antecedents, and development of 20th-century tribal colleges.

Charlotte Leforestier is an independent researcher from France. In 2012, she defended her doctoral dissertation in which she offered a comparative study of the boarding school system in the United States and Canada. She teaches English as a Second Language for law students. Her field of research now includes American Indian and First Nations education, identity, and legal issues.

E. Anne Marshall is Professor of Counselling Psychology in Educational Psychology and Leadership Studies (Faculty of Education) and Director of the Centre for Youth & Society at the University of Victoria, Canada. She is the co-developer of the Indigenous Communities Counselling Psychology graduate program, the first of its kind in Canada. Dr. Marshall's community-engaged research focuses on youth well-being, transitions, and mental health in cultural and community contexts. Much of her work involves Indigenous communities and marginalized youth. She is the co-author of *Knowledge translation in context. Indigenous, policy, and community settings* (2011), published by the University of Toronto Press.

Delilah F. O'Haynes is Professor of English at Concord University, Athens, West Virginia, where she has taught composition, world literature, creative writing, and women's and minority literature, including American Indian literature, since 1992. She is also the author of several books. Her American Indian heritage is from five woodland Iroquois and Algonquin tribes.

Jennifer Pharr is Assistant Professor in the School of Community Health Sciences' Environmental and Occupational Health Department at the University of Nevada, Las Vegas. Her research interests include barriers that impede healthy behaviors such as preventive care and disease prevention, interventions to reduce social and personal barriers to health behaviors, and the use of social marketing to promote health. She is currently researching barriers to preventing mother-to-child transmission (MTCT) of HIV, interventions to reduce MTCT of HIV, and barriers to HIV testing and retention in care for gay, lesbian and transgender young adults. Dr. Pharr was the principal investigator for the Nevada sector of the California-Nevada Public Health Training center 2013–2014.

Jon Reyhner is Professor of Education at Northern Arizona University. He previously taught at Montana State University-Billings, and before that, he taught junior high school for four years in the Navajo Nation and was a school administrator for ten years in Indian schools in Arizona, Montana, and New Mexico. He has written extensively on American Indian education and Indigenous language revitalization, including co-authoring *Language and Literacy Teaching for Indigenous Education* and *American Indian Education: A History*. He has also edited a column on issues in Indigenous education for the magazine of the National Association for Bilingual Education for over two decades. He currently maintains an American Indian Education website at http://nau.edu/aie with links to full text online copies of his co-edited books published by Northern Arizona University. The University of Oklahoma Press in 2015 published his newest edited book, *Teaching Indigenous Students: Honoring Place, Community, and Culture.*

Charles T. Saunders is chair of the Forensics and Information Systems Auditing program at Franklin University, Columbus, Ohio. He also teaches in the Master's program in Business Psychology. Saunders earned his B.A. from Wittenberg University (1971) and his MBA (1987), M.A. (2006), and Ph.D. (2011) in Workforce Development and Education from The Ohio State University. He has over 50 years of workforce experience in corporate business, the military, and academia.

Carsten Schmidtke is Assistant Professor of Human Resource and Workforce Development at the University of Arkansas, Fayetteville. His research involves the retention of American Indian students in post-secondary workforce programs, workforce access for Marshallese students, and the theoretical and philosophical foundations of workforce education.

Payden Spowart is a graduate of the Counselling Psychology program in the Department of Educational Psychology and Leadership Studies (Faculty of Education) at the University of Victoria, Canada. In Victoria, he worked at Aboriginal Child and Youth Mental Health for the British Columbia Government, and delivered outreach mental health treatment to on- and off-reserve Indigenous families living on Southern Vancouver Island. Currently, he works at a private practice in Calgary, where he continues support Indigenous families.

Linda Sue Warner (Comanche) is Special Assistant to the President on Tribal Affairs at Northeastern Oklahoma A&M College in Miami, Oklahoma. She completed her Ph.D. in general administration with an emphasis in personnel from the University of Oklahoma. Dr. Warner has over 40 years' experience working with American Indian tribal communities and higher education.

Name Index

Alexie, Sherman 15, 28
Archambault, Dave 9

Beatty, Willard 25, 47
Bordeaux, Lionel 85
Brewer, Brian V. 133
Burns, Mike 19
Bush, George W. 6

Columbus, Christopher 120–1
Cortés, Hernan 121
Crane, Leo 21
Custer, George Armstrong 124

Dagenett, Charles 23
Dewey, John 25

Eastman, Charles 2

Forbes, Jack 82
Fredenberg, Ralph 118
Freire, Paulo 16, 17

Graham, Joe L. 50
Grinnell, George Bird 21

Horne, Esther Burnett 24

Johnson, Lyndon B. 82

Kopta, Anne Phelps 23

Leupp, Francis 15
Lummis, Charles F. 21

Mankiller, Wilma 96, 111
Meriam, Lewis 24
Montgomery, Edward 6
Montezuma 121
Morgan, T.J. 21

Obama, Barack 6, 28, 116, 133, 134
Orata, Pedro A. 16, 28

Platero, Dillon 80
Pratt, Richard Henry 19, 40

Red Jacket 123
Reel, Estelle 20
Roessel, Robert Jr. 81
Roosevelt, Franklin D. 24

Sanchez, Lorenda T. 6
Standing Bear, Luther 3

Tax, Sol 80
Thomas, Elmer 118

Vizenor, Gerald 1, 2, 10

Wesley, Clarence 79

Topical Index

academic 42, 45, 50, 57, 165, 175, 194; academic achievement 111; academic aspirations 173, 178; academic attainment 50; academic career 175; academic challenges 175; academic courses 62, 68; academic curriculum 17, 19; academic education/ training 16, 28, 29, 47, 56, 57; academic enrollment 63; academic expectations 17; academic experiences 166, 175; academic institution 182; academic instruction 99; academic knowledge 154; academic performance 15, 96; academic preparation 45, 168, 195; academic programs 19, 27, 63, 64, 103, 178, 192; academic pursuits 174, 178, 193; academic services 46; academic skills 6, 57; academic study 48; academic success 111, 141, 148
academics 17, 19
accreditation 42, 43, 44, 85, 185, 186, 196, 198, 199
acculturation 41, 49, 76, 126, 140, 147, 148–9, 150, 155
adult education 76, 84
Adult Vocational Training program (AVT) 4, 5
alienation 82, 99, 128, 166
American Indian College Fund 45, 63, 65, 118
(American) Indian communities 5, 56, 59, 65, 74, 77, 78, 80, 82, 87, 92, 105, 106
American Indian Higher Education Consortium (AIHEC) 44, 62, 68, 83, 86

American Indian Movement (AIM) 27, 61, 78
American Indian Opportunities Industrialization Center 9, 120
"apple" 28
apprenticeship 4, 8, 64
aptitude 65, 143, 146
assessment 3, 4, 7, 8, 45, 79, 97, 99, 103, 148, 150, 151, 153, 167, 182, 186, 188, 196, 199
assimilation 19, 21, 26, 36, 40, 41, 55, 56, 57, 59, 60, 66–9, 70, 107, 109, 140, 141, 168, 202
Associate degree(s) 64, 87, 101

bachelor's degree 33, 37, 48, 64, 163, 193
barrier 28, 38, 42, 46, 49, 52, 140, 142–7, 148, 154, 155, 159, 165, 166–7, 168, 169, 172, 173, 174
basic skills 83
Bay Mills Community College 67, 85
Blackfeet Community College 98
boarding school 19, 21, 22, 23, 24, 26, 40, 47, 55, 57–60, 61, 65, 66, 69, 70, 162, 202; boarding school system 60, 61, 62, 68, 69, 70
Brown vs. Board of Education 26
Bureau of Indian Affairs (BIA) 5, 7, 26, 41, 47, 48, 108, 117
Bureau of Indian Education (BIE) 28, 98, 117, 133, 134

California Indian Manpower Consortium 9
capacity building 111, 196
career 32, 33, 51, 77, 139, 145, 146, 153, 156, 160, 161, 164; career actions 163,

212 Topical Index

career and technical education 47, 57, 144; career assessment 10, 143, 161
career barrier 154; career challenges 165; career choice 141, 142, 143, 144, 145, 146, 147, 150, 153, 154, 164, 171, 203; career counseling 10, 11, 141, 142, 150, 153, 154, 162; career counselor 90, 140, 164, 171; career decisions 140, 143, 146, 152; career desires 151; career expectations 167; career goal 149, 165; career guidance 139, 141, 144; career guidance counseling 144; career guidance counselor 139, 141; career knowledge 148; career maturity 140, 142, 143, 144, 145, 146, 147, 148, 149, 150, 154, 155, 156; career myth 146, 154; career opportunities 90, 116, 154, 166; career options 148, 154; career path(way) 11, 142, 145, 146, 152, 153, 154, 165, 166, 182; career plan(ning) 146, 148, 150, 163, 164, 203; career possibilities 165; career services 155; career skills 56; career success 152, 154; career transition 164
career development 11, 49, 139, 140, 142, 144, 145, 146, 149, 150, 151, 152, 153, 155, 159, 160, 161, 163, 164, 165, 186; career development counseling 139, 142, 155; career development materials 144; career development models 155; career development plan 145; career development path 151, 203; career development practice 176, 178; career development process 140, 148, 149, 153, 154; career development theories 142–3, 150, 151, 155, 162
Carl D. Perkins Vocational Education Act 57
Carlisle Indian Industrial School 19, 23, 40
certificate 64, 87, 89, 102, 170
certification 169, 190
Cherokee (Nation) 8, 36, 81, 124
child labor 19
Chilocco Indian School 22, 23

Civil Rights Movement 26, 55
collectivist 150, 152, 159, 203
Colonial Era 40–1
colonialism 172
colonization 105, 162
Commissioner of Indian Affairs 15, 21, 23, 57, 66, 125
Common Core 28
community 2, 3, 4, 10, 17, 19, 25, 26, 32, 33, 42, 44, 46, 50, 51, 52, 55, 59, 64, 65, 66, 68, 74, 75, 77, 79, 82, 83, 84, 86, 87, 88, 91, 92, 96, 140, 144, 146, 150, 151, 152, 154, 161, 164, 167, 168, 176, 177, 181, 183, 197, 203; Community Action Program (CAP) 82; community capacity 187, 189–92, 196; community college 46, 48, 50, 77, 98, 104, 105; community development 1, 75; community education 33; community expectations 162; community health 51, 182, 183, 186, 194, 196, 199; community member 51, 68, 100, 146, 150, 152, 153, 203; community membership 152, 164, 171; community needs 146; community programming 177
community service programs 44; community specific training 155; community support 77, 148, 166, 178, 203
competency 43, 48, 49, 186, 188, 189, 192, 196
completion (educational) 46, 87, 90, 99, 100, 102–3, 164, 173, 174, 175, 177–8
completion rate 175
Comprehensive Employment and Training Act 4
constructivist 98, 102, 103, 104
contextual action theory 151
continuing education 64, 190
core competencies 186
corporate trainer 116, 120
counseling 45, 64, 68, 84, 108, 171
credential 37, 168, 190, 197
cultural bias 149; cultural competence 188, 196; cultural differences 26, 126, 149, 152, 155, 167, 172; Cultural Formulation Approach 150; cultural identity 46, 83, 127, 131, 134, 141,

Topical Index 213

149, 150; cultural integrity 111, 202; cultural orientation 140, 149; cultural pluralism 60, 69; cultural preservation 65, 96, 106; cultural relevance 91; cultural renewal 75; cultural sensitivity 26, 203; cultural specificity 150, 155; cultural survival 51, 202; cultural traditions 67, 84, 98
culture-specific training 155, 156
curriculum 15, 16, 18, 19, 21, 25, 28, 41, 44, 46, 51, 64, 65, 66, 67, 74, 78, 82, 83, 84, 97, 98, 99, 100, 101, 102, 103, 104, 105, 110, 143; curriculum development 102, 104
curriculum materials 18, 49

Dawes Act 57
day school 25, 40, 61
degree completion 87, 102
desegregation 26
detribalization 66–9
Diné College 62, 99, 194
Direct Employment program (DE) 5
discordant education 39
discrimination 17, 52, 124, 143, 150, 153, 162, 166, 167, 171, 172
Division of Indian and Native American Programs (DINAP) 5, 6
Division of Workforce Development, BIA 7
dominant culture 120, 123, 124, 125, 126, 129, 130, 146, 149; dominant economic system 2; dominant society 39, 125, 126, 133, 141, 145, 146, 149, 150
dropout 27, 148, 149; dropout rate 5, 26, 27, 65, 81, 82, 85, 86, 89, 96, 132, 141

economic base 119; economic development 1, 7, 9, 10, 11, 26, 43, 49, 51, 70, 80, 96, 100, 104, 109, 111, 202, 203; economic survival 51; economic system 2, 88, 92, 202
Education Amendments of 1978 41
educational achievement 81, 141, 154, 164; educational attainment 32, 111, 159, 162,167, 185; educational opportunity/-ies 43, 62, 131, 132, 167, 184, 192; educational program(s) 24, 33, 67, 111, 126, 132, 133; educational services 41; education(al) system 56, 60, 62, 70, 82, 107, 166, 172
e-learning 190, 198
employability 8; employability skills 144
employment 4, 5, 6, 7, 8, 10, 29, 38, 43, 47, 49, 50, 51, 57, 64, 87, 99, 100, 109, 133, 144, 145, 159, 163, 164, 167, 168, 169–70, 171, 172, 174, 176, 177, 183, 203
employment expectations 165; employment experiences 165, 173; employment opportunities 48, 49, 50, 120, 132, 144, 174, 177; employment options 173, 190
employment outcomes 166; employment rate 4, 9, 88, 162, 163; employment search skills 177; employment services 6, 7, 9; employment success 159, 166, 174
employment support 177
empowerment 141, 153, 194
entrepreneurial skills 6
entrepreneurship 4, 8, 64
equal opportunity 7
ethnocentric 18, 146
ethnocentrism 49, 143

Family Education Model 77, 90, 91
family encouragement 164; family influence 152, 166; family networks 90; family support 77, 90, 148, 152, 166, 173, 203
Federal Era 40, 41
federal (U.S.) government 2, 4, 23, 24, 25, 26, 41, 47, 57, 61, 78, 82, 105, 107, 100, 116, 119, 126, 128, 183, 202
Federal Reserve Bank 9
Fond du Lac Tribal and Community College 68
formal education 47, 76, 96, 99, 105, 108, 109, 173; formal training 81, 182
"fundamental education" 17, 25
funding 5, 6, 7, 19, 26, 28, 42–4, 57–8, 63, 65–6, 69, 75, 77, 83, 85, 90–1, 116, 117, 129, 132, 133, 135, 155, 166–7, 168, 174, 177, 178, 183, 190, 191–2, 197, 198,

214 Topical Index

199; funding stream 5, 6, 174, 190; government funding 129, 192; grant funding 42, 190

geographic location 42, 167, 171, 173; geographic isolation 9, 38, 105, 190
globalization 46
graduation rate 45, 81, 86, 90, 141, 168
guidance counselor 26, 139, 140, 141, 142

Hampton Normal and Industrial Institute 56
Harvard Project 133, 135; Harvard University 38, 40
Haskell Institute/Indian Nations University 16, 23, 24, 26, 62, 69
healthcare 26, 33, 38, 64, 80, 109, 117, 182, 183, 184, 185, 187, 191
higher education 33, 34, 40, 42, 45, 51, 62, 63, 65, 66, 69, 74, 76, 78, 82, 83, 87, 88, 89, 96, 97, 98, 99, 104, 106, 109, 133, 134, 147; higher education institutions 69, 99, 104; higher education issues 107, 108; Higher Education Opportunity Act 99
higher education program 108, 111
high school diploma 37, 163; high school education 169; high school graduates 27, 164, 165, 190; high school graduation rate 141, 168
holistic approach 68, 77, 203; holistic understanding 85, 98; holistic worldview 167
home community/-ies 17, 86, 88, 90, 152, 164, 166, 167, 170, 171, 173, 177, 203
Hopi 4, 21
human capital 32, 100

Indian agent 19, 21, 22; Indian Employment, Training, and Related Services Demonstration Act 5; Indian Civilian Conservation Corps 48; Indian Country 2, 4, 5, 8, 74, 97, 100, 108, 109, 122, 183, 191, 193; Indian Education Act 41, 55, 61; Indian Health Care Improvement Act (IHCIA) 183; Indian Health Service 88, 187, 190, 191; Indian Manpower Program 4; Indian New Deal 24–5, 117; Indian Reorganization Act 41, 117, 118; Indian School Service 59; Indian Self-Determination and Assistance Act 41, 55, 62, 117, 119, 129, 183; Indian Welfare-to-Work Act (INA WtW) 5
indigenous communities 98, 107; indigenous cultures 17, 18, 116, 126; indigenous people(s) 18, 34, 39, 70, 76, 106, 107, 128, 130, 132, 133, 134, 135, 171, 194;indigenous population 15, 34, 35, 36, 197,
Industrial Revolution 56; industrial school 18, 19; industrial training 22, 56, 57
Inter Tribal Council of Arizona (ITAC) 8
internship 43, 171, 193
involuntary minorities 27

job counselors 177; job opportunities 27, 116, 129, 132, 134, 177; job requirements 167; job shadowing 148; job skills 56, 99, 203; job training 3, 49, 144, 202

Ketchikan Indian Community 8
knowledge economy 109
knowledge, skills, and abilities 97

labor 119; labor demands 87; labor force 56, 134, 135, 167; labor market 144, 166
Lakota 67
lifelong learning 102, 103
Little Big Horn College 87
Little Priest Tribal College 86
Little Wound School 17

mainstream 24, 35, 56, 75, 76, 78, 82, 83, 89, 92, 104, 109, 183, 189, 192, 197, 199
mainstream American culture 109; mainstream American society 57, 60, 125; mainstream college 100; mainstream community

Topical Index 215

186; mainstream culture 141, 146, 148; mainstream curriculum 103; mainstream economy 109, 202; mainstream education 99, 166, 167; mainstream educational institution 41, 50, 106, 108; mainstream higher education 96, 99; mainstream post-secondary institutions 66, 111; mainstream post-secondary learning 168; mainstream society 57, 65, 105; mainstream universities 26; mainstream values 146, 203
manual labor 17, 21, 170; manual training 56
marginalization 46, 162
meaning of work 163
mentor(ing) 42, 167, 190, 194, 196
Meriam Report 24
military school 21
minority 33, 43, 91, 97, 140, 142, 143; minority group 15, 140, 141; minority students 17, 29, 97, 140, 142, 147
Morrill Act 41, 56

National Aeronautics and Space Administration (NASA) 64, 101; National Center for American Indian Enterprise Development (NCAIED) 7–8; National Congress of American Indians (NCAI) 1, 2, 4; National Council for Workforce Education 77; National Indian Education Association (NIEA) 11, 15; National Indian Health Board (NIHB) 187, 195; National Indian and Native American Employment and Training Conference (NINAETC) 1, 7; National Indian Youth Council (NIYC) 80
Native Adult Education and Literacy Act 91; Native American Employment and Training Council (NAETC) 5–6; Native American Enterprise Initiative 8; Native American-Serving Non-Tribal Institution (NASNTI) 11, 96, 97, 99, 101–104

Native communities 74–5, 77, 79, 80, 85, 86, 87, 89, 91, 92, 99, 167, 171, 176, 187; Native Employment Works (NEW) 5, 8; Native language(s) 18, 51, 61, 65, 66, 87; Native Nations Institute 133–4; Native ways of knowing 97–9, 100, 101, 102–4, 109, 111
Navajo 4, 25, 27, 37, 67, 76, 80, 81, 82, 84, 85, 164; Navajo Nation 8, 164, 165; Navajo Community College 26, 62, 83–5; Navajo Community College Act 41
Nicolet College 9
Nineteen Tribal Nations Workforce Investment Board (NTNWIB) 8–9
No Child Left Behind (NCLB) 15, 28
NORSE model 102–104
Northeastern Oklahoma A&M College 101–4
North Dakota Department of Commerce 9
North Carolina Commission of Indian Affairs 9
Northwestern Indian College 67

occupation(s) 8, 9, 29, 40, 100, 142, 150, 153, 154
occupational skills 6, 8, 57
Office of Economic Opportunity (OEO) 82
Office of Indian Affairs 16, 20, 23, 24, 25
Oglala 64, 81, 84, 122, 133; Oglala Lakota College 62, 64, 84, 88
Ojibwe 37, 67, 127
Omnibus Indian Advancement Act 5
online 97, 98, 101, 103, 104, 154, 190, 198
on-the-job training 7, 8, 42
opportunities 7, 8, 15, 27, 28, 29, 42, 43, 50, 51, 62, 63, 74, 82, 88, 97, 102, 103, 104, 109, 111, 131, 132, 134, 143, 148, 166, 167, 172, 173, 174, 177, 184, 185, 192, 196, 197

pan-Indian identity 60, 61, 69
pan-indianism 10, 55, 60–2, 67, 68, 69
pan-indigenous 70

paraeconomic 1, 2; paraeconomic survival 1, 2, 4, 9, 10, 202; paraeconomic survivors 1, 10
Peace Corps 64
Phoenix Indian School 23
Pine Ridge Reservation 17, 64, 131, 133
place-based education 28, 102–104, 109
post-secondary curricula 101; post-secondary degree 102, 166, 174, 177; post-secondary education 42, 43, 51, 65, 100, 106, 109, 163, 164, 165, 166, 167–8, 173–4, 175, 178; post-secondary institution(s) 62, 66, 97, 99, 105, 111, 146
poverty 4, 15, 16, 28, 38, 43, 49, 50, 51, 52, 65, 79, 80, 81, 82, 87, 88, 106, 126, 130–133, 135, 146
practical skills 19
prejudice 19, 25, 38, 51, 116, 124, 126, 134, 135, 144, 145, 153
prevocational education 26
private sector 7, 43, 46, 132
Procurement Technical Assistance Center (PTAC) 8
professional development 8, 103, 148, 155, 193; professional education 47; professional and technical expertise 99
program design 194, 203; program development 11, 108, 203
progressive 3, 8, 25, 41; *Progressive Education Association* 25
psychology of working 162
public health worker 182, 188, 198; public health workforce 11, 181–7, 190, 192, 193, 194, 196, 197–9
public sector 132

Race to the Top 28
racism 49, 99, 143, 145, 153, 162, 167, 172
racist 17, 18
real-life/-world application 43, 102; real-world experience 48
relational theory 160–1
relocation 4, 25, 26, 41
reservation 10, 15, 18, 25, 40, 41, 42, 47, 48, 51, 52, 57, 58, 64, 65, 66, 68, 76, 78, 82, 83, 86, 87, 88, 100, 101, 105, 106, 108, 116–17, 119, 126–8, 129, 131, 141, 143, 144, 146, 148, 152, 166, 186, 187, 202, 203; reservation business 3; reservation community/-ies 8, 67, 76, 82, 104; reservation life 15, 126, 127, 131; reservation system 125
Reserve 159, 162, 164, 167, 173, 177
residential school 69, 162, 166, 168, 171
retention (student) 42, 45, 46, 75, 77, 84, 87, 89, 90, 99, 102–3, 109, 178, 190; retention rate 50, 65, 77, 81, 89, 96
retribalization 10, 55, 66–9, 70
role model(s) 43, 143, 144, 154, 166, 167, 168
Rosebud Reservation 132
Rough Rock Demonstration School 26, 82

(career) salience 140, 142, 144, 145, 146, 147, 148, 149, 150, 151, 152, 154, 155, 156
Salish Kootenai College 26, 64, 86, 88
savage (s) 18, 19, 35, 122, 123, 150,
Section 166 of the Workforce Investment Act 5, 6, 8
self-actualization 33, 78
self-determination 5, 24, 36, 41, 60, 62, 66–9, 70, 75–9, 82, 84–88, 91, 92, 96, 98, 99, 105, 109, 118, 120, 125, 129, 133, 162, 189; Self-Determination Era 40–1, 42
self-efficacy 145, 146
self-employment 6
self-sufficiency 6, 8, 9, 76, 111
service learning 148
Sherman Institute 22, 25
Sinte Gleska University 62, 83, 84, 85
Sisseton-Wahpeton Community College 86
skill 49; skill domain 186, 188–9; skill level 100, 187, 188; skill requirements 187; skill set 88
skilled workforce 6, 100, 181, 190, 202
skills 2, 3, 4, 5, 6, 8, 9, 10, 19, 24, 27, 41, 63, 64, 81, 97, 134, 140, 143, 146, 150, 154, 164, 169, 170, 177, 182, 186, 188, 189,

Topical Index 217

192, 196, 197, 198, 199; skills assessment 8; skills development 2, 202; skills-employability paradigm 3; skills training 6, 9, 202
Snyder Act 183
social cognitive career theory 153
social connection 162
social-constructionist 151, 159, 161, 178
soft skills 9
Southern California Indian Center (SCIC) 10
Southwestern Indian Polytechnic Institute (SIPI) 26, 62, 100
sovereignty 2, 3, 4, 7, 10, 11, 27, 41, 52, 62, 63, 76, 96, 100, 104–6, 109, 110, 111, 117, 119, 140, 183, 189, 202, 204
Special Senate Subcommittee on Indian Education 25
Standing Rock Community College 84, 86
State of Washington Workforce Board 9
STEM (science, technology, engineering, mathematics) 28, 64
stereotype 1, 19, 28, 38, 83, 116, 120, 124, 130, 135, 143, 150, 167, 204
Supreme Court 26
survival 2, 35, 51, 62, 70, 141, 153, 162, 170, 202; survival school 27

Talking Leaves Job Corps 8
Tea Party 28
technical education 56, 57; technical skills 4, 177; technical training 8
technology 8, 46, 56, 101, 109, 182, 184, 190, 198
termination 25, 26, 41
trade(s) 4, 22, 40, 57, 58, 165, 177; trade school 47, 168
traditional culture(s) 25, 27, 98, 126, 168; traditional knowledge 60, 163, 167, 195; traditional skills 41; traditional tribal education 99, 105, 106; traditional values 5, 85, 86
training 2, 4, 6, 7, 49, 50, 51, 56, 87, 100, 120, 134, 147, 164, 165, 169, 170, 174, 184, 187, 188, 189, 190, 198, 202; training needs 186, 188; training opportunities 8, 101, 162, 185, 190; training plan 186; training program 4, 6, 7, 9, 23, 24, 43, 99, 194, 198, 203; training session 198
tribal business 8, 192
tribal college(s) 9, 26, 33, 43, 50, 51, 55, 62–6, 67–9, 100, 190, 193, 203; Tribal College Act 44; Tribal College and University (TCU) 32–3, 42, 44, 50, 52, 62, 74–5, 77, 79–85, 85–8, 96, 98, 99; Tribal College Consortium for DevelopingMontana and North Dakota Workforce (TCC DeMaND Workforce) 9, 10
tribal college movement 74–5, 86
tribal community 7, 10, 50, 74, 92, 98, 99, 105, 109, 111, 166, 183, 186, 187, 190, 191, 192, 193, 197, 198, 202; Tribal Community College 51; Tribal community member 203
tribal critical race theory (TribalCrit) 106–7; tribal culture 99, 111, 126, 149; tribal development 66, 99, 105, 203; tribal economic development 100, 104, 109; tribal economy 2; Tribal Employment Rights Office (TERO) 6–7; tribal government 4, 9, 41, 42, 105, 108, 100, 183, 202; tribal higher education 107, 108, 111; tribal identity 61, 67, 70, 75, 76, 77, 82, 84, 99; Tribal Learning Community and Educational Exchange 128; tribal nations 70, 134, 135, 140; tribal public health services 187; tribal public health workforce 183, 184, 185, 186, 187, 190, 192, 194, 196, 198, 199; tribal resource development 4, 48; tribal traditions 151, 187
tribal values 100; Tribal Work Experience (TWEP) 5; tribal workers 189; tribal workforce 80, 185, 187, 196, 197, 198, 199
tribalism 61, 62

Tribally Controlled Community College Act 41, 42, 62
Turtle Mountain Community College 86
Tuskegee Institute 56
Two Feathers Curriculum 154

underemployment 4, 7, 141, 202
undergraduate 192; undergraduate program 199
underskilled 77
unemployment 4, 7, 10, 15, 25, 42, 43, 49, 50, 65, 76, 86, 87, 99, 106, 116, 141, 162, 202; unemployment rate(s) 4, 64, 86, 144, 159, 162–3
United Indians of All Tribes Foundation 10
United Nations Educational, Scientific and Cultural Organization (UNESCO) 16
United States Department of Agriculture (USDA) 64; United States Census Bureau 129; United States Chamber of Commerce 8; United States Civil Rights Commission 26, 119; United States Department of Education 96, 101; United States Department of Health and Human Services 5; United States Department of Labor 5, 10
United Tribes Technical College (UTTC) 9, 62, 99
unskilled 25
Ute 27

vocational and educational psychology 159; vocational and technical programs 99, 133
vocational aspirations 178; vocational courses 62, 68; vocational curriculum 19
vocational development 160, 162; vocational education 1, 3, 7, 10, 16, 17, 18, 19, 24, 26, 27, 28, 29, 41, 55, 56–7, 58, 59, 60, 64, 66, 69, 84; Vocational Education Act 57; vocational identity 146; vocational program 19, 27, 63; vocational training 4, 7, 8, 48, 56, 80, 85, 133

Wahpeton Indian School 24
Western education practices 98
white-collar 143
work-based learning (WBL) 144
work environment 166, 167, 172; work experience 169, 173; work experiences 159, 169, 170, 171, 172, 175, 177; work goals 170; work life 161, 164; 2ork-life transition 161; work plan 171; work program 48; work transition 168
workforce 38, 47, 49, 75, 77, 80, 81, 82, 83, 88, 92, 109, 110, 116, 126, 134, 139, 170, 181, 187, 189, 192, 197, 202; workforce competency 188, 192, 199; workforce development 5, 6, 7, 8, 9, 32, 41, 42, 43, 46, 47, 49, 50, 51, 74–5, 77, 78, 80, 81, 82, 83, 87, 96, 97, 98, 109, 186, 190, 192, 196; workforce development planning 188; workforce education 1, 2, 3, 7, 56, 74–5, 77, 78, 79, 82–8, 89, 91, 92, 97, 108, 120, 130, 192, 193, 202, 204; workforce education philosophy 84; workforce education plan 116, 118, 124, 125, 128, 129, 130, 131, 134, 135; workforce education program 120, 126, 127, 131, 132, 133, 134; workforce educational design 125; workforce educator 122; workforce goals 88, 134; Workforce Innovation and Opportunity Act (WIOA) 6, 7; Workforce Investment Act (WIA) 5, 91; workforce needs 100, 185, 187, 199; workforce planning 108; workforce preparation 10, 109; workforce priorities 197; workforce program 118, 120, 122, 126, 131, 203; workforce training 4, 133, 184, 185, 189, 190, 197, 198, 203
working landscape 160
workplace 47, 50, 144, 146; workplace learning 109; workplace rules 9; workplace skill development 202; workplace skills 203
World War II 25, 26, 40, 41, 47